Cases and Materials on
The Law of Tort

Authors

The Tort Law Team at BPP

Consultant Editor

Kate Smith

First edition July 2010

Fourth edition July 2015

Published ISBN: 9781 4727 3388 7

Previous ISBN: 9781 4727 2115 0

British Library Cataloguing-in-Publication Data
A catalogue record for this book is available
from the British Library

Published by
BPP Learning Media Ltd
BPP House, Aldine Place
London W12 8AA
www.bpp.com/learningmedia

Printed in the United Kingdom by
Charlesworth Press

Flanshaw Way
Flanshaw Lane
Wakefield
WF2 9LP

Your learning materials, published by BPP
Learning Media Ltd, are printed on paper
sourced from sustainable, managed forests.

Contents

Index of Cases

A

B

C

D

E

F

G

H

L

M

S

T

U

V

W

Y

Z

1

Trespass to the Person

Topic List

Introduction

Trespass to the person is an ancient tort, which predates negligence by centuries. The tort of negligence was originally considered a sub species of trespass. The two torts are now completely separate. Trespass to the person is actionable *per se*, while actual damage must be proved in a claim for negligence. Also trespass to the person involves an intentional act, whereas a negligence claim could only arise from an unintentional accident. The three forms of trespass to the person are battery, assault and false imprisonment. There is also a residuary tort under the rule in *Wilkinson v Downton* [1897] 2 QB 57.

Many of the cases cited here are criminal cases. The principles from these cases can be applied to the tort of trespass to the person. There is a scarcity of tort cases in this area as it is rare in practice to sue. The assailant may be unknown, or, if known, unlikely to have insurance against the possibility of him attacking somebody! The usual way to obtain compensation in this type of claim is via the Criminal Injuries Compensation Authority, the details of which are beyond the scope of this book.

1.1 Battery

The current definition of battery has developed from a long line of cases dating back to the eighteenth century. Battery can now be formulated as an intentional and direct application of force by the defendant to the claimant without lawful justification.

1.1.1 Intention

Letang v Cooper [1965] 1 QB 232

Panel: Lord Denning MR, Dankwerts and Diplock LJJ

Facts: The claimant was sunbathing in the car park belonging to the Ponosmere Hotel, in Perranporth, Cornwall. The defendant drove over the claimant's legs with his Jaguar car. For technical reasons relating to the time limit on legal actions, the claim was for trespass to the person, rather than negligence.

At first instance, Elwes J held, *inter alia*, that the defendant was liable for trespass to the person. The defendant appealed to the Court of Appeal.

The Court of Appeal allowed the appeal, and held that there was no trespass to the person as the defendant's act was not intentional.

> LORD DENNING MR
>
> ...Instead of dividing actions for personal injuries into trespass (direct damage) or case (consequential damage), we divide the causes of action now according as the defendant did the injury intentionally or unintentionally. If one man intentionally applies force directly to another, the plaintiff has a cause of action in assault and battery, or, if you so please to describe it, in trespass to the person. "The least touching of another in anger is a battery," per Holt C.J. in *Cole v. Turner* ...

Lord Denning MR's decision was partly founded upon an earlier case, *Fowler v Lanning* [1959] 1 QB 426, in which the statement of claim merely stated that 'The defendant shot the plaintiff'. There was no allegation either of intention, which would give rise to an action in trespass, or carelessness, which may have led to a negligence action.

Fowler v Lanning [1959] 1 QB 426

Panel: Diplock J

MR JUSTICE DIPLOCK

...I can summarise the law as I understand it from my examination of the cases as follows:

(1) Trespass to the person does not lie if the injury to the plaintiff, although the direct consequence of the act of the defendant, was caused unintentionally and without negligence on the defendant's part.

... If, as I have held, the onus of proof of intention or negligence on the part of the defendant lies upon the plaintiff, then, under the modern rules of pleading, he must allege either intention on the part of the defendant, or, if he relies upon negligence, he must state the facts which he alleges constitute negligence. Without either of such allegations the bald statement that the defendant shot the plaintiff in unspecified circumstances with an unspecified weapon in my view discloses no cause of action.

The intention requirement relates only to the original touching. The claimant does not need to prove that the defendant intended harm to result from his actions.

1.1.2 The Act must be Direct

In *Letang v Cooper* Lord Denning MR discusses the distinction between an indirect act (negligence) and a direct act (trespass to the person).

The courts have been prepared to exercise some flexibility regarding this requirement, as in the case described below.

Fagan v Commissioner of Metropolitan Police [1969] 1 QB 439

Panel: Lord Parker CJ, James and Bridge JJ

Facts: This was a criminal case. Police Constable Morris, who was standing at the side of a road, indicated to the defendant, Mr Fagan, to pull his car in towards the kerb. In doing so, Fagan unintentionally drove his car onto PC Morris's foot. When asked to move, Fagan initially refused, and turned off his engine. After being requested to move several times, he reluctantly acquiesced.

It was held, *inter alia*, that (1) battery could be inflicted through the medium of a weapon (in this case, a car) and that (2) although the original act was unintentional, it became a criminal act and would also be tortious from the moment of the necessary intention to inflict unlawful force.

MR JUSTICE JAMES

... On the facts found the action of the appellant may have been initially unintentional, but the time came when knowing that the wheel was on the officer's foot the appellant (1) remained seated in the car so that his body through the medium of the car was in contact with the officer, (2) switched off the ignition of the car, (3) maintained the wheel of the car on the foot and (4) used words indicating the intention of keeping the wheel in that position. For our part we cannot regard such conduct as mere omission or inactivity.

There was an act constituting a battery which at its inception was not criminal because there was no element of intention but which became criminal from the moment the intention was formed to produce the apprehension which was flowing from the continuing act...

This case illustrates two things well. The first is that a battery can result from an unintentional act which, upon continuance, becomes intentional. The second is that the requirement that battery is a direct act does not mean that the defendant has to use his body to inflict the battery, but can use something else, in this case, a car.

An early example of the court's relaxed attitude in relation to the 'directness requirement' is *Scott v Shepherd* (1773) 2 Bl R 892 in which the defendant was found to have committed a battery against the victim by throwing a lighted firework onto another person's market stall. The firework was actually thrown from stall to stall before eventually landing on the stall of the unfortunate victim, against whom the court found the defendant had committed a battery, owing to the chain of events.

1.1.3 There must be an Application of Force

Any physical contact amounts to 'force' in this context. See Lord Denning MR's comments in *Letang v Cooper*. In R v Cotesworth (1704) 6 Mod 172, spitting was held to be an application of force.

1.1.4 Extra requirement of hostility

In *Wilson v Pringle* [1987] QB 237 the Court of Appeal introduced a further requirement of hostility. In an appeal against an order for summary judgment (where judgment had been given in favour of the defendant on the grounds that he had no defence, as battery had clearly been committed), the court decided that the matter was not straightforward, as the defendant should be allowed to defend on the basis that his action lacked hostility. The facts are clearly stated in the judgment.

Wilson v Pringle **[1987] QB 237**

Panel: O'Connor, Croom-Johnson and Balcombe LJJ

LORD JUSTICE CROOM-JOHNSON

On 4 December 1980 the plaintiff and defendant were both schoolboys aged 13. On that day at school the plaintiff had a fall which caused an injury to his left hip, from which he still suffers. In the statement of claim it is alleged:

> "the defendant jumped on the plaintiff, causing him to suffer personal injury, loss and damage.... The matters aforesaid constitute a trespass to the person of the plaintiff and/or were caused by the defendant's negligence."

...The defendant put in a defence. It is there denied that the defendant jumped on the plaintiff. Trespass to the person and negligence are both denied. The defendant's version of what happened is set out in paragraph 5, as follows:

> "The defendant will aver that... after the Maths class which both plaintiff and defendant had attended, the plaintiff was in front of the defendant in a corridor and was carrying his school bag over his right shoulder. The bag was of the hand grip type, and the plaintiff was holding the handle in his right hand and holding the bag over his shoulder so that the bag hung down over his back. The defendant on this occasion pulled the bag off the plaintiff's shoulder. The defendant will aver that this act was one of ordinary horseplay as between pupils in the same school and the same class, and that it was induced by the plaintiff because it was a school regulation that bags should not be carried over the shoulder."

...*Tuberville v. Savage* (1669) 1 Mod. 3 was an action for assault. The defendant clapped his hand upon his sword and said to the plaintiff, "If it were not assize-time, I would not take such language." The court ruled that there was no threat, and accordingly no assault. This case is authority that there must be not only a deliberate threat (in an assault) or a deliberate touching (in battery) but also hostile behaviour. If the intention is obviously hostile, that will suffice, but it was recognised that there are many circumstances in life where contact with one's fellow men is not only unavoidable but even if deliberate may also be innocent.

... A more recent authority is *Collins v. Wilcock* [1984] 1 W.L.R. 1172 . This case was not cited to the judge. It had not been reported at the time of the hearing of the Order 14 appeal. The facts were that a woman police officer, suspecting that a woman was soliciting contrary to the Street Offences Act 1959, tried to question her. The woman walked away, and was followed by the police officer. The officer took hold of her arm in order to restrain her. The woman scratched the officer's arm. She was arrested, charged with assaulting a police officer in the execution of her duty, and convicted. On appeal by case stated, the appeal was allowed, on the ground that the officer had gone beyond the scope of her duty in detaining the woman in circumstances short of arresting her. The officer had accordingly committed a battery.

... Nevertheless, it still remains to indicate what is to be proved by a plaintiff who brings an action for battery. Robert Goff L.J.'s judgment [in *Collins v. Wilcock*] is illustrative of the considerations which underlie such an action, but it is not practicable to define a battery as "physical contact which is not generally acceptable in the ordinary conduct of daily life."

In our view, the authorities lead one to the conclusion that in a battery there must be an intentional touching or contact in one form or another of the plaintiff by the defendant. That touching must be proved to be a hostile touching. That still leaves unanswered the question "when is a touching to be called hostile?" Hostility cannot be equated with ill-will or malevolence. It cannot be governed by the obvious intention shown in acts like punching, stabbing or shooting. It cannot be solely governed by an expressed intention, although that may be strong evidence. But the element of hostility, in the sense in which it is now to be considered, must be a question of fact for the tribunal of fact. It may be imported from the circumstances. Take the example of the police officer in *Collins v. Wilcock*. She touched the woman deliberately, but without an intention to do more than restrain her temporarily. Nevertheless, she was acting unlawfully and in that way was acting with hostility. She was acting contrary to the woman's legal right not to be physically restrained. We see no more difficulty in establishing what she intended by means of question and answer, or by inference from the surrounding circumstances, than there is in establishing whether an apparently playful blow was struck in anger...Where the immediate act of touching does not itself demonstrate hostility, the plaintiff should plead the facts which are said to do so.

As the court did not define 'hostility', other than to say that 'it cannot be equated to ill-will or malevolence', it is not entirely clear what this requirement adds to the traditional formula. One possible interpretation is that the act must be something to which the claimant would not have consented, although this does not seem far removed from what Lord Goff was expressing in *Collins v Wilcock* disapproved of in *Wilson v Pringle*. The view that 'hostility' simply means doing something to a claimant to which he would not consent has also caused some difficulty for the courts. Consider the contrasting cases of *R v Wilson* [1997] QB 47 and *R v Brown* [1992] QB 491.

R v Wilson [1997] QB 47

Panel: Russell LJ, Bracewell J and Judge Capstick QC

LORD JUSTICE RUSSELL

On 16 May 1995 the appellant, Alan Thomas Wilson, was convicted by the verdict of the jury, in the Crown Court at Doncaster before Judge Crabtree. The charge was one of assault occasioning actual bodily harm contrary to section 47 of the Offences Against the Person Act 1861, the particulars being that on 14 May 1994 the appellant assaulted Julie Anne Wilson, thereby occasioning her actual bodily harm. The so-called victim was the wife of the appellant.

The police informed the appellant that his wife had been medically examined and that marks had been observed on both her buttocks. On the right buttock, as the photographs before the court disclose, there was a fading scar in the form of a capital letter "W," and on the left buttock, a more pronounced and more recent scar in the form of a capital letter "A." The two letters "A" and "W" were the initials of the appellant.

He at once admitted that he was responsible for the marks. He told the police:

> "I put them there. . . . She wanted a tattoo and I didn't know how to do a tattoo, but she wanted my name tattooing on her bum and I didn't know how to do it; so I burned it on with a hot knife. It wasn't life threatening, it wasn't anything, it was done for love. She loved me. She wanted me to give her - put my name on her body. As I say, she asked me originally if I would tattoo my name on her. She wanted me to do it on her breasts and I talked her out of that because I didn't know how to do a tattoo. Then she said, 'Well, there must be some way. If you can't do a tattoo, there must be some way' she says..."

...In the court below, and before us, reference was predictably made to *Rex v. Donovan* [1934] 2 K.B. 498 , a decision of the Court of Criminal Appeal, and to *Reg. v. Brown (Anthony)* [1994] 1 A.C. 212, a decision of the House of Lords. They are the two authorities to which the trial judge referred in the observations we have cited.

In *Rex v. Donovan* [1934] 2 K.B. 498 the appellant, in private, beat a girl of 17 years of age for the purposes of sexual gratification, with her consent. The act had about it an aggressive element. The court held that consent was immaterial. In *Reg. v. Brown* [1994] 1 A.C. 212 the appellants engaged in sado-masochism of the grossest kind, involving inter alia, physical torture, and as Lord Templeman pointed out, at p. 236D: "obvious dangers of serious personal injury and blood infection." The facts of the case were truly extreme.

We are abundantly satisfied that there is no factual comparison to be made between the instant case and the facts of either *Rex v. Donovan* [1934] 2 K.B. 498 or *Reg. v. Brown* [1994] 1 A.C. 212: Mrs. Wilson not only consented to that which the appellant did, she instigated it. There was no aggressive intent on the part of the appellant. On the contrary, far from wishing to cause injury to his wife, the appellant's desire was to assist her in what she regarded as the acquisition of a desirable piece of personal adornment, perhaps in this day and age no less understandable than the piercing of nostrils or even tongues for the purposes of inserting decorative jewellery.

...For our part, we cannot detect any logical difference between what the appellant did and what he might have done in the way of tattooing. The latter activity apparently requires no state authorisation, and the appellant was as free to engage in it as anyone else. We do not think that we are entitled to assume that the method adopted by the appellant and his wife was any more dangerous or painful than tattooing. There was simply no evidence to assist the court on this aspect of the matter.

Does public policy or the public interest demand that the appellant's activity should be visited by the sanctions of the criminal law? The majority in *Reg. v. Brown* clearly took the view that such considerations were relevant. If that is so, then we are firmly of the opinion that it is not in the public interest that activities such as the appellant's in this appeal should amount to criminal behaviour. Consensual activity between husband and wife, in the privacy of the matrimonial home, is not, in our judgment, normally a proper matter for criminal investigation, let alone criminal prosecution. Accordingly we take the view that the judge failed to have full regard to the facts of this case and misdirected himself in saying that *Rex v. Donovan* [1934] 2 K.B. 498 and *Reg. v. Brown* [1994] 1 A.C. 212 constrained him to rule that consent was no defence.

In this field, in our judgment, the law should develop upon a case by case basis rather than upon general propositions to which, in the changing times in which we live, exceptions may arise from time to time not expressly covered by authority.

We shall allow the appeal and quash the conviction.

In the earlier case of *R v Brown* referred to, the court had refused to accept that the victims consented to extreme sado-masochistic practices, even though the whole event was consensual, as it was considered that it offended public decency to accept the defence of consent to such deeds. When *Wilson* was heard, the court was at pains to distinguish it from *Brown*, even to the extent of likening branding somebody's buttocks to the lawful activity of tattooing! The cases are hard to reconcile, and whether consent will be accepted as a defence to battery when the defendant has committed what would normally be a criminal activity is unclear, but the more extreme the activity in which the parties are engaged, the less likely it is that consent would be accepted as a defence.

Consent is highly relevant in the field of medical treatment. If a patient is capable of consent, and consent is not obtained before treatment, any treatment will constitute a battery. Hostility is not a requirement for battery in this context.

Chatterton v Gerson [1981] QB 432

Panel: Bristow J

Facts: The claimant was treated by the defendant performing a pain relieving operation. She had two operations within ten months. After the second operation she lost the sensation in her leg, and her original pain had not been cured. She alleged that the risks had not been fully explained to her, and that this vitiated her consent, so that the treatment she received was a battery.

In relation to the battery issue, it was held that the claimant understood the general nature of the operations and it was this that she had consented to, so the operations were not a battery.

MR JUSTICE BRISTOW

...In my judgment once the patient is informed in broad terms of the nature of the procedure which is intended, and gives her consent, that consent is real, and the cause of the action on which to base a claim for failure to go into risks and implications is negligence, not trespass. Of course if information is withheld in bad faith, the consent will be vitiated by fraud. Of course if by some accident, as in a case in the 1940's in the Salford Hundred Court where a boy was admitted to hospital for tonsillectomy and due to administrative error was circumcised instead, trespass would be the appropriate cause of action against the doctor, though he was as much the victim of the error as the boy...

In this case in my judgment even taking the plaintiff's evidence at its face value she was under no illusion as to the general nature of what an intrathecal injection of phenol solution nerve block would be, and in the case of each injection her consent was not unreal. I should add that getting the patient to sign a pro forma expressing consent to undergo the operation "the effect and nature of which have been explained to me," as was done here in each case, should be a valuable reminder to everyone of the need for explanation and consent. But it would be no defence to an action based on trespass to the person if no explanation had in fact been given. The consent would have been expressed in form only, not in reality.

Therefore if the patient has been given an explanation as to what is involved, their consent will be real, although they may have recourse to a claim in negligence.

To conclude, in order to establish a claim in battery, the claimant must prove that there has been a direct and intentional application of force, arguably with some degree of hostility, to which the claimant has not consented.

1.2 Assault

The second type of trespass to the person is assault. Drawing from the Offences Against the Person Act 1861, Lord Lane CJ, defines assault thus, in *R v Dennis John Beasley* (1981) 73 Cr App R 44:

"any act by which D intentionally or recklessly, causes P to apprehend immediate and unlawful personal violence".

Note that assault requires the claimant only to apprehend 'personal violence' (or force), whereas battery requires the claimant to have had force used against them.

That which constitutes an assault has been the subject of much debate and questions have arisen as to whether words alone or are actions also needed for an assault; and whether an assault can be committed through silence.

R v Ireland [1997] 3 WLR 534

Panel: Lord Goff of Chievley, Lord Slynn of Hadley, Lord Steyn, Lord Hope of Craighead and Lord Hutton

Statute: Offences Against the Person Act 1861 s 47

Facts: The appellant, Mr Ireland, made numerous telephone calls to three women, during which he either remained silent or breathed heavily. He was convicted of assault occasioning actual bodily harm under the Offences against the Person Act 1861 s 47. His appeal against conviction was dismissed by the Court of Appeal (Criminal Division).

The House of Lords also dismissed the appeal, holding that assault could be committed by words or gestures alone, or even silent telephone calls where these caused the victim to fear immediate and unlawful violence.

LORD STEYN

... That brings me to the critical question whether a silent caller may be guilty of an assault. The answer to this question seems to me to be 'Yes, depending on the facts.' It involves questions of fact within the province of the jury. After all, there is no reason why a telephone caller who says to a woman in a menacing way 'I will be at your door in a minute or two' may not be guilty of an assault if he causes his victim to apprehend immediate personal violence. Take now the case of the silent caller. He intends by his silence to cause fear and he is so understood. The victim is assailed by uncertainty about his intentions. Fear may dominate her emotions, and it may be the fear that the caller's arrival at her door may be imminent. She may fear the possibility of immediate personal violence. As a matter of law the caller may be guilty of an assault: whether he is or not will depend on the circumstance and in particular on the impact of the caller's potentially menacing call or calls on the victim.

LORD HOPE OF CRAIGHEAD

...In my opinion silent telephone calls of this nature are just as capable as words or gestures, said or made in the presence of the victim, of causing an apprehension of immediate and unlawful violence.

Their lordships in *R v Ireland* confirmed that a menacing silence can amount to assault where it causes the victim to apprehend immediate harm, through this medium of direct communication. Lord Hope also cited the case of *R v Wilson* [1955] 1 WLR 493, in which a gamekeeper was threatened by a poacher shouting to his fellow poachers, 'Get out the knives'. Here, it was argued by the defendant that words alone could not constitute an assault, and that some form of threatening action accompanying the words was required. The Court of Criminal Appeal found that the words in themselves were sufficient to constitute an assault.

From the cases of *R v Ireland* and *R v Wilson*, we can see that an assault can arise not only from actions, and words, but also from a threatening silence.

For an assault there must be an immediate threat. Contrast the following cases of *Stephens v Myers* (1830) 172 ER 735 where it was held that there was an assault, with *Thomas and Others v National Union of Mineworkers (South Wales Area) and Others* [1986] Ch. 20, where there was no assault.

Stephens v Myers (1830) 172 ER 735

Panel: Tindal CJ

Facts: The plaintiff was chairing a meeting of the local parish council. Matters became rather heated, and the defendant, who was seated at the same table as the plaintiff with about 6 people between them, became very vociferous. A motion to remove the defendant from the meeting was carried. However, the defendant said that he would rather pull the plaintiff out of his chair than leave the meeting. He advanced towards the plaintiff with a clenched fist, but was stopped by the churchwarden. Witnesses confirmed that they thought he would have hit the plaintiff if the churchwarden had not intervened.

In this case, although the defendant was stopped from reaching the plaintiff to carry out his threat, this was only because of the intervention of a third party. The judge therefore considered that his 'advancing with intent' would amount to an assault, if it could be carried out immediately.

In contrast, consider *Thomas v NUM*, a case involving the miners' strike of the 1980s.

Thomas and Others v National Union of Mineworkers (South Wales Area) and Others [1986] Ch 20

Panel: Scott J

Facts: The claimants were being transported by bus through the picket line at their colliery. The bus was protected from the pickets by a police cordon.

MR JUSTICE SCOTT

... Assault is defined in Clerk & Lindsell on Torts, 15th ed. (1982), para. 14-10 as "an overt act indicating an immediate intention to commit a battery, coupled with the capacity to carry that intention into effect." The tort of assault is not, in my view, committed, unless the capacity in question is present at the time the overt act is committed. Since the working miners are in vehicles and the pickets are held back from the vehicles, I do not understand how even the most violent of threats or gestures could be said to constitute an assault.

Whether the threat is looked at as objectively likely to cause fear has been the subject of debate. It is generally considered that the view of the reasonable person is taken into account, and that a neurotic individual may not be able to sustain a claim of assault if the defendant's words or actions would not have caused others to fear them (for obvious policy reasons). This is borne out by *Thomas v NUM*, as a reasonable person would not have considered that the threats could lead to immediate harm to someone protected within a vehicle.

1.3 Residuary Trespass – The rule in *Wilkinson v Downton*

Where a defendant says something with the intention of harming the claimant, but with no threat of violence, can a claim be made for trespass to the person?

Wilkinson v Downton [1897] 2 QB 57

Panel: Wright J

Facts: The defendant, as a practical joke, told the claimant that her husband had been seriously injured in a coaching accident, breaking both his legs. He said that he was lying at a public house, and that she should go at once and take him some pillows to bring him home. The claimant suffered nervous shock. It was held that the defendant must pay damages to the claimant.

MR JUSTICE WRIGHT

...The defendant has, as I assume for the moment, wilfully done an act calculated to cause physical harm to the plaintiff—that is to say, to infringe her legal right to personal safety, and has in fact thereby caused physical harm to her. That proposition without more appears to me to state a good cause of action, there being no justification alleged for the act. This wilful injuria is in law malicious, although no malicious purpose to cause the harm which was caused nor any motive of spite is imputed to the defendant.

This has since become known as 'the rule in *Wilkinson v Downton*', or 'residuary trespass'. If somebody says or does something with intention to cause physical harm to another, and that person suffers harm, the tort of residuary trespass will have been committed. The rule imposes a requirement of damage, unlike the other forms of trespass to the person which are actionable *per se*.

In the case of *Janvier v Sweeney* [1919] 2 KB 316, the defendants, private detectives, wished to obtain some letters to which they believed the claimant, a maid, had access. In order to coerce the claimant into obtaining these letters, one of the defendants falsely told her that she was wanted for questioning, as she had been corresponding with a German spy, (she had in fact been visiting and writing to her German boyfriend who had become imprisoned during World War I in the Isle of Man). This false statement caused her to be very frightened and she suffered illness as a result. Applying the rule in *Wilkinson v Downton* the defendants were liable.

The more recent case of *Wainwright v Home Office* [2002] QB 1334 is an interesting demonstration of an application of the rule defeating a claim.

Wainwright v Home Office **[2002] QB 1334**

Panel: Lord Woolf CJ, Mummery and Buxton LJJ

Facts: The claimants were a mother and her son who suffered from learning difficulties. Both had gone to visit the mother's other son at Armley Prison in Leeds. They were taken to one side to be searched on suspicion of smuggling in drugs. The mother was strip searched in front of an uncovered window, which was overlooked by a neighbouring building. Her son reported that there had been close inspection of his penis. Both claimants had suffered emotional distress. As both had consented to be searched, they could not claim that they had a cause of action in battery. Applying the *Wilkinson v Downton* rule, the judge at first instance awarded damages to both claimants. The Home Office appeal was allowed.

LORD WOOLF CJ

49 The limiting factor to the "tort" is the intention to cause harm which harm is in fact then caused or recklessness as to whether that harm would be caused. While the tort is not conventional trespass it is closer to trespass than negligence. I personally have no difficulty with the statement in Salmond & Heuston on Torts, 21st ed (1996), p 215 that "one who by extreme and outrageous conduct intentionally or recklessly causes severe emotional distress to another is liable for such emotional distress, provided that bodily

harm results from it". This passage accepts that emotional distress by itself does not suffice. It requires bodily harm to have resulted. It presumably is intended to recognise that emotional distress although severe may not be classifiable by psychiatrists as a psychiatric illness. It therefore requires, in lay terms, that the severe emotional distress has caused bodily harm. It also requires that this is what the defendant intended to be the consequence or was reckless as to whether this would be the consequence.

50 Both as a matter of principle and authority I regard it appropriate that there should be a right to compensation in these circumstances. We are here concerned with an intentional tort and intended harm. In such a situation, unlike negligence, problems as to foreseeability do not arise. If the conduct is actionable then compensation should be payable for the intended harm. For this general approach there is general support in Winfield & Jolowicz on Tort, 15th ed (1998), pp 86-87.

51 In this jurisdiction I consider that *Wilkinson v Downton* [1897] 2 QB 57 should be so limited. This provides the proper justification for distinguishing the cause of action from negligence. On that basis I would not seek to doubt the correctness of the decision in *Wilkinson v Downton*. However, so understood *Wilkinson v Downton* cannot be relied upon by the claimants in the present case. The judge made no finding that the prison officers were intending to cause or were reckless as to whether they caused harm. Furthermore the findings which he did make were inconsistent with such a conclusion. Had the facts been otherwise and harm had been intended or if there had been recklessness then I would have upheld the decision of the judge. I would have concluded that on the judge's findings the complainants had suffered the necessary damage.

A limit was placed on the rule by Lord Woolf CJ. It is not sufficient to show that a claimant had been caused harm by such words or actions. As with the other forms of trespass to the person, intention is required. Here, the prison officers were careless and did not follow the statutory requirements in relation to strip-searching. However, there was no evidence that their actions were calculated to cause the claimants harm, so the claim was defeated.

Therefore, if a defendant has done or said something, intending that the claimant should suffer harm, but which falls short of battery or assault, the rule in *Wilkinson v Downton* may fill the gap and afford the claimant a remedy.

1.4 False Imprisonment

The final form of trespass to the person is false imprisonment. This is an act which is direct and intentional and which causes the complete restriction of a person's freedom without lawful justification.

The elements which need to be proved are: that the act is direct and intentional (therefore, accidentally locking somebody in a building without realising that they were there would not suffice), that the restriction is complete with no alternative means of escape, and that there is no lawful justification (such as lawfully arresting a criminal or enforcement of a contractual right).

1.4.1 Complete Restriction

Bird v Jones (1845) 115 ER 668

Panel: Lord Denman CJ, Patteson, Coleridge and Williams JJ

Facts: The facts are set out in the following judgment.

> PATTESON J
>
> Now the facts of this case appear to be as follows. A part of Hammersmith Bridge which is ordinarily used as a public footway was appropriated for seats to view a regatta on the river, and separated for that purpose from the carriage way by a temporary fence. The plaintiff insisted on passing along the part so appropriated, and attempted to climb over the fence. The defendant, being clerk of the Bridge Company, seized his coat, and tried to pull him back: the plaintiff, however, succeeded in climbing over the fence. The defendant then stationed two policemen to prevent and, they did prevent, the plaintiff from proceeding forwards along the footway; but he was told that he might go back into the carriage way, and proceed to the other side of the bridge, if he pleased. The plaintiff would not do so, but remained where he was above half an hour: and then, on the defendant still refusing to suffer him to go forwards along the footway, he endeavoured to force his way, and, in so doing, assaulted the defendant: whereupon he was taken into custody.

As the claimant had an alternative means of crossing the bridge, his route was not completely restricted, and his claim for false imprisonment failed. The decision was not unanimous, as Lord Denman CJ dissented, being of the opinion that the lawfulness of the restriction should not be determined by whether a claimant has another option or not. However, later cases confirm that there must be a full restriction of the claimant's freedom for the tort to be established.

Whether a person could complain of false imprisonment if he was unaware of it at the time was neatly explained (albeit *obiter*) in the following case, in which the claimant failed in her claim for false imprisonment.

Murray v Ministry of Defence [1988] 1 WLR 692

Panel: Lord Keith of Kinkel, Lord Templeman, Lord Griffiths, Lord Oliver of Aylmerton and Lord Jauncey of Tullichettle

Facts: The claimant was suspected of raising money for arms for the IRA. The army attended her house at 7am to arrest her. A female corporal accompanied her while she dressed in her bedroom, during which time other officers rounded up the rest of the family and held them in the sitting room. When the claimant asked if she was under arrest, the corporal did not reply. Before leaving the house at 7.30 am, the corporal, correctly – according to the terrorism legislation at that time – told the claimant that she was under arrest. Part of the claim was based on the fact that the claimant was not told that she was under arrest until 7.30, and that her restraint until then was false imprisonment as she did not know that she was to be arrested. This was not accepted by the court. Her false imprisonment claim failed at first instance and her appeals to the Court of Appeal and the House of Lords were dismissed.

> **LORD GRIFFITHS**
>
> [quoting Atkin LJ in *Meering v Grahame-White Aviation* (1919) 122 LT 44] "It appears to me that a person could be imprisoned without his knowing it. I think a person can be imprisoned while he is asleep, while he is in a state of drunkenness, while he is unconscious, and while he is a lunatic. Those are cases where it seems to me that the person might properly complain if he were imprisoned, though the imprisonment began and ceased while he was in that state. Of course, the damages might be diminished and would be affected by the question whether he was conscious of it or not. So a man might in fact, to my mind, be imprisoned by having the key of a door turned against him so that he is imprisoned in a room in fact although he does not know that the key has been turned. It may be that he is being detained in that room by persons who are anxious to make him believe that he is not in fact being imprisoned, and at the same time his captors outside that room may be boasting to persons that he is imprisoned, and it seems to me that if we were to take this case as an instance supposing it could be proved that Prudence had said while the plaintiff was waiting: 'I have got him detained there waiting for the detective to come in and take him to prison' — it appears to me that that would be evidence of imprisonment. It is quite unnecessary to go on to show that in fact the man knew that he was imprisoned. If a man can be imprisoned by having the key turned upon him without his knowledge, so he can be imprisoned if, instead of a lock and key or bolts and bars, he is prevented from, in fact, exercising his liberty by guards and warders or policemen. They serve the same purpose. Therefore it appears to me to be a question of fact. It is true that in all cases of imprisonment so far as the law of civil liability is concerned that 'stone walls do not a prison make,' in the sense that they are not the only form of imprisonment, but any restraint within defined bounds which is a restraint in fact may be an imprisonment."

Lord Griffiths refers to the case of *Meering v Grahame-White Aviation*, in which the claimant was oblivious to the fact that the room in which he was sitting was guarded, pending the arrival of the Metropolitan Police. Even though he did not know that he could not leave, this amounted to false imprisonment.

1.4.2 Without Lawful Justification

There are occasions when a claim for false imprisonment will fail because the defendant has lawful authority to restrict the freedom of the claimant, for example if the claimant is in breach of contract and the defendant is attempting to enforce his contractual rights (although it may be a risky self-help strategy!).

In *Archibald Nugent Robinson v Balmain New Ferry Company, Limited* [1910] AC 29, the claimant paid one penny to enter a wharf to catch a ferry. The claimant, upon deciding not to wait twenty minutes for the ferry, tried to leave the wharf. There was a requirement that a further penny be paid to leave the wharf. The officer in charge of the wharf tried to restrain him from leaving without paying, and succeeded for some minutes, until the claimant managed to squeeze past the turnstile and escape. The claimant sued the defendant company for false imprisonment. The claim failed on the basis that the defendant was entitled to resist the claimant's evasion of his contractual obligation.

1.5 Defences to the Tort of Trespass to the Person

A full discussion on defences can be found in Chapter 8.

The general defences of *volenti non fit injuria*; contributory negligence; *ex turpi causa*, as well as inevitable accident (act of God) and statutory authority apply here.

In the context of trespass to the person, *volenti* is more commonly referred to as 'consent'. A case that we have already considered deals with the defence of consent in a medical context. Referring again to the case of *Chatterton v Gerson* Bristow J said:

"It is clear law that in any context in which consent of the injured party is a defence to what would otherwise be a crime or a civil wrong, the consent must be real. Where for example a woman's consent to sexual intercourse is obtained by fraud, her apparent consent is no defence to a charge of rape. It is not difficult to state the principle or to appreciate its good sense. As so often, the problem lies in its application."

The case of *In Re F* [1990] 2 AC 1 also deals with the issue of consent in a medical context. The case was heard in the House of Lords, but the extract below is from the Court of Appeal judgment.

In Re F [1990] 2 AC 1

Panel: Lord Donaldson of Lymington MR, Neill and Butler-Sloss LJJ

Facts: This complex case involved the issue of whether a sterilisation operation should be performed on a woman who lacked mental capacity. The House of Lords upheld the decision of the judge at first instance, which had been upheld by the Court of Appeal, to grant a declaration that such an operation would not be unlawful by reason of the lack of consent. Whether such an operation would be lawful would depend upon the best interests of the patient and the public interest.

LORD JUSTICE NEILL

...Accordingly, provided the consent was properly obtained and the scope of the operation did not exceed the ambit of the consent, a patient over the age of 16 cannot bring an action for trespass to the person against the surgeon who carried out the operation to which he gave his consent. Treatment or surgery which would otherwise be unlawful as a trespass is made lawful by the consent of the patient. It is to be noted, however, that in certain circumstances consent does not provide an answer to an allegation of assault. Thus it was held in *Attorney-General's Reference (No 6 of 1980)* [1981] Q.B. 715 that a person who had caused actual bodily harm to another in the course of a fight in which they had both agreed to take part was guilty of a criminal assault notwithstanding the consent of the person injured. In the words of Lord Lane CJ, at p. 719: "it is not in the public interest that people should try to cause, or should cause, each other actual bodily harm for no good reason." It is true, of course, that Lord Lane CJ was referring to the criminal law but it seems to me that in such a case the act is tortious as well as criminal though the injured participant would probably be unable to recover any damages because of the rule ex turpi causa non oritur actio. It is apparent therefore that the defence of consent is not a complete answer if to give effect to such consent would be against the public interest. The determination of the public interest is a matter for the courts, applying, subject to any statutory provisions which may be relevant, the common law. In this field, as in many others, the common law is capable of moving with the times to meet changing conditions so that as far as possible it reflects the acceptable standards of the day...

In addition to the general defences, there are also defences which apply specifically to the tort of trespass to the person. These include: necessity, reasonable chastisement and self defence.

Necessity rarely works in relation to trespass to the person, as the situations in which one can justify violating another will be very rare. It will therefore hardly ever be encountered outside the narrow field of medical law.

In relation to children, smacking by parents is not unlawful under English law, but reasonable chastisement will not act as a defence to an action for assault occasioning actual bodily harm, due to the Children Act 2004 s 58. Physical punishment in schools is unlawful – Education Act 1996 s 548. Finally, let us consider self-defence.

Lane v Holloway [1968] 1 QB 379

Panel: Lord Denning MR, Salmon and Winn LJJ

Facts: This case involved an altercation between a 23-year old male defendant, and a 64 year old male claimant. The older man verbally abused the defendant's wife. Upon the claimant striking the defendant, the defendant retaliated with such force that the claimant required hospitalisation after sustaining a serious eye injury. In defence to a claim for battery, the defendant pleaded *ex turpi causa* and *volenti non fit injuria*, as well as self-defence. He was unsuccessful as his reaction had been out of proportion to the attack upon him by the elderly claimant.

LORD DENNING MR

On July 21, 1966, the peace of the ancient borough of Dorchester was disturbed. Mr. Lane, the plaintiff, was a retired gardener aged 64. He was living in a quiet court just off High East Street. Backing onto that court there was a café which was run by a young man, Mr. Holloway, the defendant, aged 23. The people in the court did not like the sound of a juke-box from the café. They also objected because the customers relieved themselves at night in the courtyard. To meet their objection Mr. Holloway began to build some lavatories. But relations were strained. On July 21, 1966, at about 11 o'clock at night Mr. Lane, the 64-year-old, came back from the public-house. He stopped outside his door and started talking to his neighbour, Mrs. Brake. Mr.

Holloway was in bed drinking a cup of coffee. His wife, hearing Mr. Lane and Mrs. Brake talking, called out to them: "You bloody lot." Mr. Lane replied: "Shut up, you monkey-faced tart." Mr. Holloway sprang up and said: "What did you say to my wife?" He said it twice. Mr. Lane said: "I want to see you on your own," implying a challenge to fight. Whereupon Mr. Holloway came out in his pyjamas and dressing-gown. He walked up the courtyard to the place where Mr. Lane was standing at his door. He moved up close to Mr. Lane in a manner which made Mr. Lane think that he might himself be struck by Mr. Holloway. Whereupon Mr. Lane threw a punch at Mr. Holloway's shoulder. Then Mr. Holloway drew his right hand out of his pocket and punched Mr. Lane in the eye, a very severe blow. Mr. Holloway said: "You hit me first." Mr. Lane said: "If I had two good pins you would not have done this. I shall make a case of it." Mr. Lane was taken to hospital. It was indeed a very severe wound. It needed 19 stitches. He had also to have an operation. He was in hospital for a month…

Mr. Holloway in anger went much too far. He gave a blow out of proportion to the occasion for which he must answer in damages…

Although *volenti* would normally be a defence if two people are engaged in a fist fight, the elderly man was not considered to have volunteered to run the risk of such a savage attack, nor to have been engaged in a mutual illegal activity which would give rise to the *ex turpi* defence, nor to have been contributorily negligent just by virtue of being abusive and cantankerous. Neither could the defendant prove self-defence.

Therefore, in order to establish a claim for trespass to the person, it is necessary to prove battery, assault or false imprisonment, or that the tort of 'residuary trespass' has been committed. The act must have been intentional. Once established, the action may still be lost if there is a defence, but an over-reaction by the defendant may defeat any such defence.

Further Reading

Vera Birmingham and Carol Brennan, *Tort Law Directions*, Oxford University Press, 2008, Chapter 3 (3.1 to 3.4)

Mark Lunney and Ken Olliphant, *Tort Law Text and Materials*, (3rd edition), Oxford University Press, 2008, Chapter 2

2

General Negligence
and the Duty of Care I

Topic List

Introduction

Negligence is a tort that, although developed only relatively recently, has come to dominate tort law. To establish the tort of negligence the claimant must show that a duty was owed, which was breached and resulted in damage. They must also establish that the damage was caused by the defendant's breach and that it was not too remote.

This chapter will focus on cases that trace the development of the test for the duty of care and look at recent developments in applying the test, as well as specific situations such as when a duty of care is owed by the police, public services and lawyers.

2.1 Development

M'Alister (or Donoghue) (Pauper) Appellant v Stevenson Respondent [1932] AC 562

Panel: Lord Buckmaster, Lord Atkin, Lord Tomlin, Lord Thankerton and Lord Macmillan

Facts: The appellant drank a bottle of ginger beer which was bought for her by her friend. The bottle was opaque and after she had drunk most of it she discovered it contained the remains of a decomposed snail. The appellant was unable to sue the retailer as there was no privity of contract between them. The appellant instead sought to sue the manufacturer, alleging that she had suffered shock and severe gastro-enteritis as a result.

The House of Lords (by a majority of 3 to 2) held that a manufacturer was under a duty to the final purchaser or consumer to take reasonable care to ensure the article was free from any defect which would be injurious.

> LORD ATKIN
>
> ...The question is whether the manufacturer of an article of drink sold by him to a distributor, in circumstances which prevent the distributor or the ultimate purchaser or consumer from discovering by inspection any defect, is under any legal duty to the ultimate purchaser or consumer to take reasonable care that the article is free from defect likely to cause injury to health.
>
> ...The liability for negligence, whether you style it such or treat it as in other systems as a species of "culpa," is no doubt based upon a general public sentiment of moral wrongdoing for which the offender must pay. But acts or omissions which any moral code would censure cannot in a practical world be treated so as to give a right to every person injured by them to demand relief. In this way rules of law arise which limit the range of complainants and the extent of their remedy. The rule that you are to love your neighbour becomes in law, you must not injure your neighbour; and the lawyer's question, Who is my neighbour? receives a restricted reply. You must take reasonable care to avoid acts or omissions which you can reasonably foresee would be likely to injure your neighbour. Who, then, in law is my neighbour? The answer seems to be - persons who are so closely and directly affected by my act that I ought reasonably to

 **Decipher**
The test Lord Atkin sets out for foreseeability is an objective one.

have them in contemplation as being so affected when I am directing my mind to the acts or omissions which are called in question.

...There will no doubt arise cases where it will be difficult to determine whether the contemplated relationship is so close that the duty arises. But in the class of case now before the Court I cannot conceive any difficulty to arise.

Lord Buckmaster (dissenting) had pointed out how it would be very difficult for trade to be carried out, were an action for negligence to be established in these circumstances and raised the floodgates policy argument. Note how in Lord Atkin's judgment above, he is keen to allay any fears of the floodgates argument, and limits the situations when a duty would be likely to arise.

LORD TOMLIN

...First, I think that if the appellant is to succeed it must be upon the proposition that every manufacturer or repairer of any article is under a duty to every one who may thereafter legitimately use the article to exercise due care in the manufacture or repair. It is logically impossible to stop short of this point. There can be no distinction between food and any other article. Moreover, the fact that an article of food is sent out in a sealed container can have no relevancy on the question of duty; it is only a factor which may render it easier to bring negligence home to the manufacturer.

The above case establishes negligence as a tort in its own right. However, the decision only allowed the consumer to sue the manufacturer directly if the product caused physical injury. If the claim was that the goods were faulty, the only claim would be in contract.

Note that the claim was finally settled out of court for £100 and the existence of a snail in the ginger beer was never conclusively proven.

As the years progressed the courts recognised that a duty of care existed between previously established categories and would apply the relevant precedent. When a novel situation arose, the courts had to formulate a satisfactory test to establish whether a duty of care existed between the parties. The 'neighbour test' set out above by Lord Atkin formed the cornerstone of that test. The case below shows how the courts were willing, for a time, to go even further when establishing a test for the duty of care. Note that the case below has now been over-ruled. Nevertheless, it is still very important in terms of the development of the test for a duty of care.

Anns and Others Respondents and Merton London Borough Council Appellants [1978] AC 728

Panel: Lord Wilberforce, Lord Diplock, Lord Simon of Glaisdale, Lord Salmon and Lord Russell of Killowen

Facts: The case involved a block of maisonettes which had suffered damage as a result of the foundations being too shallow. The subsequent occupiers of the flat alleged negligence on the part of the local authority whom they claimed owed them a duty of care and should have carried out a competent inspection. The Court of Appeal allowed the claim of the lessees and leave was given to appeal to the House of Lords. One of the questions the House of Lords had to decide was whether a duty was owed by the local authority to the respondents. The decision of the Court of Appeal was affirmed.

LORD WILBERFORCE

...In these circumstances I take the questions in this appeal to be:

1. Whether the defendant council was under: (a) a duty of care to the plaintiffs to carry out an inspection of the foundations (which did not arise in Dutton's case); (b) a duty, if any inspection was made, to take reasonable care to see that the byelaws were complied with (as held in Dutton's case); (c) any other duty including a duty to ensure that the building was constructed in accordance with the plans, or not to allow the builder to construct the dwelling house upon foundations which were only 2 feet 6 inches deep instead of 3 feet or deeper (as pleaded)...

Through the trilogy of cases in this House – *Donoghue v. Stevenson* [1932] A.C. 562, *Hedley Byrne & Co. Ltd. v. Heller & Partners Ltd.* [1964] A.C. 465, and *Dorset Yacht Co. Ltd. v. Home Office* [1970] A.C. 1004, the position has now been reached that in order to establish that a duty of care arises in a particular situation, it is not necessary to bring the facts of that situation within those of previous situations in which a duty of care has been held to exist. Rather the question has to be approached in two stages. First one has to ask whether, as between the alleged wrongdoer and the person who has suffered damage there is a sufficient relationship of proximity or neighbourhood such that, in the reasonable contemplation of the former, carelessness on his part may be likely to cause damage to the latter - in which case a prima facie duty of care arises. Secondly, if the first question is answered affirmatively, it is necessary to consider whether there are any considerations which ought to negative, or to reduce or limit the scope of the duty or the class of person to whom it is owed or the damages to which a breach of it may give rise: see Dorset Yacht case [1970] A.C. 1004, per Lord Reid at p. 1027. Examples of this are Hedley Byrne's case [1964] A.C. 465 where the class of potential plaintiffs was reduced to those shown to have relied upon the correctness of statements made, and *Weller & Co. v. Foot and Mouth Disease Research Institute* [1966] 1 Q.B. 569; and (I cite these merely as illustrations, without discussion) cases about "economic loss" where, a duty having been held to exist, the nature of the recoverable damages was limited: see *S.C.M. (United Kingdom) Ltd. v. W. J. Whittall & Son Ltd.* [1971] 1 Q.B. 337 and *Spartan Steel & Alloys Ltd. v. Martin & Co. (Contractors) Ltd.* [1973] Q.B. 27.

... My Lords, I believe that the conception of a general duty of care, not limited to particular accepted situations, but extending generally over all relations of sufficient proximity, and even pervading the sphere of statutory functions of public bodies... Indeed it may well be that full recognition of the impact of *Donoghue v. Stevenson* in the latter sphere only came with the decision of this House in *Dorset Yacht Co. Ltd. v. Home Office* [1970] A.C. 1004...

...There are many questions here which do not directly arise at this stage and which may never arise if the actions are tried. But some conclusions are necessary if we are

Alert

This is the two-stage test which resulted in a huge expansion of the duty of care.

Decipher

Lord Wilberforce is referring here to policy reasons – for example the floodgates argument, or factors deciding whether society benefits as a whole.

to deal with the issue as to limitation. The damages recoverable include all those which foreseeably arise from the breach of the duty of care which, as regards the council, I have held to be a duty to take reasonable care to secure compliance with the byelaws. Subject always to adequate proof of causation, these damages may include damages for personal injury and damage to property. In my opinion they may also include damage to the dwelling house itself; for the whole purpose of the byelaws in requiring foundations to be of a certain standard is to prevent damage arising from weakness of the foundations which is certain to endanger the health or safety of occupants.

To allow recovery for such damage to the house follows, in my opinion, from normal principle. If classification is required, the relevant damage is in my opinion material, physical damage, and what is recoverable is the amount of expenditure necessary to restore the dwelling to a condition in which it is no longer a danger to the health or safety of persons occupying and possibly (depending on the circumstances) expenses arising from necessary displacement.

Note that the two-stage test formulated by Lord Wilberforce resulted in a massive expansion of the situations where a duty of care was held to exist. This was because one could establish first that a duty arose, and only then consider whether policy considerations should limit it. The courts became gradually more critical of the test, until the case was finally overruled in *Murphy v Brentwood* [1990] 2 All ER 908.

2.2 The Incremental Approach

In the case of *Caparo Industries plc v Dickman and others* [1990] 2 AC 605 Lord Bridge summarises the competing approaches to establishing a duty of care. This case sets out the modern approach of the courts, which has been duly developed.

Caparo Industries plc v Dickman and others [1990] 2 AC 605

Panel: Lord Bridge of Harwich, Lord Roskill, Lord Ackner, Lord Oliver of Aylmerton and Lord Jauncey of Tullichettle

Facts: The key question in this case was whether the defendants (auditors) owed a duty of care to potential investors (plaintiffs), who made a successful takeover bid for a company, based on the erroneous accounts of the auditors. The issue was whether the auditors owed a duty of care to shareholders or potential investors, to carry out an audit using reasonable care and skill.

The Court of Appeal held that the auditors owed a duty of care to shareholders to prepare the audit with reasonable care and skill, but not to potential investors. The auditors appealed to the House of Lords against the decision that they owed a duty of care to shareholders. The respondents also appealed (a cross-appeal) to the House of Lords against the decision that no duty was owed to them as potential investors. The appeal was allowed and the cross-appeal dismissed

LORD BRIDGE OF HARWICH

...But since Anns's case a series of decisions of the Privy Council and of your Lordships' House, notably in judgments and speeches delivered by Lord Keith, have emphasised the inability of any single general principle to provide a practical test which can be applied to every situation to determine whether a duty of care is owed and, if so, what is its scope: see *Peabody Donation Fund v Sir Lindsay Parkinson & Co Ltd* [1984] 3 All ER 529 at 533–534, [1985] AC 210 at 239–241, *Yuen Kun-yeu v A-G of Hong Kong* [1987] 2 All ER 705 at 709–712, [1988] AC 175 at 190–194, *Rowling v Takaro Properties Ltd* [1988] 1 All ER 163 at 172, [1988] AC 473 at 501 and *Hill v Chief Constable of West Yorkshire* [1988] 2 All ER 238 at 241, [1989] AC 53 at 60. What emerges is that, in addition to the foreseeability of damage, necessary ingredients in any situation giving rise to a duty of care are that there should exist between the party owing the duty and the party to whom it is owed a relationship characterised by the law as one of 'proximity' or 'neighbourhood' and that the situation should be one in which the court considers it fair, just and reasonable that the law should impose a duty of a given scope on the one party for the benefit of the other. But it is implicit in the passages referred to that the concepts of proximity and fairness embodied in these additional ingredients are not susceptible of any such precise definition as would be necessary to give them utility as practical tests, but amount in effect to little more than convenient labels to attach to the features of different specific situations which, on a detailed examination of all the circumstances, the law recognises pragmatically as giving rise to a duty of care of a given scope. Whilst recognising, of course, the importance of the underlying general principles common to the whole field of negligence, I think the law has now moved in the direction of attaching greater significance to the more traditional categorisation of distinct and recognisable situations as guides to the existence, the scope and the limits of the varied duties of care which the law imposes. We must now, I think, recognise the wisdom of the words of Brennan J in the High Court of Australia in *Sutherland Shire Council v Heyman* (1985) 60 ALR 1 at 43–44, where he said:

'It is preferable in my view, that the law should develop novel categories of negligence incrementally and by analogy with established categories, rather than by a massive extension of a prima facie duty of care restrained only by indefinable "considerations which ought to negative, or to reduce or limit the scope of the duty or the class of person to whom it is owed".'

One of the most important distinctions always to be observed lies in the law's essentially different approach to the different kinds of damage which one party may have suffered in consequence of the acts or omissions of another...

...It is never sufficient to ask simply whether A owes B a duty of care. It is always necessary to determine the scope of the duty by reference to the kind of damage from which A must take care to save B harm less:

'The question is always whether the defendant was under a duty to avoid or prevent that damage, but the actual nature of the damage suffered is relevant to the existence and extent of any duty to avoid or prevent it.'

 Alert

This is the test which is referred to as the 'Caparo Test'.

(See *Sutherland Shire Council v Heyman* (1985) 60 ALR 1 at 48 per Brennan J)

Assuming for the purpose of the argument that the relationship between the auditor of a company and individual shareholders is of sufficient proximity to give rise to a duty of care, I do not understand how the scope of that duty can possibly extend beyond the protection of any individual shareholder from losses in the value of the shares which he holds. As a purchaser of additional shares in reliance on the auditor's report, he stands in no different position from any other investing member of the public to whom the auditor owes no duty.

I would allow the appeal and dismiss the cross-appeal.

Although Lord Bridge seemed to be emphasising the need to examine the facts on an incremental approach rather than using a 'set test', his judgment is now treated as the 'three stage test' to determine whether a duty of care exists in a situation where there is no precedent to rely upon.

Applying the test, one needs to establish 1) foreseeability; 2) proximity and 3) whether it is fair, just and reasonable to recognise a duty in the circumstances.

Lord Bridge's test for a duty of care, where policy factors are considered to decide whether a duty arises, can be contrasted with Lord Wilberforce's approach in *Anns* where a *prima facie* duty arose, based on foreseeability, and policy reasons are only then considered when deciding whether they should limit such a duty from arising.

After the decision in *Murphy v Brentwood*, (the case which over-ruled *Anns*) the courts continued to cautiously expand the situations when a duty of care could be imposed. Examples can be seen from cases such as *Watson v British Boxing Board of Control* [2001] QB 1134. *White v Jones* [1995] 2 AC 207 below, is an example where the courts used the incremental approach, but also discussed the need to achieve 'practical justice' in the outcome.

White and another v Jones and others [1995] 2 AC 207

Panel: Lord Keith of Kinkel, Lord Goff of Chieveley, Lord Browne-Wilkinson, Lord Mustill and Lord Nolan

Facts: The plaintiffs were two daughters who were bringing an action against the defendants, their late father's solicitors. The daughters had previously quarreled with their father and he had written a new will which had cut them out of his estate as a result. They were then reconciled and the father called his solicitors to ask them to change his will to give his daughters each £9,000 as had previously been the case. Despite calling to remind his solicitor two months later, the will was not altered in time, and the father died. The plaintiffs brought an action in negligence against the solicitors alleging that a duty of care was owed to them. The Court of Appeal found for the plaintiffs, and the solicitors appealed to the House of Lords arguing that no duty of care existed in these situations.

LORD GOFF OF CHIEVELEY

...The impulse to do practical justice

Before addressing the legal questions which lie at the heart of the present case, it is, I consider, desirable to identify the reasons of justice which prompt judges and academic writers to conclude, like Megarry V-C in Ross v Caunters, that a duty should be owed by the testator's solicitor to a disappointed beneficiary. The principal reasons are, I believe, as follows.

(1) In the forefront stands the extraordinary fact that, if such a duty is not recognised, the only persons who might have a valid claim (ie the testator and his estate) have suffered no loss, and the only person who has suffered a loss (ie the disappointed beneficiary) has no claim: see *Ross v Caunters* [1979] 3 All ER 580 at 583, [1980] Ch 297 at 303 per Megarry V-C. It can therefore be said that, if the solicitor owes no duty to the intended beneficiaries, there is a lacuna in the law which needs to be filled. This I regard as being a point of cardinal importance in the present case...

The question therefore arises whether it is possible to give effect in law to the strong impulse for practical justice which is the fruit of the foregoing considerations. For this to be achieved, I respectfully agree with Nicholls V-C when he said that the court will have to fashion 'an effective remedy for the solicitor's breach of his professional duty to his client' in such a way as to repair the injustice to the disappointed beneficiary (see [1993] 3 All ER 481 at 489, [1993] 3 WLR 730 at 739...

...The tortious solution

I therefore return to the law of tort for a solution to the problem. For the reasons I have already given, an ordinary action in tortious negligence on the lines proposed by Megarry V-C in *Ross v Caunters* [1979] 3 All ER 580, [1980] Ch 297 must, with the greatest respect, be regarded as inappropriate, because it does not meet any of the conceptual problems which have been raised. Furthermore, for the reasons I have previously given, the Hedley Byrne principle cannot, in the absence of special circumstances, give rise on ordinary principles to an assumption of responsibility by the testator's solicitor towards an intended beneficiary. Even so, it seems to me that it is open to your Lordships' House, as in *Linden Gardens Trust Ltd v Lenesta Sludge Disposals Ltd* [1993] 3 All ER 417, [1994] 1 AC 85, to fashion a remedy to fill a lacuna in the law and so prevent the injustice which would otherwise occur on the facts of cases such as the present. In the Lenesta Sludge case, as I have said, the House made available a remedy as a matter of law to solve the problem of transferred loss in the case before them. The present case is, if anything, a fortiori, since the nature of the transaction was such that, if the solicitors were negligent and their negligence did not come to light until after the death of the testator, there would be no remedy for the ensuing loss unless the intended beneficiary could claim. In my opinion, therefore, your Lordships' House should in cases such as these extend to the intended beneficiary a remedy under the Hedley Byrne principle by holding that the assumption of responsibility by the solicitor towards his client should be held in law to extend to the intended beneficiary who (as the solicitor can reasonably foresee) may, as a result of the solicitor's negligence, be deprived of his intended legacy in circumstances in which neither the testator nor his estate will have a remedy against the solicitor. Such liability will not of course arise in cases in which the defect in the will comes to light before the death of the testator, and the testator either leaves the will as it is or otherwise continues to exclude the previously intended beneficiary from the relevant benefit. I only wish to add that, with the benefit of experience during the 15 years in which Ross v Caunters has been regularly applied, we can say with some confidence that a direct remedy by the intended beneficiary against the solicitor appears to create no problems in practice. That is therefore the solution which I would recommend to your Lordships.

...Conclusion

For these reasons I would dismiss the appeal with costs.

Note how Lord Goff stresses the need to achieve practical justice, but bases his decision on a line of cases, stressing equally the need for an incremental approach.

2.3 The Duty of Care in Specific Situations

Having explored the way in which case law has evolved, using *Caparo v Dickman* to accommodate novel duty situations, we will now look in particular at circumstances where, (usually for policy reasons), the duty of care is restricted. This can be seen most clearly where the defendant is a public body (including lawyers, the police and the emergency services) or a rescuer.

2.3.1 Lawyers

It had originally been the case that advocates were immune from suit in respect of the way they conducted a case, or in the way they dealt with matters closely related to it. However, this was changed in the following case, which then brought lawyers into line with other professionals.

Arthur J S Hall & Co (a firm) v Simons; Barratt v Ansell and others (trading as Woolf Seddon (a firm)); Harris v Scholfield Roberts & Hill (a firm) and another [2002] 1 AC 615

Panel: Lord Steyn, Lord Browne-Wilkinson, Lord Hoffmann, Lord Hope of Craighead, Lord Hutton, Lord Hobhouse of Woodborough and Lord Millett

Facts: The three separate cases involved claims for negligence by clients against their former solicitors. The claims were originally struck out on the basis that advocates were immune from claims of negligence. The Court of Appeal, however, held that the claims should not have been struck out, and the solicitors appealed to the House of Lords. The House of Lords was unanimous in the decision to remove immunity from suit regarding negligent civil cases, but there were strong dissenting arguments on the decision to remove immunity from suit regarding negligent conduct of *criminal* cases, namely from Lords Hope, Hutton and Hobhouse.

LORD HOBHOUSE OF WOODBOROUGH

All of your Lordships are in favour of dismissing the appeals; the solicitors are not entitled to the immunity which they claim in the present cases. Your Lordships agree that on any view the immunity claimed in these cases falls outside the recognised immunity afforded to advocates. The Court of Appeal arrived at the right conclusion. Further, all your Lordships would be prepared to arrive at the same conclusion on the basis that there is no longer an adequate justification for continuing to recognise a general immunity for advocates engaged in civil litigation.

But that is the limit of the unanimity. Some of your Lordships would be prepared to declare that the immunity should also no longer be recognised for advocates engaged in criminal litigation. Other of your Lordships, among whom I number myself, would not be prepared to take that step on the present appeals. These cases, unlike *Rondel v Worsley* [1967] 3 All ER 993, [1969] 1 AC 191 (but like *Saif Ali v Sydney Mitchell & Co (a firm) (P, third party)* [1978] 3 All ER 1033, [1980] AC 198), do not concern criminal litigation and your Lordships have not heard any argument upon the distinctions that might, still less, should, be made between civil and criminal litigation beyond the generalised discussion arising from the case of *Hunter v Chief Constable of West Midlands* [1981] 3 All ER 727, [1982] AC 529. That there is room for a difference of opinion on this point cannot be doubted. Further, it is clear that it is not necessary for this difference to be resolved for the purpose of deciding the present appeals. In my judgment, that resolution will have to await a case in which it does arise for decision.

2.3.2 The Police

The courts had previously recognised a distinction between policy matters and operational matters in regards to when the police owe a duty of care in the case of *Rigby v Chief Constable of Northamptonshire* [1985] 1 WLR 1242. The courts were willing to recognise a duty of care in the latter situation, but rarely in the former. In *Hill v Chief Constable of Yorkshire* [1989] AC 53 the mother of a victim of the Yorkshire Ripper sued the police, alleging that the victim was owed a duty of care by the police. The House of Lords held that there was insufficient proximity between the parties, and also that as a general rule that they would not impose a duty upon the police in the investigation of a crime on policy grounds. The case law in this area was examined more recently in the case below.

Brooks v Commissioner of Police for the Metropolis and others [2005] UKHL 24, [2005] 1 WLR 1495

Panel: Lord Bingham of Cornhill, Lord Nicholls of Birkenhead, Lord Steyn, Lord Rodger of Earlsferry and Lord Brown of Eaton-under-Heywood

Facts: The case involved the friend of Stephen Lawrence, who was murdered in a racist attack in 1993. The claimant was also attacked and abused and suffered from his traumatic experience. He brought a claim against the police, containing allegations that their treatment of him and their investigation into the incident had resulted in him suffering from severe post-traumatic stress disorder. The court had to establish, among other things, whether a duty of care was owed by the police in the circumstances alleged.

LORD STEYN

...The claim in negligence alleged that the [Commissioner] and/or those for whom he is vicariously responsible owed [Mr Brooks] ... duties of care, namely to:

1 take reasonable steps to assess whether [Mr Brooks] was a victim of crime and then to accord him reasonably appropriate protection, support, assistance and treatment if he was so assessed ("the first duty");

2 take reasonable steps to afford [Mr Brooks] the protection, assistance and support commonly afforded to a key eye-witness to a serious crime of violence ("the second duty");

3 afford reasonable weight to the account that [Mr Brooks] gave and to act upon it accordingly ("the third duty");

...[18] Counsel for Mr Brooks did not in any way challenge the decision in Hill but submitted that it does not stand in the way of his arguments. His central submission was that the Police owe a duty of care not to cause by positive acts or omissions harm to victims of serious crime, or witnesses to serious crime, with whom they have contact. He said that the first, second and third pleaded duties of care were concrete manifestations of this general duty.

XI. The Case Law

[19] *Hill v Chief Constable* is an important decision. The claim in that case was that the Police had been negligent by failing properly to investigate the crimes committed by the Yorkshire Ripper before the murder of his last victim. The mother of the victim brought the claim. With the express agreement of three Law Lords, and the support of a concurring speech by another, Lord Keith of Kinkel observed [at 59B-59I]:

"There is no question that a police officer, like anyone else, may be liable in tort to a person who is injured as a direct result of his acts or omissions. So he may be liable in damages for assault, unlawful arrest, wrongful imprisonment and malicious prosecution, and also for negligence. Instances where liability for negligence has been established are *Knightley v Johns* [1982] 1 WLR 349 and *Rigby v Chief Constable of Northamptonshire* [1985] 1 WLR 1242. Further, a police officer may be guilty of a criminal offence if he wilfully fails to perform a duty which he is bound to perform by common law or by statute: see *R v Dytham* [1979] QB 722, where a constable was convicted of wilful neglect of duty because, being present at the scene of a violent assault resulting in the death of the victim, he had taken no steps to intervene..."

XIII. The Status of Hill

[27] Since the decision in Hill there have been developments which affect the reasoning of that decision in part. In Hill the House relied on the barrister's immunity enunciated in *Rondel v Worsley* [1969] 1 AC 191, [1967] 3 All ER 993.

That immunity no longer exists: *Arthur J S Hall & Co (A Firm) v Simons* [2002] 1 AC 615, [2000] 3 All ER 673. More fundamentally since the decision of the European Court of Human Rights in *Z and others v United Kingdom* 34 EHRR 97, para 100, it would be best for the principle in *Hill* to be reformulated in terms of the absence of a duty of care rather than a blanket immunity.

[28] With hindsight not every observation in *Hill* can now be supported. Lord Keith of Kinkel observed that "From time to time [the police] make mistakes in the exercise of that function, but it is not to be doubted that they apply their best endeavours to the performance of it": 63D. Nowadays, a more sceptical approach to the carrying out of all public functions is necessary....

[30] But the core principle of *Hill* has remained unchallenged in our domestic jurisprudence and in European jurisprudence for many years. If a case such as the Yorkshire Ripper case, which was before the House in *Hill*, arose for decision today I have no doubt that it would be decided in the same way. It is, of course, desirable that police officers should treat victims and witnesses properly and with respect: compare the Police Conduct regs 2004 (No. 645). But to convert that ethical value into general legal duties of care on the police towards victims and witnesses would be going too far. The prime function of the police is the preservation of the Queen's peace. The police must concentrate on preventing the commission of crime; protecting life and property; and apprehending criminals and preserving evidence...A retreat from the principle in *Hill* would have detrimental effects for law enforcement. Whilst focusing on investigating crime, and the arrest of suspects, police officers would in practice be required to ensure that in every contact with a potential witness or a potential victim time and resources were deployed to avoid the risk of causing harm or offence. Such legal duties would tend to inhibit a robust approach in assessing a person as a possible suspect, witness or victim. By placing general duties of care on the police to victims and witnesses the police's ability to perform their public functions in the interests of the community, fearlessly and with despatch, would be impeded. It would, as was recognised in *Hill*, be bound to lead to an unduly defensive approach in combating crime.

...

[36] I would allow the appeal of the Commissioner.

Appeal allowed.

2.3.3 Emergency Services

The treatment of the fire brigade can be seen from the decision where the three cases below were heard in the Court of Appeal.

Capital and Counties plc v Hampshire County Council and others; Digital Equipment Co Ltd v Hampshire County Council and others; John Munroe (Acrylics) Ltd v London Fire and Civil Defence Authority and others; Church of Jesus Christ of Latter Day Saints (Great Britain) v West Yorkshire Fire and Civil Defence Authority [1997] QB 1004

Panel: Stuart-Smith, Potter and Judge LJJ

Facts: These were three separate cases brought by the owners/occupiers of premises, alleging negligence on the part of the fire brigade. In the first one, a fire-fighter, while fighting a fire, had ordered that a sprinkler system be turned off. In the second case it was alleged that the fire brigade had left the scene of the fire before the fire was fully extinguished. In the third case, the fire was exacerbated due to the fact that the fire brigade had failed to ensure that there was an adequate water supply to the scene of the fire. The court had to decide, among other things, whether a fire brigade owed a duty of care to the owner/occupier of premises.

The Court of Appeal held that although generally the fire brigade is under no duty to respond to calls or extinguish a fire, a duty was owed in the first case, where the actions of the fire brigade had positively exacerbated the situation, but no duty could arise from an omission to act.

LORD JUSTICE STUART-SMITH

...In our judgment the fire brigade are not under a common law duty to answer the call for help and are not under a duty to take care to do so. If therefore they fail to turn up or fail to turn up in time because they have carelessly misunderstood the message, got lost on the way or run into a tree, they are not liable.

Does the fire brigade owe a duty of care to the owner of property on fire, or anyone else to whom the fire may spread, once they have arrived at the fire ground and started to fight the fire?

...[W]here the rescue/protective service itself by negligence creates the danger which caused the plaintiff's injury there is no doubt in our judgment the plaintiff can recover. There are many examples of this. In *Rigby v Chief Constable of Northamptonshire* [1985] 2 All ER 985, [1985] 1 WLR 1242 the plaintiff's gun shop was at risk from a lunatic. The police came to deal with the situation; they fired a CS canister of gas into the shop, though it caused a high risk of fire, without ensuring that the fire engine which had previously been available was there to put out any fire that resulted. In *Knightley v Johns* [1982] 1 All ER 851, [1982] 1 WLR 349 in the course of traffic control following an accident two police constables were instructed to take a course which involve them riding against the traffic flow round a blind bend causing a collision in which the plaintiff was injured. In *Home Office v Dorset Yacht Co Ltd* [1970] 2 All ER 294, [1970] AC 1004 the defendant's prison officers had brought the borstal boys who had a known propensity to escape into the locality where the yachts were moored and so had created a potential situation of danger for the owners of those yachts, in which they failed to exercise proper supervision over the boys...

These are all cases, however, where a new or different danger has been created from that which the police were seeking to guard against, except perhaps in Alcock. A comparable situation would be if, on arrival at the scene of a fire, the fire engine was negligently driven into the owner's car parked in the street. But it seems to us that there is no difference in principle if, by some positive negligent act, the rescuer/protective service substantially increases the risk; he is thereby creating a fresh danger, albeit of the same kind or of the same nature, namely fire. The judge held that at the time the sprinkler systems were turned off, the fire was being contained, but that once they were turned off it rapidly went out of control, spreading to blocks B and C which had been deprived of their own sprinkler protection.

...In our judgment, a fire brigade does not enter into a sufficiently proximate relationship with the owner or occupier of premises to come under a duty of care merely by attending at the fire ground and fighting the fire; this is so, even though the senior officer actually assumes control of the fire-fighting operation.

Kent v Griffiths and Others [2001] QB 36

Panel: Lord Woolf MR, Aldous and Laws LJJ

Facts: The claimant was a pregnant woman who suffered an asthma attack while at home. A doctor attended and called for an ambulance using the emergency 999 service. They then waited for the ambulance, instead of driving to hospital in her husband's car. The ambulance took 40 minutes to arrive during which time the claimant had suffered a respiratory arrest. She subsequently brought an action for negligence against the ambulance service. The ambulance service appealed against the finding of Turner J that a duty was owed to the claimant. The ambulance service relied on cases which showed that the police and fire service did not owe a duty when answering 999 calls.

The Court of Appeal held that in certain circumstances an ambulance could owe a duty of care to the person who made the 999 call, if it accepted the call and then failed to arrive within a reasonable time due to negligence.

LORD WOOLF MR

...4. The claimant is an asthmatic. On 16 February 1991 she suffered an asthma attack. The first defendant attended at her home. At 1625 the first defendant telephoned the LAS, gave the claimant's name, address and age and indicated that she was suffering from bronchial asthma and asked for an ambulance to take her 'immediately please' to casualty where she was expected. The control replied 'okay doctor'. By 1638 the ambulance had not arrived so the claimant's husband made a second call. The LAS's response was 'Yes. They are well on their way to you ... give them another 7 or 8 minutes'. At 1654 the first defendant made a second call as the ambulance had still not arrived. The response was 'Well it should be a couple of minutes'. The ambulance did not arrive, as the judge found, until 1705. The claimant arrived at the hospital at 1717.

5. The record prepared by a member of the ambulance crew indicated that the time of arrival at the claimant's home was not 1705 but 1647. The judge found that there had been contemporary falsification of the records by the member of the ambulance crew. He considered that he had not been given any satisfactory explanation for the ambulance taking 34 minutes to travel 6.5 miles from its base to the claimant's home. The judge was satisfied that the crew member had 'withheld the true reason, whatever it might have been, why it took so long for the ambulance to reach the claimant's house'. The crew member 'knew full well just how critical was going to be the record which he made' of the time of arrival. In the absence of any reasonable excuse for the delay, the judge was 'driven to conclude that the delay was culpable'. The ambulance did not reach the claimant's home within a reasonable time. It could and should have arrived at the claimant's home at least 14 minutes sooner than it did. If it had arrived in a reasonable time, as it should have done, there was a high probability that the respiratory arrest, from which the claimant suffered, would have been averted. The judge also made criticisms as to the information communicated by the LAS to the ambulance crew, which would also amount to carelessness, but he did not base his decision on this additional finding.

...The ambulance service is part of the health service. Its care functions include transporting patients to and from hospital when the use of an ambulance for this purpose is desirable. It is therefore appropriate to regard the LAS as providing services of the category provided by hospitals and not as providing services equivalent to those rendered by the police or the fire service. Situations could arise where there is a conflict between the interests of a particular individual and the public at large. But in the case of the ambulance service in this particular case, the only member of the public who could be adversely affected was the claimant. It was the claimant alone for whom the ambulance had been called.

...An important feature of this case is that there is no question of an ambulance not being available or of a conflict in priorities. Again I recognise that where what is being attacked is the allocation of resources, whether in the provision of sufficient ambulances or sufficient drivers or attendants, different considerations could apply. There then could be issues which are not suited for resolution by the courts. However, once there are available, both in the form of an ambulance and in the form of manpower, the resources to provide an ambulance on which there are no alternative demands, the ambulance service would be acting perversely 'in circumstances such as arose in this case', if it did not make those resources available. Having decided to provide an ambulance an explanation is required to justify a failure to attend within reasonable time.

49. So in my judgment here. The fact that it was a person who foreseeably would suffer further injuries by a delay in providing an ambulance, when there was no reason why it should not be provided, is important in establishing the necessary proximity and thus duty of care in this case. In other words, as there were no circumstances which made it unfair or unreasonable or unjust that liability should exist, there is no reason

 Decipher

Note the important caveat being inserted here – the ambulance service would still be free to prioritise calls.

why there should not be liability if the arrival of the ambulance was delayed for no good reason. The acceptance of the call in this case established the duty of care. On the findings of the judge it was delay which caused the further injuries. If wrong information had not been given about the arrival of the ambulance, other means of transport could have been used.

53. I would dismiss this appeal.

2.3.4 Omissions

Generally it can be said there is no positive duty to act, (in other words, there is no liability for an omission). However, there are exceptions to this general rule. This rule and its exceptions are shown clearly in the case below:

Smith and Others v Littlewoods Organisation Ltd (Chief Constable, Fife Constabulary, third party) and conjoined appeal [1987] AC 241

Panel: Lord Keith of Kinkel, Lord Brandon of Oakbrook, Lord Griffiths, Lord Mackay of Clashfern and Lord Goff of Chieveley

Facts: Littlewoods owned a disused cinema. The cinema was broken into and a fire started. The question arose as to whether Littlewoods could be liable for an omission to act and failing to prevent the fire.

LORD GOFF OF CHIEVELEY

...Why does the law not recognise a general duty of care to prevent others from suffering loss or damage caused by the deliberate wrongdoing of third parties? The fundamental reason is that the common law does not impose liability for what are called pure omissions...

That there are special circumstances in which a defender may be held responsible in law for injuries suffered by the pursuer through a third party's deliberate wrongdoing is not in doubt. For example, a duty of care may arise from a relationship between the parties which gives rise to an imposition or assumption of responsibility on or by the defender, as in *Stansbie v Troman* [1948] 1 All ER 599, [1948] 2 KB 48, where such responsibility was held to arise from a contract. In that case a decorator, left alone on the premises by the householder's wife, was held liable when he went out leaving the door on the latch and a thief entered the house and stole property. Such responsibility might well be held to exist in other cases where there is no contract, as for example where a person left alone in a house has entered as a licensee of the occupier. Again, the defender may be vicariously liable for the third party's act; or he may be held liable as an occupier to a visitor on his land. Again, as appears from the dictum of Dixon J in *Smith v Leurs* (1945) 70 CLR 256 at 262, a duty may arise from a special relationship between the defender and the third party, by virtue of which the defender is responsible for controlling the third party: see, for example, *Home Office v Dorset Yacht Co Ltd.* More pertinently, in a case between adjoining occupiers of land, there may be liability in nuisance if one occupier causes or permits persons to gather on his land, and they impair his neighbour's enjoyment of his land. Indeed, even if such persons come onto his land as trespassers, the occupier may, if they constitute a nuisance, be under an affirmative duty to abate the nuisance. As I pointed out in *P Perl (Exporters) Ltd v Camden London BC* [1983] 3 All ER 161 at 172, [1984] QB 342 at 359, there may well be other cases.

These are all special cases. But there is a more general circumstance in which a defender may be held liable in negligence to the pursuer, although the immediate cause of the damage suffered by the pursuer is the deliberate wrongdoing of another. This may occur where the defender negligently causes or permits to be created a source of danger, and it is reasonably foreseeable that third parties may interfere with it and, sparking off the danger, thereby cause damage to persons in the position of the pursuer. The classic example of such a case is, perhaps, *Haynes v Harwood* [1935] 1 KB 146, [1934] All ER Rep 103, where the defendant's carter left a horse-drawn van unattended in a crowded street and the horses bolted when a boy threw a stone at them. A police officer who suffered injury in stopping the horses before they injured a woman and children was held to be entitled to recover damages from the defendant. There, of course, the defendant's servant had created a source of danger by leaving his horses unattended in a busy street. Many different things might have caused them to bolt, a sudden noise or movement, for example, or, as happened, the deliberate action of a mischievous boy. But all such events were examples of the very sort of thing which the defendant's servant ought reasonably to have foreseen and to have guarded against by taking appropriate precautions. In such a case, Lord Sumner's dictum in *Weld-Blundell v Stephens* [1920] AC 956 at 986, [1920] All ER Rep 32 at 47 can have no application to exclude liability.

Haynes v Harwood was a case concerned with the creation of a source of danger in a public place. We are concerned in the present case with an allegation that the defenders should be held liable for the consequences of deliberate wrongdoing by others who were trespassers on the defenders' property. In such a case it may be said that the defenders are entitled to use their property as their own and so should not be held liable if, for example, trespassers interfere with dangerous things on their land. But this is, I consider, too sweeping a proposition. It is well established that an occupier of land may be liable to a trespasser who has suffered injury on his land; though in *British Rlys Board v Herrington* [1972] 1 All ER 749, [1972] AC 877, in which the nature and scope of such liability was reconsidered by your Lordships' House, the standard of care so imposed on occupiers was drawn narrowly so as to take proper account of the rights of occupiers to enjoy the use of their land. It is, in my opinion, consistent with the existence of such liability that an occupier who negligently causes or permits a source of danger to be created on his land, and can reasonably foresee that third parties may trespass on his land and, interfering with the source of danger, may spark it off, thereby causing damage to the person or property of those in the vicinity, should be held liable to such a person for damage so caused to him. It is useful to take the example of a fire hazard, not only because that is the relevant hazard which is alleged to have existed in the present case, but also because of the intrinsically dangerous nature of fire hazards as regards neighbouring property. Let me give an example of circumstances in which an occupier of land might be held liable for damage so caused. Suppose that a person is deputed to buy a substantial quantity of fireworks for a village fireworks display on Guy Fawkes night. He stores them, as usual, in an unlocked garden shed abutting onto a neighbouring house. It is well known that he does this. Mischievous boys from the village enter as trespassers and, playing with the fireworks, cause a serious fire which spreads to and burns down the neighbouring house. Liability might well be imposed in such a case; for, having regard to the dangerous and tempting nature of fireworks, interference by naughty children was the very thing which, in the circumstances, the purchaser of the fireworks ought to have guarded against.

But liability should only be imposed under this principle in cases where the defender has negligently caused or permitted the creation of a source of danger on his land, and where it is foreseeable that third parties may trespass on his land and spark it off, thereby damaging the pursuer or his property. Moreover, it is not to be forgotten that, in ordinary households in this country, there are nowadays many things which might be described as possible sources of fire if interfered with by third parties, ranging from matches and firelighters to electric irons and gas cookers and even oil-fired central heating systems. These are commonplaces of modern life; and it would be quite wrong if householders were to be held liable in negligence for acting in a socially acceptable manner. No doubt the question whether liability should be imposed on defenders in a case where a source of danger on his land has been sparked off by the deliberate wrongdoing of a third party is a question to be decided on the facts of each case, and it would, I think, be wrong for your Lordships' House to anticipate the manner in which the law may develop; but I cannot help thinking that cases where liability will be so imposed are likely to be very rare.

There is another basis on which a defender may be held liable for damage to neighbouring property caused by a fire started on his (the defender's) property by the deliberate wrongdoing of a third party. This arises where he has knowledge or means of knowledge that a third party has created or is creating a risk of fire, or indeed has started a fire, on his premises, and then fails to take such steps as are reasonably open to him (in the limited sense explained by Lord Wilberforce in *Goldman v Hargrave* [1966] 2 All ER 989 at 995–996, [1967] 1 AC 645 at 663–664) to prevent any such fire from damaging neighbouring property. If, for example, an occupier of property has knowledge, or means of knowledge, that intruders are in the habit of trespassing on his property and starting fires there, thereby creating a risk that fire may spread to and damage neighbouring property, a duty to take reasonable steps to prevent such damage may be held to fall on him.

...Turning to the facts of the present case, I cannot see that the defenders should be held liable... First, I do not consider that the empty cinema could properly be described as an unusual danger in the nature of a fire hazard...

...Nor can I see that the defenders should be held liable for having failed to take reasonable steps to abate a fire risk created by third parties on their property without their fault. If there was any such fire risk, they had no means of knowing that it existed. If anybody (for example, the police) considered that there was such a risk they could and should have contacted the defenders (a well-known public company, whose particulars were given on a notice outside the cinema) by telephone to warn them of the situation; but they did not do so. But in any event, on the evidence, the existence of such a risk was not established.

...I would dismiss these appeals.

Further Reading

Mark Lunney and Ken Olliphant, *Tort Law Text and Materials: A Fundamental Restatement*, (3rd edition) Oxford University Press 2008, Chapter 3

3

Duty of Care II – Psychiatric Injury ('Nervous Shock')

Topic List

Introduction

This chapter will explore a type of loss for which claimants may seek to claim in a negligence action, namely psychiatric damage, or 'nervous shock'. Cases in this area tend to focus on whether a duty of care ought to be owed by defendant to claimant. However, it should be noted that the claim does not end at the duty stage. A claimant, having successfully demonstrated that they ought to be owed a duty by the defendant for their loss, would still need to satisfy the other elements of a negligence claim, for example, breach, causation, etc). The courts have always been reluctant to allow an open-ended duty of care generally, and this is one such area where claims are heavily restricted, for policy reasons, for example, to prevent floodgates opening and to ensure unmeritorious claims are kept away from trial. Therefore, no successful claims were brought for nervous shock until the early twentieth century.

3.1 Psychiatric Injury 'Nervous shock'

Dulieu v White & Sons [1901] 2 KB 669

Panel: Kennedy and Phillimore JJ

Facts: Mrs Dulieu was a barmaid in Bethnal Green. She working behind the bar when a coach and horses, driven by an employee of White & Sons, ploughed into the building. Mrs Dulieu was pregnant at the time, and although the coach did not hit her, the shock of the near miss caused her to miscarry. Mrs Dulieu sued for her injury. White & Sons' defence was that her nervous shock was too remote for her to claim. The court disagreed and held that a claim in negligence, for damage caused by nervous shock, could succeed.

> **MR JUSTICE PHILLIMORE**
>
> I think there may be cases in which A. owes a duty to B. not to inflict a mental shock on him or her, and that in such a case, if A. does inflict such a shock upon B.—as by terrifying B.—and physical damage thereby ensues, B. may have an action for the physical damage, though the medium through which it has been inflicted is the mind.

Hambrook v Stokes Brothers [1925] 1 KB 141

Panel: Bankes, Atkin and Sargant LJJ

Facts: Mrs Hambrook was walking her three children to school. As they rounded a bend, Mrs Hambrook left them to continue on their own and she started to return home. While she was on her way back, she saw and heard a lorry owned by Stokes Brothers career out of control down Dover Street, crashing into a house before it reached her. She knew that her children may have been struck by the lorry, as the vehicle was large and the street narrow. She went back to the scene and asked if anyone was injured. She was told a little girl with glasses - her youngest daughter - had been taken away. Mrs Hambrook immediately went to the hospital where she saw her daughter had been seriously injured.

Like Mrs Dulieu, Mrs Hambrook was pregnant, and like Mrs Dulieu, the shock of the incident and injury caused Mrs Hambrook to miscarry. Tragically, complications from Mrs Hambrook's injury resulted in more serious haemorrhaging, from which Mrs Hambrook died. Mr Hambrook therefore brought a claim against Stokes Brothers for negligently causing the death of his wife. Under the law at the time he could only succeed if he showed that Mrs Hambrook had suffered a nervous shock as a result of Stokes Brothers' negligence. Stokes Brothers argued that *Dulieu* only allowed a claim for nervous shock when the claimant was concerned for their own personal safety, rather than anyone else's safety. The court disagreed.

LORD JUSTICE BANKES

Upon the authorities as they stand, the defendant ought to have anticipated that if his lorry ran away down this narrow street, it might terrify some woman to such an extent, through fear of some immediate bodily injury to herself, that she would receive such a mental shock as would injure her health. Can any real distinction be drawn from the point of view of what the defendant ought to have anticipated and what, therefore, his duty was, between that case and the case of a woman whose fear is for her child, and not for herself? Take a case in point as a test. Assume two mothers crossing this street at the same time when this lorry comes thundering down, each holding a small child by the hand. One mother is courageous and devoted to her child. She is terrified, but thinks only of the damage to the child, and not at all about herself. The other woman is timid and lacking in the motherly instinct. She also is terrified, but thinks only of the damage to herself and not at all about her child. The health of both mothers is seriously affected by the mental shock occasioned by the fright. Can any real distinction be drawn between the two cases? Will the law recognize a cause of action in the case of the less deserving mother, and none in the case of the more deserving one?

Does the law say that the defendant ought reasonably to have anticipated the non-natural feeling of the timid mother, and not the natural feeling of the courageous mother? I think not. In my opinion the step which the Court is asked to take, under the circumstances of the present case, necessarily follows from an acceptance of the decision in *Dulieu v. White & Sons...* .

The court found that a claim for damage caused by nervous shock could be brought by someone in fear of their own physical safety (later called a primary victim), and by someone in fear of someone else's physical safety (later called a secondary victim), so long as there was a sufficient link between the claimant and the "victim" of the negligence.

The court, however, had not found that a claim could be brought by someone who was not closely linked to the victim. Indeed this question was specifically left open.

LORD JUSTICE ATKIN

I should accept the view that the duty extended to the duty to take care to avoid threatening personal injury to a child in such circumstances as to cause damage by shock to a parent or guardian then present, and that the duty was owned to the parent or guardian; but I confess that upon this view of the case I should find it difficult to explain why the duty was confined to the case of parent or guardian and child, and did not extend to other relations of life also involving intimate associations; and why it did not eventually extend to bystanders.

The question remained open until 1943.

Bourhill v Young [1943] AC 92

Panel: Lord Thankerton, Lord Russell of Killowen, Lord Macmillan, Lord Wright and Lord Porter

Facts: Mrs Bourhill had just got off a tram and was picking up her basket when she heard a crash. A motorcyclist - John Young - had sped past and collided with a car. Mr Young was killed; Mrs Bourhill went to see what had happened and the sight of blood on the road caused her to suffer a nervous shock. Like Mrs Dulieu and Mrs Hambrook, Mrs Bourhill too was pregnant, and the shock caused her to miscarry. She sued Mr Young's estate for his causing her nervous shock through his negligent riding. Mrs Bourhill did not see the crash and was in no danger of physical harm. She did not know Mr Young so could not, as a matter of law, be concerned for his safety. Therefore, she could only succeed if a claimant could show the nervous shock was caused by worry for the safety of an unknown third party.

The court dismissed her claim. It held that there was no general duty of care owed to bystanders.

LORD PORTER

... The duty is not to the world at large. It must be tested by asking with reference to each several complainant: Was a duty owed to him or her? If no one of them was in such a position that direct physical injury could reasonably be anticipated to them or their relations or friends normally I think no duty would be owed, and if, in addition, no shock was reasonably to be anticipated to them as a result of the defender's negligence, the defender might, indeed, be guilty of actionable negligence to others but not of negligence towards them. In the present case the appellant was never herself in any bodily danger nor reasonably in fear of danger either for herself or others. She was merely a person who, as a result of the action, was emotionally disturbed and rendered physically ill by that emotional disturbance. The question whether emotional disturbance or shock, which a defender ought reasonably to have anticipated as likely to follow from his reckless driving, can ever form the basis of a claim is not in issue. It is not every emotional disturbance or every shock which should have been foreseen. The driver of a car or vehicle, even though careless, is entitled to assume that the ordinary frequenter of the streets has sufficient fortitude to endure such incidents as may from time to time be expected to occur in them, including the noise of a collision and the sight of injury to others, and is not to be considered negligent towards one who does not possess the customary phlegm.]

 Alert

The court did not entirely dismiss the chances of a bystander, but made it clear that only one with "customary phlegm" who would reasonably have been expected to suffer nervous shock would be able to succeed. As subsequent case law shows, this test is a very high one to meet.

The law on nervous shock was becoming clear. A claimant could bring a claim if they witnessed a sudden incident that caused them to fear either for their own safety, or for the safety of someone with whom they had a close relationship. In two medical negligence cases, the court clarified the suddenness further; in *North Glamorgan NHS Trust v Walters* [2002] EWCA Civ 1792, [2002] PIQR P16 it was held that a 36 hour deterioration in the health of a baby was sufficiently short to be sudden, whereas in *Sion v Hampstead Health Authority* [1994] 5 Med LR 170 a two-week deterioration in the health of a boy was held to be too long to be a single event.

The next logical developments after *Bourhill* concerned claimants who had not witnessed the incident itself, but dealt with its aftermath.

Chadwick v British Railways Board [1967] 1 WLR 912

Panel: Waller J

Facts: A train crash at Lewisham killed 90 people. Mr Chadwick, a local resident, went to the scene to see if he could help. He remained on site for 14 hours, taking food, water and medicine to those trapped in the wreckage. Although Mr Chadwick was not physically harmed, the sights and sounds of those dead and injured played upon Mr Chadwick's mind and he suffered neurotic anxiety. After his death (which was unconnected with the train crash) his wife brought a claim for damages on his behalf. The court considered that Mr Chadwick was entitled to recover, as there was a danger that the carriages could collapse on him.

MR JUSTICE WALLER

In the present case, the defendants were negligent towards their passengers. As a result, passengers were injured and put in peril. All of that could reasonably have been foreseen. It could also be foreseen that somebody might try to rescue passengers and suffer injury in the process, and in my opinion the defendants owed a duty to Mr. Chadwick, who was within the area of contemplation.

The lack of physical harm was irrelevant.

I do not see any objection in principle to damages being recoverable for shock caused other than by fear for one's own safety or for the safety of one's children. One only too frequently comes across the case of a man with a trivial industrial injury which subsequently produces genuine neurotic symptoms not due to fear but due to other causes. It would seem anomalous if serious mental illness accompanied by a trivial injury would entitle a man to compensation but if there were no trivial injury it would not.

The case confirmed beyond doubt that physical harm as a result of the nervous shock was an unnecessary ingredient. Pure psychological damage was enough to found an action. With legal hindsight, we can see that Mr Chadwick was viewed as a primary victim, and that this was the basis for the duty. In other words, he suffered nervous shock, and was in reasonable fear for his physical safety, although in the event he did not suffer physical injury.

McLoughlin v O'Brian and others [1983] 1 AC 410

Panel: Lord Wilberforce, Lord Edmund-Davies, Lord Russell of Killowen, Lord Scarman and Lord Bridge of Harwich

Facts: Two miles from Mrs McLoughlin's home, her husband and three children were seriously injured in a road accident. An articulated lorry had crashed into their car. A neighbour gave Mrs McLoughlin the news two hours later and took her straight to the hospital. Mrs McLoughlin saw her children screaming in pain and her husband still covered in mud and oil from the accident. She learned that her youngest daughter had been killed outright. The shock of what she had seen and heard resulted in severe depression and she brought a claim. The defendants - two separate lorry drivers and their employers - claimed that she had not witnessed the incident, nor had she come upon the immediate aftermath; there was a two hour gap between the crash and her perception.

LORD WILBERFORCE

... If one continues to follow the process of logical progression, it is hard to see why the present plaintiff also should not succeed. She was not present at the accident, but she came very soon after upon its aftermath. If, from a distance of some 100 yards..., she had found her family by the roadside, she would have come within principle 4 [allowing her to claim for having seen the immediate aftermath] above. Can it make any difference that she comes upon them in an ambulance, or, as here, in a nearby hospital, when, as the evidence shows, they were in the same condition, covered with oil and mud, and distraught with pain? If Mr. Chadwick can recover when, acting in accordance with normal and irresistible human instinct, and indeed moral compulsion, he goes to the scene of an accident, may not a mother recover if, acting under the same motives, she goes to where her family can be found? ... As regards proximity to the accident, it is obvious that this must be close in both time and space. It is, after all, the fact and consequence of the defendant's negligence that must be proved to have caused the "nervous shock." Experience has shown that to insist on direct and immediate sight or hearing would be impractical and unjust and that under what may be called the "aftermath" doctrine one who, from close proximity, comes very soon upon the scene should not be excluded.

 Alert

Therefore the "immediate aftermath" could be extended to two hours after the incident. The court, however, emphasised that Mrs McLoughlin had seen the direct effects on her family. She had experienced the full effects of the incident with her own senses.

The question of whether a claimant could claim for nervous shock as a result of seeing an incident on television was therefore still open. It was answered in the seminal case brought following the Hillsborough disaster. This case is particularly relevant when considering secondary victims, (i.e. a claimant who suffers nervous shock as a result of witnessing a traumatic event which happens to someone else).

Alcock and others v Chief Constable of South Yorkshire Police [1992] 1 AC 310

Panel: Lord Keith of Kinkel, Lord Ackner, Lord Oliver of Aylmerton, Lord Jauncey of Tullichettle and Lord Lowry

Facts: At the FA Cup semi-final between Liverpool and Nottingham Forest, held at the Hillsborough stadium, 96 supporters were crushed to death. They had been standing in a pen behind one of the goals surrounded by tall metal fencing. The overcrowding had been caused by the police directing spectators into the pen, even though it was already filled. The disaster was covered on live television. Although the broadcast did not show any identifiable victim, many people suspected, or knew, that their friends or relatives would have been standing in that location. As a result they suffered nervous shock.

Sixteen claimants brought claims against the police for their shock. The claimants were in different situations: two had been at the ground itself, others had seen it on television, others had heard it on the radio. The court heard all the cases together and dismissed all the claims.

LORD ACKNER

Of course it is common ground that it was clearly foreseeable by the defendant that the scenes at Hillsborough would be broadcast live and that amongst those who would be watching would be parents and spouses and other relatives and friends of those in the pens behind the goal at the Leppings Lane end. However he would also know of the code of ethics which the television authorities televising this event could be expected to follow, namely that they would not show pictures of suffering by recognisable individuals. Had they done so, Mr. Hytner accepted that this would have been a "novus actus" breaking the chain of causation between the defendant's alleged breach of duty and the psychiatric illness. As the defendant was reasonably entitled to expect to be the case, there were no such pictures. Although the television pictures certainly gave rise to feelings of the deepest anxiety and distress, in the circumstances of this case the simultaneous television broadcasts of what occurred cannot be equated with the "sight or hearing of the event or its immediate aftermath". Accordingly shocks sustained by reason of these broadcasts cannot found a claim.

 Alert

LORD KEITH OF KINKELL

In neither of these cases was there any evidence of particularly close ties of love or affection with the brothers or brother-in-law. In my opinion the mere fact of the particular relationship was insufficient to place the plaintiff within the class of persons to whom a duty of care could be owed by the defendant as being foreseeably at risk of psychiatric illness by reason of injury or peril to the individuals concerned. The same is true of other plaintiffs who were not present at the ground and who lost brothers, or in one case a grandson. I would, however, place in the category to members of which risk of psychiatric illness was reasonably foreseeable Mr. and Mrs. Copoc, whose son was killed, and Alexandra Penk, who lost her fiancée. In each of these cases the closest ties of love and affection fall to be presumed from the fact of the particular relationship, and there is no suggestion of anything which might tend to rebut that presumption. ...

LORD ACKNER

The quality of brotherly love is well known to differ widely - from Cain and Abel to David and Jonathan. I assume that Mr. Harrison's relationship with his brothers was not an abnormal one. His claim was not presented upon the basis that there was such a close and intimate relationship between them, as gave rise to that very special bond of affection which would make his shock-induced psychiatric illness reasonably foreseeable by the defendant. Accordingly, the judge did not carry out the requisite close scrutiny of their relationship. Thus there was no evidence to establish the necessary proximity which would make his claim reasonably foreseeable and, subject to the other factors, to which I have referred, a valid one. The other plaintiff who was present at the ground, Robert Alcock, lost a brother-in-law. He was not, in my judgment, reasonably foreseeable as a potential sufferer from shock-induced psychiatric illness, in default of very special facts and none was established.

Lord Ackner went on to state that the secondary victim's perception of the incident must be:

...[A] sudden appreciation by sight or sound of a horrifying event which violently agitated the mind.

Therefore, the court dismissed all the claims, on two different grounds. Firstly, 14 of the claimants were not at the ground. They were too remote in time and place to have experienced the full horror of the event. Secondly, the two claimants who were at the ground did not show they had a close enough relationship with those who had died. The relationships were that of brother and brother-in-law, yet the court would not presume that those relationships were close enough. Lord Ackner held that there was insufficient proximity for those who were not at the ground itself and had only witnessed the event on television.

Therefore, to bring a claim for nervous shock, a claimant needs to perceive the actual incident – or its immediate aftermath – with their own unaided senses. *Alcock* also confirmed that seeing the victim's body nine hours after the incident was insufficiently close in time. We seem, therefore, to have a gap where the claimant has arrived between two and nine hours after the incident within which a claim may be possible.

A secondary victim can only establish a duty of care, then, if:

- they saw the incident, or were involved in the immediate aftermath;
- they have a sufficiently close relationship of love and affection with the primary victim; and
- they suffer a nervous shock from a single event.

There were further claims brought arising from the Hillsborough disaster. Although the tragedy had been caused by the negligence of the police, the individual officers dealing with the disaster were not to blame; the fault lay at an operational level. Several officers had been mentally scarred by having to deal with 95 deaths at the ground and one victim who died after several years in a coma.

The police therefore brought claims against their employer.

White v Chief Constable of South Yorkshire [1999] 2 AC 455

Panel: Lord Browne-Wilkinson, Lord Griffiths, Lord Goff of Chieveley, Lord Steyn and Lord Hoffmann

Facts: Various officers who had dealt with the aftermath of the Hillsborough disaster claimed against their employer for negligence. All were on duty at the stadium but none were in any personal danger. All suffered serious psychological harm. The claimants claimed that *Chadwick* showed there was a general principle that "rescuers" should be treated as primary victims. Therefore it was foreseeable that they would suffer psychiatric harm as a result of dealing with the tragedy.

LORD STEYN

...I too would accept that the *Chadwick* case was correctly decided. But it is not authority for the proposition that a person who never exposed himself to any personal danger and never thought that he was in personal danger can recover pure psychiatric injury as a rescuer. In order to recover compensation for pure psychiatric harm as rescuer it is not necessary to establish that his psychiatric condition was caused by the perception of personal danger. And Waller J. rightly so held. But in order to contain the concept of rescuer in reasonable bounds for the purposes of the recovery of compensation for pure psychiatric harm the plaintiff must at least satisfy the threshold requirement that he objectively exposed himself to danger or reasonably believed that he was doing so. Without such limitation one would have the unedifying spectacle that, while bereaved relatives are not allowed to recover as in the Alcock case, ghoulishly curious spectators, who assisted in some peripheral way in the aftermath of a disaster, might recover.

 Alert

LORD HOFFMANN

There does not seem to me to be any logical reason why the normal treatment of rescuers on the issues of foreseeability and causation should lead to the conclusion that, for the purpose of liability for psychiatric injury, they should be given special treatment as primary victims when they were not within the range of foreseeable physical injury and their psychiatric injury was caused by witnessing or participating in the aftermath of accidents which caused death or injury to others. ...

 Alert

The court, by a majority of 4-1, rejected the claims. Lord Steyn held that *Chadwick* did not outline a general rescue principle, but confirmed that a claimant had to be in personal danger to make a claim.

This confirmed that there was no general rescue principle for those who had suffered nervous shock as a result of assisting at an accident. That is not to say that rescuers can never succeed; if they are in danger of personal injury, such as in *Chadwick*, or the later case of *Cullin v London Fire and Civil Defence Authority* [1999] PIQR P314 (where a fireman was able to bring a claim for attending a disaster where two of his colleagues died, on the basis that he was within the danger area), a claim is possible on conventional *Dulieu* lines.

The court has been careful to confirm that the categories of negligence are not closed. It is possible that a claimant may be able to show a duty of care is owed to them for other reasons. Two cases - *Dooley v Cammell Laird* [1951] 1 Lloyd's Rep 271 and *W v Essex CC* [2001] 2 AC 692 - suggest that claimants who are led to believe that they are to blame for causing death or serious injury, and as a result of which suffer nervous shock at the consequences of their actions, are able to bring a claim against the actual negligent party. Nevertheless, it is clear that a primary victim must be in the range of physical harm in order to bring a claim. Lord Steyn's dicta in *Alcock* suggested that it was possible for a claimant to bring a claim if they "reasonably believed" that they were in physical danger. However, a subsequent decision has cast doubt on that proposition.

McFarlane v E.E. Caledonia Ltd [1994] 2 All ER 1

Panel: Ralph Gibson, Stuart-Smith and McCowan LJJ

Facts: Mr McFarlane worked on oil rigs and was on board a ship near the Piper Alpha rig when a fire broke out on the rig. The ship went to offer assistance. Mr McFarlane was not involved in the rescue, and the ship was never in actual physical danger, but Mr McFarlane suffered psychiatric harm as a result of the experience.

LORD JUSTICE STUART-SMITH

[The ship] never was in actual danger. This was [the ship's captain]'s appreciation at the time and it is borne out by events. She sustained no damage, save minimal paint blistering on the crane which projected nearest the platform; no debris fell on her; although there was one incident when a fireball may have approached fairly near, her heat shield was never turned to steam. No one sustained any physical injury, and there is no evidence that anyone other than the plaintiff sustained psychiatric injury. In my judgment it cannot be said that the defendants ought reasonably to have foreseen that the plaintiff or other non-essential personnel on board her would suffer such injury.

[The ship] was a well found vessel, equipped with a heat shield, and under the control of an experienced and competent captain. If indeed the plaintiff had felt himself to be in any danger, he could have taken refuge in or behind the helicopter hangar, which was where non-essential personnel were required to muster. The Judge thought it was entirely understandable that the plaintiff and other non-essential personnel should wish to see what was happening on *Piper Alpha*. I agree with this. What I do not agree with, is that someone who as in truth in fear of his life from spread of the fire and falling debris should not take shelter. Only someone who is rooted to the spot through fear would be unable to do so. The plaintiff never suggested that; he accepted that he had moved about quite freely and could have taken shelter had he wished.

This principle was approved in *Hegarty v EE Caledonia Ltd* [1997] 2 Lloyd's Rep 259 arising out of the same facts.

Consequently, the test as to whether someone is in physical danger is *objective*; if a claimant, as a matter of fact, is *not* in physical danger, they cannot bring a claim. The claimant's only recourse is to persuade the court that a bystander of customary phlegm would be affected by such an incident, which as we see above is a very high barrier to a claim.

However, if a claimant can cross the threshold of danger and bring a claim on the basis that physical injury were foreseeable, the claimant can succeed in claiming for all nervous shock, whether foreseeable or not. In other words, you take your primary victim as you find them.

Page v Smith [1996] AC 155

Panel: Lord Keith of Kinkel, Lord Ackner, Lord Jauncey of Tullichettle, Lord Browne-Wilkinson and Lord Lloyd of Berwick

Facts: Mr Smith was driving along a road when he suddenly cut across the traffic to turn into a side road. Mr Page, driving on the other side of the road, was unable to avoid Mr Smith's car and there was a collision. It was of a minor nature, and Mr Page was not physically injured. However, the shock caused Mr Page to suffer a recurrence of chronic fatigue syndrome, which had lain dormant in him for some time. As a direct result of this outbreak, Mr Page was unable to work again and he sued Mr Smith for loss of wages. The issue for the court was whether Mr Page should be able to claim for the full extent of his psychiatric injury even though it was not foreseeable.

LORD LLOYD OF BERWICK

In the case of physical injury ... [t]he negligent defendant, or more usually his insurer, takes his victim as he finds him. The same should apply in the case of psychiatric injury. There is no difference in principle, as Geoffrey Lane J. pointed out in *Malcolm v Broadhurst* [1970] 3 All ER 508, between an eggshell skull and an eggshell personality. Since the number of potential claimants is limited by the nature of the case, there is no need to impose any further limit by reference to a person of ordinary phlegm. Nor can I see any justification for doing so. ... it was enough to ask whether the defendant should have reasonably foreseen that the plaintiff might suffer physical injury as a result of the defendant's negligence, so as to bring him within the range of the defendant's duty of care. It was unnecessary to ask, as a separate question, whether the defendant should reasonably have foreseen injury by shock; and it is irrelevant that the plaintiff did not, in fact, suffer any external physical injury.

 Alert

For secondary victims, the foreseeability of physical injury is, of course, irrelevant; if such an injury is foreseeable, the claimant becomes a primary victim.

At the heart of any claim for nervous shock is the nature of the damage itself. It must be recognised psychiatric injury; nothing less will do. In the following case, the court allowed the claim on the basis that the damage went beyond 'mere' grief.

Vernon v Bosley (No. 1) [1997] 1 All ER 577

Panel: Stuart-Smith, Evans and Thorpe LJJ

Facts: Ms Bosley was the nanny to Mr and Mrs Vernon's children and crashed while driving with them as passengers. Her car slid down a slope into a river and although she escaped, the children were trapped. The Vernons were working nearby and the police called them to the scene. Despite their best efforts, the children drowned. The shock of seeing their bodies being rescued caused Mr Vernon to fall into a deep depression and he was unable to work again. He sued Ms Bosley for loss of earnings. Ms Bosley alleged that Mr Vernon was not of "customary phlegm"; naturally he suffered grief as a result of the deaths of his children, but that was a normal human emotion, for which a claim was impossible. Therefore, Mr Vernon's pathological illness demonstrated that he did not have sufficient mental backbone to be able to bring a claim. The court dismissed this argument.

LORD JUSTICE EVANS

In principle, damages are recoverable for injury caused partly by the negligence of the defendant, even if there was another cause and the negligence was only a contributory cause: *Bonnington Castings v. Wardlaw* [1956] AC 613 (this leads to the proposition that the plaintiff is entitled to recover damages for an injury caused *or contributed to* by the negligence of the defendant, provided that it was a "substantial" or "significant" contributory cause). Mental illness, as distinct from grief and other emotional sufferings resulting from bereavement, is a kind of injury which is recognised by the law. Therefore, I would hold that damages are recoverable for mental illness caused or at least contributed to by actionable negligence of the defendant, *i.e.* in breach of a duty of care, notwithstanding that the illness may also be regarded as a pathological consequence of the bereavement which the plaintiff, where the primary victim was killed, must inevitably have suffered.

Therefore, so long as some significant mental illness is foreseeable, the claimant can claim for all losses caused by all mental illness.

Further Reading

Dyer, Simon: 'Negligence: no sticks, no stones', PILJ. 2001, 1 (Nov) 5-7

Teff, Harvey: 'Liability for negligently inflicted psychiatric harm: justifications and boundaries', CLJ. 1998 57(1) 91 – 122

4

Duty of Care III – Pure Economic Loss and Negligent Misstatement

Topic List

Introduction

In the law of tort, losses fit into one of three categories: physical damage (to persons or property), consequential economic loss and pure economic loss. The general rule is that no duty will be owed where the loss suffered is held to be pure economic loss. Obvious policy reasons underpin this rationale, for example, a fear of crushing liability on the defendant. Also, claims for pure economic loss can often be dealt with within the realm of contract law (an area outside the scope of this chapter).

If the claimant has suffered no physical damage to his property or person then the loss will ordinarily be regarded as pure economic loss and therefore not be recoverable. Similarly, where the claimant suffers loss as a result of damage to property in which they have no proprietary interest, then the loss will also be considered pure economic loss as can be seen in the following case.

Weller & Co. and Another v Foot and Mouth Disease Research Institute. [1966] 1 QB 569

Panel: Widgery J

Facts: The defendants were the occupiers of premises upon which they carried out experimental work in connection with foot and mouth disease. Nearby cattle became infected with the disease and, as a result, two markets in the area were closed. During the closure, the plaintiffs were unable to auction cattle at those markets and they brought claims against the defendants for damages for loss of business.

MR JUSTICE WIDGERY

In the present case, the defendants' duty to take care to avoid the escape of the virus was due to the foreseeable fact that the virus might infect cattle in the neighbourhood and cause them to die. The duty of care is accordingly owed to the owners of cattle in the neighbourhood, but the plaintiffs are not owners of cattle and have no proprietary interest in anything which might conceivably be damaged by the virus if it escaped. Even if the plaintiffs have a proprietary interest in the premises known as Farnham market, these premises are not in jeopardy. In my judgment, therefore, the plaintiffs' claim in negligence fails even if the assumptions of fact most favourable to them are made.

4.1 Pure Economic Loss and Consequential Economic Loss

The distinction between pure economic loss and consequential economic loss was considered in the following case.

Spartan Steel & Alloys Ltd. v Martin & Co. (Contractors) Ltd. [1973] QB 27

Panel: Lord Denning MR, Edmund Davies and Lawton LJJ

Facts: The plaintiffs were engaged in the manufacturing of stainless steel alloys, a process which required continuous power to maintain the temperature in the furnace. The defendant's employee, who was working nearby to the factory damaged the cable that supplied electricity to the plaintiffs' factory, which required the power to be shut off for 14½ hours. The plaintiffs claimed damages for the reduction in value of the melt which had to be removed from the furnace, the loss of profit that they would have made from that melt had the power not been shut off and the loss of profit from another four melts which they would have made during the time the power was shut off. The Court of Appeal, by a majority, held that only the first two heads of claim were recoverable and that the third constituted pure economic loss.

LORD DENNING MR

At bottom I think the question of recovering economic loss is one of policy. Whenever the courts draw a line to mark out the bounds of *duty,* they do it as matter of policy so as to limit the responsibility of the defendant. Whenever the courts set bounds to the *damages* recoverable - saying that they are, or are not, too remote - they do it as matter of policy so as to limit the liability of the defendant.

In many of the cases where economic loss has been held not to be recoverable, it has been put on the ground that the defendant was under no *duty* to the plaintiff. Thus where a person is injured in a road accident by the negligence of another, the negligent driver owes a duty to the injured man himself, but he owes no duty to the servant of the injured man - see *Best v. Samuel Fox & Co. Ltd.* [1952] A.C. 716 , 731: nor to the master of the injured man - *Inland Revenue Commissioners v. Hambrook* [1956] 2 Q.B. 641, 660: nor to anyone else who suffers loss because he had a contract with the injured man - see *Simpson & Co. v. Thomson* (1877) 3 App.Cas. 279, 289: nor indeed to anyone who only suffers economic loss on account of the accident: see *Kirkham v. Boughey* [1958] 2 Q.B. 338, 341. Likewise, when property is damaged by the negligence of another, the negligent tortfeasor owes a duty to the owner or possessor of the chattel, but not to one who suffers loss only because he had a contract entitling him to use the chattel or giving him a right to receive it at some later date: see *Elliott Steam Tug Co. Ltd. v. Shipping Controller* [1922] 1 K.B. 127, 139 and *Margarine Union G.m.b.H. v. Cambay Prince Steamship Co. Ltd.* [1969] 1 Q.B. 219, 251-252.

In other cases, however, the defendant seems clearly to have been under a duty to the plaintiff, but the economic loss has not been recovered because it is *too remote.* Take the illustration given by Blackburn J. in *Cattle v. Stockton Waterworks Co.* (1875) L.R. 10 Q.B. 453, 457, when water escapes from a reservoir and floods a coal mine where many men are working. Those who had their tools or clothes destroyed could recover: but those who only lost their wages could not. Similarly, when the defendants' ship negligently sank a ship which was being towed by a tug, the owner of the tug lost his remuneration, but he could not recover it from the negligent ship: though the same duty (of navigation with reasonable care) was owed to both tug and tow: see *Société Anonyme de Remorquage à Hélice v. Bennetts* [1911] 1 K.B. 243, 248. In such cases if the plaintiff or his property had been physically injured, he would have recovered:

but, as he only suffered economic loss, he is held not entitled to recover. This is, I should think, because the loss is regarded by the law as too remote: see *King v. Phillips* [1953] 1 Q.B. 429, 439-440.

On the other hand, in the cases where economic loss by itself has been held to be recoverable, it is plain that there was a duty to the plaintiff and the loss was not too remote. Such as when one ship negligently runs down another ship, and damages it, with the result that the cargo has to be discharged and reloaded. The negligent ship was already under a duty to the cargo owners: and they can recover the cost of discharging and reloading it, as it is not too remote: see *Morrison Steamship Co. Ltd. v. Greystoke Castle* (Cargo Owners) [1947] A.C. 265 . Likewise, when a banker negligently gives a reference to one who acts on it, the duty is plain and the damage is not too remote: see *Hedley Byrne & Co. Ltd. v. Heller & Partners Ltd.* [1964] A.C. 465.

The more I think about these cases, the more difficult I find it to put each into its proper pigeon-hole. Sometimes I say: "There was no duty." In others I say: "The damage was too remote." So much so that I think the time has come to discard those tests which have proved so elusive. It seems to me better to consider the particular relationship in hand, and see whether or not, as a matter of policy, economic loss should be recoverable, or not. Thus in *Weller & Co. v. Foot and Mouth Disease Research Institute* [1966] 1 Q.B. 569 it was plain that the loss suffered by the auctioneers was not recoverable, no matter whether it is put on the ground that there was no duty or that the damage was too remote. Again in *Electrochrome Ltd. v. Welsh Plastics Ltd.* [1968] 2 All E.R. 205, it is plain that the economic loss suffered by the plaintiffs' factory (due to the damage to the fire hydrant) was not recoverable, whether because there was no duty or that it was too remote.

So I turn to the relationship in the present case. It is of common occurrence. The parties concerned are: the electricity board who are under a statutory duty to maintain supplies of electricity in their district; the inhabitants of the district, including this factory, who are entitled by statute to a continuous supply of electricity for their use; and the contractors who dig up the road. Similar relationships occur with other statutory bodies, such as gas and water undertakings. The cable may be damaged by the negligence of the statutory undertaker, or by the negligence of the contractor, or by accident without any negligence by anyone: and the power may have to be cut off whilst the cable is repaired. Or the power may be cut off owing to a short-circuit in the power house: and so forth. If the cutting off of the supply causes economic loss to the consumers, should it as matter of policy be recoverable? and against whom?

The first consideration is the position of the statutory undertakers. If the board do not keep up the voltage or pressure of electricity, gas or water, likewise, if they shut it off for repairs - and thereby cause economic loss to their consumers, they are not liable in damages, not even if the cause of it is due to their own negligence. The only remedy (which is hardly ever pursued) is to prosecute the board before the magistrates. Such is the result of many cases, starting with a water board - *Atkinson v. Newcastle & Gateshead Waterworks Co.* (1877) 2 Ex.D. 441; going on to a gas board - *Clegg, Parkinson & Co. v. Earby Gas Co.* [1896] 1 Q.B. 592; and then to an electricity company - *Stevens v. Aldershot Gas, Water & District Lighting Co. Ltd* best reported in

(1932) 31 L.G.R. 48; also in 102 L.J.K.B. 12. In those cases the courts, looking at the legislative enactments, held that Parliament did not intend to expose the board to liability for damages to the inhabitants en masse: see what Lord Cairns L.C. said in *Atkinson v. Newcastle & Gateshead Waterworks Co.*, 2 Ex.D. 441, 445 and Wills J. in *Clegg, Parkinson & Co. v. Earby Gas Co.* [1896] 1 Q.B. 592, 595. In those cases there was indirect damage to the plaintiffs, but it was not recoverable. There is another group of cases which go to show that, if the board, by their negligence in the conduct of their supply, cause direct physical damage or injury to person or property, they are liable: see *Milnes v. Huddersfield Corporation* (1886) 11 App.Cas. 511, 530 by Lord Blackburn; *Midwood & Co. Ltd. v. Manchester Corporation* [1905] 2 K.B. 597; *Heard v. Brymbo Steel Co. Ltd.* [1947 K.B. 692 and *Hartley v. Mayoh & Co.* [1954] 1 Q.B. 383. But one thing is clear: the statutory undertakers have never been held liable for economic loss only. If such be the policy of the legislature in regard to electricity boards, it would seem right for the common law to adopt a similar policy in regard to contractors. If the electricity boards are not liable for economic loss due to negligence which results in the cutting off the supply, nor should a contractor be liable.

The second consideration is the nature of the hazard, namely, the cutting of the supply of electricity. This is a hazard which we all run. It may be due to a short circuit, to a flash of lightning, to a tree falling on the wires, to an accidental cutting of the cable, or even to the negligence of someone or other and when it does happen, it affects a multitude of persons: not as a rule by way of physical damage to them or their property, but by putting them to inconvenience, and sometimes to economic loss. The supply is usually restored in a few hours, so the economic loss is not very large. Such a hazard is regarded by most people as a thing they must put up with - without seeking compensation from anyone. Some there are who install a stand-by system. Others seek refuge by taking out an insurance policy against breakdown in the supply. But most people are content to take the risk on themselves. When the supply is cut off, they do not go running round to their solicitor. They do not try to find out whether it was anyone's fault. They just put up with it. They try to make up the economic loss by doing more work next day. This is a healthy attitude which the law should encourage.

The third consideration is this: if claims for economic loss were permitted for this particular hazard, there would be no end of claims. Some might be genuine, but many might be inflated, or even false. A machine might not have been in use anyway, but it would be easy to put it down to the cut in supply. It would be well-nigh impossible to check the claims. If there was economic loss on one day, did the claimant do his best to mitigate it by working harder next day? and so forth. Rather than expose claimants to such temptation and defendants to such hard labour - on comparatively small claims - it is better to disallow economic loss altogether, at any rate when it stands alone, independent of any physical damage.

The fourth consideration is that, in such a hazard as this, the risk of economic loss should be suffered by the whole community who suffer the losses - usually many but comparatively small losses - rather than on the one pair of shoulders, that is, on the contractor on whom the total of them, all added together, might be very heavy.

The fifth consideration is that the law provides for deserving cases. If the defendant is guilty of negligence which cuts off the electricity supply and causes actual physical damage to person or property, that physical damage can be recovered: see *Baker v. Crow Carrying Co. Ltd.* (unreported) February 1, 1960; Bar Library Transcript No. 45, referred to by Buckley L.J. in *S.C.M. (United Kingdom) Ltd. v. W. J. Whittall & Son Ltd.* [1971] 1 Q.B. 337, 356; and also any economic loss truly consequential on the material damage: see *British Celanese Ltd. v. A. H. Hunt (Capacitors) Ltd.* [1969] 1 W.L.R. 959 and *S.C.M. (United Kingdom) Ltd. v. W. J. Whittall & Son Ltd.* [1971] 1 Q.B. 337. Such cases will be comparatively few. They will be readily capable of proof and will be easily checked. They should be and are admitted.

These considerations lead me to the conclusion that the plaintiffs should recover for the physical damage to the one melt (£368), and the loss of profit on that melt consequent thereon (£400): but not for the loss of profit on the four melts (£1,767), because that was economic loss independent of the physical damage. I would, therefore, allow the appeal and reduce the damages to £768.

4.2 Defective Items

While it is possible to bring a claim in tort where property has been damaged by another's negligence, it is not possible to bring a claim for the costs of repairing an inherently defective item, as such losses have been categorised as pure economic loss. (The appropriate claim here would be in the law of contract.) However, this has not always been the position. Following *Hedley Byrne & Co. Ltd v Heller & Partners Ltd.* [1963] 3 WLR 101 and until *Caparo Industries plc. v Dickman and others* [1990] 2 WLR 358 discussed below, there was a significant period of expansion for pure economic loss.

The 'high water mark' came with *Junior Books Ltd. v Veitchi Co. Ltd.* [1983] 1 AC 520.

Junior Books Ltd. v Veitchi Co. Ltd. [1983] 1 AC 520

Panel: Lord Fraser of Tullybelton, Lord Russell of Killowen, Lord Keith of Kinkel, Lord Roskill and Lord Brandon of Oakbrook

Facts: The defendants, a specialist floor company, were subcontracted to lay a floor at the plaintiffs' factory, designed to support heavy machinery. The floor was however laid defectively and had to be re-laid. The plaintiffs successfully claimed damages in negligence against the defendants, despite there being no threat to health and safety or any risk to the actual fabric of the building. The claim was for pure economic loss to include the cost of relaying the floor and their lost profits arising out of the delay in commencing production.

LORD ROSKILL

...Turning back to the present appeal I therefore ask first whether there was the requisite degree of proximity so as to give rise to the relevant duty of care relied on by the respondents. I regard the following facts as of crucial importance in requiring an affirmative answer to that question. (1) The appellants were nominated sub-contractors.

(2) The appellants were specialists in flooring. (3) The appellants knew what products were required by the respondents and their main contractors and specialised in the production of those products. (4) The appellants alone were responsible for the composition and construction of the flooring. (5) The respondents relied upon the appellants' skill and experience. (6) The appellants as nominated sub-contractors must have known that the respondents relied upon their skill and experience. (7) The relationship between the parties was as close as it could be short of actual privity of contract. (8) The appellants must be taken to have known that if they did the work negligently (as it must be assumed that they did) the resulting defects would at some time require remedying by the respondents expending money upon the remedial measures as a consequence of which the respondents would suffer financial or economic loss.

My Lords, reverting to Lord Devlin's speech in *Hedley Byrne & Co. Ltd. v. Heller & Partners Ltd.* [1964] A.C. 465, it seems to me that all the conditions existed which give rise to the relevant duty of care owed by the appellants to the respondents.

I then turn to Lord Wilberforce's second proposition. On the facts I have just stated, I see nothing whatsoever to restrict the duty of care arising from the proximity of which I have spoken. During the argument it was asked what the position would be in a case where there was a relevant exclusion clause in the main contract. My Lords, that question does not arise for decision in the instant appeal, but in principle I would venture the view that such a clause according to the manner in which it was worded might in some circumstances limit the duty of care just as in the Hedley Byrne case the plaintiffs were ultimately defeated by the defendants' disclaimer of responsibility. But in the present case the only suggested reason for limiting the damage (ex hypothesi economic or financial only) recoverable for the breach of the duty of care just enunciated is that hitherto the law has not allowed such recovery and therefore ought not in the future to do so. My Lords, with all respect to those who find this a sufficient answer, I do not. I think this is the next logical step forward in the development of this branch of the law. I see no reason why what was called during the argument "damage to the pocket" simpliciter should be disallowed when "damage to the pocket" coupled with physical damage has hitherto always been allowed. I do not think that this development, if development it be, will lead to untoward consequences. The concept of proximity must always involve, at least in most cases, some degree of reliance - I have already mentioned the words "skill" and "judgment" in the speech of Lord Morris of Borth-y-Gest in *Hedley Byrne* [1964] A.C. 465, 503. These words seem to me to be an echo, be it conscious or unconscious, of the language of section 14 (1) of the Sale of Goods Act 1893. My Lords, though the analogy is not exact, I do not find it unhelpful for I think the concept of proximity of which I have spoken and the reasoning of Lord Devlin in the Hedley Byrne case involve factual considerations not unlike those involved in a claim under section 14 (1); and as between an ultimate purchaser and a manufacturer would not easily be found to exist in the ordinary everyday transaction of purchasing chattels when it is obvious that in truth the real reliance was upon the immediate vendor and not upon the manufacturer.

The court found that the defendant held a position of special skill, had assumed responsibility for the condition of the floor and that the plaintiffs had relied upon this. The decision was controversial at the time and has since been distinguished to the extent that it now stands on its own restricted to its own facts.

4.3 Exceptions: Negligent Misstatements

The general rule provides that damages in tort for pure economic loss are not recoverable. However, there are a number of exceptions to this rule. The most important one is negligent misstatement.

Until approximately 1964, liability in tort was only possible for losses caused by fraudulent rather than negligent statements. It was a requirement of the tort of deceit that the defendant knowingly or recklessly made a statement with the intent that the claimant should act upon it. *Hedley Byrne & Co. Ltd v Heller & Partners Ltd.* [1964] AC 465 was a landmark decision that provided the House of Lords an opportunity to reassess the position. The case also put in place the basis for the most important exception to the rule governing duty for pure economic loss. Where that loss is caused by a negligent misstatement, and where the circumstances of that loss fit those prescribed in *Hedley Byrne*, then the claimant may be able to establish a duty of care.

Hedley Byrne & Co. Ltd v Heller & Partners Ltd. [1964] AC 465

Panel: Lord Reid, Lord Morris of Borth-Y-Gest, Lord Hodson, Lord Devlin and Lord Pearce

Facts: The plaintiffs were an advertising agency, seeking information as to the financial status of a company with which it was considering entering into a number of contracts. The plaintiffs requested financial references from the company's bankers, Heller and Partners. The references were supplied confirming that the company was creditworthy, and containing a disclaimer excluding liability on the part of the bank. The plaintiffs, on the strength of the references, entered into the contracts and lost £17,000 when the company went into liquidation. The plaintiffs brought a claim against the bankers (it being futile to attempt to claim against the company) on the basis that they had been negligent when preparing the credit references. The House of Lords held that in view of the disclaimer there was no liability. However, they stated *obiter* that a duty of care could arise in situations where advice was given, even where the only damage was pure economic loss.

LORD MORRIS OF BORTH-Y-GEST

...My Lords, I consider that it follows and that it should now be regarded as settled that if someone possessed of a special skill undertakes, quite irrespective of contract, to apply that skill for the assistance of another person who relies upon such skill, a duty of care will arise. The fact that the service is to be given by means of or by the instrumentality of words can make no difference. Furthermore, if in a sphere in which a person is so placed that others could reasonably rely upon his judgment or his skill or upon his ability to make careful inquiry, a person takes it upon himself to give information or advice to, or allows his information or advice to be passed on to, another person who, as he knows or should know, will place reliance upon it, then a duty of care will arise...

I shall therefore content myself with the proposition that wherever there is a relationship equivalent to contract, there is a duty of care. Such a relationship may be either general or particular. Examples of a general relationship are those of solicitor and client and of banker and customer. For the former *Nocton v. Lord Ashburton* has long stood as the authority and for the latter there is the decision of Salmon J. in *Woods v. Martins Bank Ltd.* which I respectfully approve. There may well be others yet to be established. Where there is a general relationship of this sort, it is unnecessary to do more than prove its existence and the duty follows. Where, as in the present case, what is relied on is a particular relationship created ad hoc, it will be necessary to examine the particular facts to see whether there is an express or implied undertaking of responsibility.

I regard this proposition as an application of the general conception of proximity. Cases may arise in the future in which a new and wider proposition, quite independent of any notion of contract, will be needed. There may, for example, be cases in which a statement is not supplied for the use of any particular person, any more than in *Donoghue v. Stevenson* the ginger beer was supplied for consumption by any particular person; and it will then be necessary to return to the general conception of proximity and to see whether there can be evolved from it, as was done in Donoghue v. Stevenson, a specific proposition to fit the case. When that has to be done, the speeches of your Lordships today as well as the judgment of Denning L.J. to which I have referred - and also, I may add, the proposition in the American Restatement of the Law of Torts, Vol. III, p. 122, para. 552, and the cases which exemplify it - will afford good guidance as to what ought to be said. I prefer to see what shape such cases take before committing myself to any formulation, for I bear in mind Lord Atkin's warning, which I have quoted, against placing unnecessary restrictions on the adaptability of English law. I have, I hope, made it clear that I take quite literally the dictum of Lord Macmillan, so often quoted from the same case, that "the categories of negligence are never closed." English law is wide enough to embrace any new category or proposition that exemplifies the principle of proximity...

LORD PEARCE

The reason for some divergence between the law of negligence in word and that of negligence in act is clear. Negligence in word creates problems different from those of negligence in act. Words are more volatile than deeds. They travel fast and far afield. They are used without being expended and take effect in combination with innumerable facts and other words. Yet they are dangerous and can cause vast financial damage. How far they are relied on unchecked (by analogy with there being no probability of intermediate inspection - see *Grant v. Australian Knitting Mills Ltd.* must in many cases be a matter of doubt and difficulty. If the mere hearing or reading of words were held to create proximity, there might be no limit to the persons to whom the speaker or writer could be liable. Damage by negligent acts to persons or property on the other hand is more visible and obvious; its limits are more easily defined...

How wide the sphere of the duty of care in negligence is to be laid depends ultimately upon the courts' assessment of the demands of society for protection from the carelessness of others. Economic protection has lagged behind protection in physical matters where there is injury to person and property. It may be that the size and the width of the range of possible claims has acted as a deterrent to extension of economic protection…

Was there such a special relationship in the present case as to impose on the defendants a duty of care to the plaintiffs as the undisclosed principals for whom the National Provincial Bank was making the inquiry? The answer to that question depends on the circumstances of the transaction. If, for instance, they disclosed a casual social approach to the inquiry, no such special relationship or duty of care would be assumed (see *Fish v. Kelly*) To import such a duty the representation must normally, I think, concern a business or professional transaction whose nature makes clear the gravity of the inquiry and the importance and influence attached to the answer… A most important circumstance is the form of the inquiry and of the answer. Both were here plainly stated to be without liability. Mr. Gardiner argues that those words are not sufficiently precise to exclude liability for negligence. Nothing, however, except negligence could, in the facts of this case, create a liability (apart from fraud, to which they cannot have been intended to refer and against which the words would be no protection, since they would be part of the fraud). I do not, therefore, accept that even if the parties were already in contractual or other special relationship the words would give no immunity to a negligent answer. But in any event they clearly prevent a special relationship from arising. They are part of the material from which one deduces whether a duty of care and a liability for negligence was assumed. If both parties say expressly (in a case where neither is deliberately taking advantage of the other) that there shall be no liability, I do not find it possible to say that a liability was assumed.

While stated in *obiter*, it can be seen that the House of Lords did accept that a duty of care could arise in situations where advice was given, even where the only harm caused was one of pure economic loss, but that this was limited to situations were the following conditions were met:

- There was a special relationship between the parties, of trust and confidence; and

- The party preparing the advice had **voluntarily assumed the risk**; and

- There had been **reliance on the advice** prepared by the other party; and

- That **such reliance was reasonable** in the circumstances.

4.3.1 Special Relationship

There is unlikely to be a special relationship if the parties were on an equal footing. For a time, the position seemed to be that the claimant needed to show that the defendant was involved in the business, about which they were giving advice. However, the Court of Appeal in *Esso Petroleum Co Ltd v Mardon* [1976] QB 801 stated that there was no need for the defendant to be in the business of giving advice. This approach was more recently affirmed in the case of *Chaudhry v Prabhakar and Another* [1989] 1 WLR 29.

Chaudhry v Prabhakar and Another [1989] 1 WLR 29

Panel: May, Stocker and Stuart-Smith LJJ

Facts: The plaintiff asked the first defendant, a close friend, to find a suitable second-hand car for her to buy, stipulating that it should not have been involved in an accident. He agreed to do so for no payment. He was not a mechanic but was regarded by the plaintiff as knowing much more about cars than she did. He found a car which the second defendant, a car sprayer and panel beater, whom the first defendant had not previously met, had for sale.

The first defendant realised that the bonnet had been crumpled and straightened or replaced, but he did not ask the second defendant if it had been in an accident and told the plaintiff that it was in very good condition and that he highly recommended it. He told her that the second defendant was a friend and when she asked if the car had been in an accident he said that it had not and that she need not have it examined by a mechanic.

Relying on those assurances, the plaintiff bought the car. It was subsequently discovered that the car had been involved in an accident and was unroadworthy and worthless. The plaintiff obtained judgment against the second defendant on the basis that he had been in breach of the implied term that the car was of merchantable quality, and against the first defendant on the basis that he had owed the plaintiff a duty of care to inquire if the car had been in an accident, and that he had been in breach of that duty.

LORD JUSTICE STUART-SMITH

...[W]here, as in this case, the relationship of principal and agent exists, such that a contract comes into existence between the principal and the third party, it seems to me that, at the very least, this relationship is powerful evidence that the occasion is not a purely social one, but, to use Lord Reid's expression, is in a business connection. Indeed the relationship between the parties is one that is equivalent to contract, to use the words of Lord Devlin, at p. 530, save only for the absence of consideration.

It seems to me that all the necessary ingredients are here present. The plaintiff clearly relied upon the first defendant's skill and judgment, and, although it may not have been great, it was greater than hers and was quite sufficient for the purpose of asking the appropriate questions of the second defendant. The first defendant also knew that the plaintiff was relying on him; indeed he told her that she did not need to have it inspected by a mechanic and she did not do so on the strength of his recommendation. It was clearly in a business connection, because he knew that she was there and then going to commit herself to buying the car for £4,500 through his agency.

If, as I think, the duty of care in this case can equally be said to arise under the Hedley Byrne principle, then logically the standard of care, or the nature and extent of the duty, should be the same as that required of an unpaid agent. And this is an additional reason why I prefer to state the duty as I have, namely, to take such care as is reasonably to be expected of him in all the circumstances.

Was there a breach of this duty? Mr. Scott submits that this is a question of fact and one to be decided by the jury, had there been one, and that we should not interfere with the judge's decision. Where the conclusion depends upon an issue of primary fact, this court will not normally interfere; the judge has seen and heard the witnesses and is in a far better position to decide such issue than this court. But where, as here, the conclusion that the appellant has been negligent depends upon inferences drawn from the primary facts, this court may well conclude that the judge has drawn the wrong inference or imposed too high a standard. But for my part I wholly agree with the judge's conclusion. It seems to me that, whatever standard of care is required, the first defendant fell below it. The plaintiff had stipulated that the car had not been involved in an accident. The first defendant never asked the second defendant about this; and in answer to the plaintiff's question he assured her that it had not. When he was asked about this in evidence he said that, since he had no knowledge of the matter, he said "No;" and he went on to tell her that she need not have the car examined by a mechanic. I do not think that this answer and advice can possibly be justified simply on the basis that the first defendant honestly thought that it had not been so involved because the car looked nice and well got up. When one adds to this the judge's finding that the first defendant was put on notice by the crumpled bonnet, the case against him was in my judgment a powerful one.

I must however deal with two arguments advanced by Mr. Hoyle. First, he submits that the question whether the car had been involved in an accident was far too vague. It might cover a scratch or a bump going in or out of the garage, or minor damage resulting from a slight collision which could easily be put right. I am not impressed with this argument. The plaintiff's stipulation must be given a reasonable interpretation. It is common knowledge that sometimes attempts are made to stitch together motor cars that have been involved in serious collisions affecting their roadworthiness; unless the repairs are done scrupulously, there is a serious risk that the value, performance or roadworthiness of the rehabilitated car will be affected. To my mind this is what the plaintiff's stipulation and inquiry was directed to and was so understood.

Secondly, Mr. Hoyle submitted that, if the first defendant had asked the second defendant the question whether the vehicle had been involved in an accident, he would have received a negative answer. In the light of the judge's findings that the second defendant's purpose in carrying out the repairs in the way he did was to conceal the true state of the vehicle, I am prepared to accept that as a matter of probability, though not certainty, this is so. If the first defendant had asked the question and reasonably believed the answer, then in my view he would have discharged his duty to the plaintiff. I emphasise the words " reasonably believed" because it seems to me that the first defendant showed a remarkable degree of naïveté when dealing with an unknown second-hand car dealer, whose trade was that of panel beater and paint sprayer. But I do not think it is helpful to speculate upon this question. The fact is that the first defendant did not ask the question and the judge has held, rightly in my judgment, that the plaintiff bought the car in reliance upon what the first defendant did and said.

In *Caparo Industries plc. v Dickman and others* [1990] 2 AC 605 the House of Lords provided detail about situations in which a special relationship may arise.

Caparo Industries plc. v Dickman and others [1990] 2 AC 605

Panel: Lord Bridge of Harwich, Lord Roskill, Lord Ackner, Lord Oliver of Aylmerton and Lord Jauncey of Tullichettle

Facts: For a summary of the facts, see Chapter 2, Section 2.

LORD BRIDGE OF HARWICH

The salient feature of all these cases is that the defendant giving advice or information was fully aware of the nature of the transaction which the plaintiff had in contemplation, knew that the advice or information would be communicated to him directly or indirectly and knew that it was very likely that the plaintiff would rely on that advice or information in deciding whether or not to engage in the transaction in contemplation. In these circumstances the defendant could clearly be expected, subject always to the effect of any disclaimer of responsibility, specifically to anticipate that the plaintiff would rely on the advice or information given by the defendant for the very purpose for which he did in the event rely on it. So also the plaintiff, subject again to the effect of any disclaimer, would in that situation reasonably suppose that he was entitled to rely on the advice or information communicated to him for the very purpose for which he required it. The situation is entirely different where a statement is put into more or less general circulation and may foreseeably be relied on by strangers to the maker of the statement for any one of a variety of different purposes which the maker of the statement has no specific reason to anticipate. To hold the maker of the statement to be under a duty of care in respect of the accuracy of the statement to all and sundry for any purpose for which they may choose to rely on it is not only to subject him, in the classic words of Cardozo C.J. to 'liability in an indeterminate amount for an indeterminate time to an indeterminate class:' see *Ultramares Corporation v. Touche* (1931) 174 N.E. 441, 444; it is also to confer on the world at large a quite unwarranted entitlement to appropriate for their own purposes the benefit of the expert knowledge or professional expertise attributed to the maker of the statement. Hence, looking only at the circumstances of these decided cases where a duty of care in respect of negligent statements has been held to exist, I should expect to find that the 'limit or control mechanism . . . imposed upon the liability of a wrongdoer towards those who have suffered economic damage in consequence of his negligence' rested in the necessity to prove, in this category of the tort of negligence, as an essential ingredient of the 'proximity' between the plaintiff and the defendant, that the defendant knew that his statement would be communicated to the plaintiff, either as an individual or as a member of an identifiable class, specifically in connection with a particular transaction or transactions of a particular kind (e.g. in a prospectus inviting investment) and that the plaintiff would be very likely to rely on it for the purpose of deciding whether or not to enter upon that transaction or upon a transaction of that kind.

...Some of the speeches in the *Hedley Byrne* case derive a duty of care in relation to negligent statements from a voluntary assumption of responsibility on the part of the maker of the statements. In his speech in *Smith v. Eric S. Bush* [1990] 1 A.C. 831, 862, Lord Griffiths emphatically rejected the view that this was the true ground of liability and concluded that:

'The phrase 'assumption of responsibility' can only have any real meaning if it is understood as referring to the circumstances in which the law will deem the maker of the statement to have assumed responsibility to the person who acts upon the advice.' I do not think that in the context of the present appeal anything turns upon the difference between these two approaches.

These considerations amply justify the conclusion that auditors of a public company's accounts owe no duty of care to members of the public at large who rely upon the accounts in deciding to buy shares in the company. If a duty of care were owed so widely, it is difficult to see any reason why it should not equally extend to all who rely on the accounts in relation to other dealings with a company as lenders or merchants extending credit to the company. A claim that such a duty was owed by auditors to a bank lending to a company was emphatically and convincingly rejected by Millett J. in *Al Saudi Banque v. Clarke Pixley* [1990] Ch. 313. The only support for an unlimited duty of care owed by auditors for the accuracy of their accounts to all who may foreseeably rely upon them is to be found in some jurisdictions in the United States of America where there are striking differences in the law in different states. In this jurisdiction I have no doubt that the creation of such an unlimited duty would be a legislative step which it would be for Parliament, not the courts, to take.

...It is never sufficient to ask simply whether A owes B a duty of care. It is always necessary to determine the scope of the duty by reference to the kind of damage from which A must take care to save B harm. 'The question is always whether the defendant was under a duty to avoid or prevent that damage, but the actual nature of the damage suffered is relevant to the existence and extent of any duty to avoid or prevent it:' see *Sutherland Shire Council v. Heyman*, 60 A.L.R. 1, 48, *per* Brennan J. Assuming for the purpose of the argument that the relationship between the auditor of a company and individual shareholders is of sufficient proximity to give rise to a duty of care, I do not understand how the scope of that duty can possibly extend beyond the protection of any individual shareholder from losses in the value of the shares which he holds. As a purchaser of additional shares in reliance on the auditor's report, he stands in no different position from any other investing member of the public to whom the auditor owes no duty.

LORD OLIVER OF AYLMERTON

...The extension of the concept of negligence since the decision of this House in *Hedley Byrne & Co. Ltd. v. Heller & Partners Ltd.* [1964] A.C. 465 to cover cases of pure economic loss not resulting from physical damage has given rise to a considerable and as yet unsolved difficulty of definition. The opportunities for the infliction of pecuniary loss from the imperfect performance of everyday tasks upon the proper performance of which people rely for regulating their affairs are illimitable and the effects are far reaching. A defective bottle of ginger beer may injure a single consumer but the damage stops there. A single statement may be repeated endlessly with or without the permission of its author and may be relied upon in a different way by many different people. Thus the postulate of a simple duty to avoid any harm that is, with hindsight, reasonably capable of being foreseen becomes untenable without the imposition of some intelligible limits to keep the law of negligence within the bounds of common sense and practicality. Those limits have been found by the requirement of what has been called a 'relationship of proximity' between plaintiff and defendant and by the imposition of a further requirement that the attachment of liability for harm which has occurred be 'just and reasonable.' But although the cases in which the courts have imposed or withheld liability are capable of an approximate categorisation, one looks in vain for some common denominator by which the existence of the essential relationship can be tested. Indeed it is difficult to resist a conclusion that what have been treated as three separate requirements are, at least in most cases, in fact merely facets of the same thing, for in some cases the degree of foreseeability is such that it is from that alone that the requisite proximity can be deduced, whilst in others the absence of that essential relationship can most rationally be attributed simply to the court's view that it would not be fair and reasonable to hold the defendant responsible. 'Proximity' is, no doubt, a convenient expression so long as it is realised that it is no more than a label which embraces not a definable concept but merely a description of circumstances from which, pragmatically, the courts conclude that a duty of care exists.

As I have already mentioned, it is almost always foreseeable that someone, somewhere and in some circumstances, may choose to alter his position upon the faith of the accuracy of a statement or report which comes to his attention and it is always foreseeable that a report - even a confidential report - may come to be communicated to persons other than the original or intended recipient. To apply as a test of liability only the foreseeability of possible damage without some further control would be to create a liability wholly indefinite in area, duration and amount and would open up a limitless vista of uninsurable risk for the professional man...

In my judgment, accordingly, the purpose for which the auditors' certificate is made and published is that of providing those entitled to receive the report with information to enable them to exercise in conjunction those powers which their respective proprietary interests confer upon them and not for the purposes of individual speculation with a view to profit. The same considerations as limit the existence of a duty of care also, in my judgment, limit the scope of the duty and I agree with O'Connor L.J. that the duty of care is one owed to the shareholders as a body and not to individual shareholders.

To widen the scope of the duty to include loss caused to an individual by reliance upon the accounts for a purpose for which they were not supplied and were not intended would be to extend it beyond the limits which are so far deducible from the decisions of this House. It is not, as I think, an extension which either logic requires or policy dictates and I, for my part, am not prepared to follow the majority of the Court of Appeal in making it. In relation to the purchase of shares of other shareholders in a company, whether in the open market or as a result of an offer made to all or a majority of the existing shareholders, I can see no sensible distinction, so far as a duty of care is concerned, between a potential purchaser who is, vis-à-vis the company, a total outsider and one who is already the holder of one or more shares. I accordingly agree with what has already fallen from my noble and learned friend, Lord Bridge of Harwich, and with the speech to be delivered by my noble and learned friend, Lord Jauncey of Tullichettle, which have had the advantage of reading, and I, too, would allow the appeal and dismiss the cross-appeal.

In the subsequent case of *James McNaughton Paper Group Ltd. v Hicks Anderson & Co.* [1991] 2 QB 113, an auditor's duty of care was held not to exist when a party to a take over bid relied upon a company's draft accounts, as they had not been prepared for that purpose.

On appeal, the Court of Appeal made it clear that the special relationship depended upon whether or not the claimant was relying upon a statement made for a particular purpose. If a claimant uses a statement for a different purpose than that for which it was originally intended then liability should not arise.

4.3.2 Reasonable Reliance

The claimant must show that he relied upon the statement, advice or information and that it caused him to act, to his detriment. That reliance must have been reasonable.

As can been seen from *Caparo v Dickman*, it was held that the reliance on the audited accounts was not reasonable, given the context in which they had been made. As there was no reasonable reliance, no special relationship could arise between the parties. In *James McNaughton Paper Group Ltd. v Hicks Anderson & Co* [1991] 2 QB 113, in which it was found that it was not reasonable for the claimants to rely upon the draft accounts, Neill LJ set out a list of factors to consider in determining whether a duty of care arises in relation to negligent misstatements. The criteria will not be relevant in every case and there is a high degree of overlap between them.

James McNaughton Paper Group Ltd. v Hicks Anderson & Co [1991] 2 QB 113

Panel: Neill, Nourse and Balcombe LJJ

Facts: The plaintiffs instructed the defendants, their accountants, to prepare accounts during negotiations that were taking place for the take-over of a group of companies. The defendants submitted the accounts as "final drafts" showing a net loss for the year and, in reply to a question put by the plaintiffs, said that the group were "breaking even or doing marginally worse". Subsequently, the plaintiffs completed the take-over and discovered a number of errors in the accounts. The plaintiffs brought a claim in negligence against the defendants for the loss and damage suffered as a result of the take-over.

NEILL LJ

The purpose for which the statement was made

In some cases the statement will have been prepared or made by the "adviser" for the express purpose of being communicated to the "advisee," to adopt the labels used by Lord Oliver. In such a case it may often be right to conclude that the advisee was within the scope of the duty of care. In many cases, however, the statement will have been prepared or made, or primarily prepared or made, for a different purpose and for the benefit of someone other than the advisee. In such cases it will be necessary to look carefully at the precise purpose for which the statement was communicated to the advisee.

The purpose for which the statement was communicated

Under this heading it will be necessary to consider the purpose of, and the circumstances surrounding, the communication. Was the communication made for information only? Was it made for some action to be taken and, if so, what action and by whom? Who requested the communication to be made? These are some of the questions which may have to be addressed.

The relationship between the adviser, the advisee and any relevant third party

Where the statement was made or prepared in the first instance to or for the benefit of someone other than the advisee it will be necessary to consider the relationship between the parties. Thus it may be that the advisee is likely to look to the third party and through him to the adviser for advice or guidance. Or the advisee may be wholly independent and in a position to make any necessary judgments himself.

The size of any class to which the advisee belongs

Where there is a single advisee or he is a member of only a small class it may sometimes be simple to infer that a duty of care was owed to him. Membership of a large class, however, may make such an inference more difficult, particularly where the statement was made in the first instance for someone outside the class.

The state of knowledge of the adviser

The precise state of knowledge of the adviser is one of the most important matters to examine. Thus it will be necessary to consider his knowledge of the purpose for which the statement was made or required in the first place and also his knowledge of the purpose for which the statement was communicated to the advisee. In this context knowledge includes not only actual knowledge but also such knowledge as would be attributed to a reasonable person in the circumstances in which the adviser was placed. On the other hand any duty of care will be limited to transactions or types of transactions of which the adviser had knowledge and will only arise where

"the adviser knows or ought to know that [the statement or advice] will be relied upon by a particular person or class of persons in connection with that transaction:" *per* Lord Oliver in the Caparo case [1990] 2 A.C. 605, 641.

It is also necessary to consider whether the adviser knew that the advisee would rely on the statement without obtaining independent advice.

Reliance by the advisee

In cases where the existence of a duty of care is in issue it is always useful to examine the matter from the point of view of the plaintiff. As I have ventured to say elsewhere the question "Who is my neighbour?" prompts the response "Consider first those who would consider you to be their neighbour." One should therefore consider whether and to what extent the advisee was entitled to rely on the statement to take the action that he did take. It is also necessary to consider whether he did in fact rely on the statement, whether he did use or should have used his own judgment and whether he did seek or should have sought independent advice. In business transactions conducted at arms' length it may sometimes be difficult for an advisee to prove that he was entitled to act on a statement without taking any independent advice or to prove that the adviser knew, actually or inferentially, that he would act without taking such advice.

...Since preparing this judgment I have had the opportunity of reading the speeches of the House of Lords in *Murphy v. Brentwood District Council* [1991] 1 A.C. 398 . There is nothing in any of these speeches which alters what was said earlier this year in the Caparo case. Indeed it may be noted (a) that Lord Keith of Kinkel referred again, at p. 461, to the judgment of Brennan J. in the Shire of Sutherland case, 157 C.L.R. 424, where Brennan J. emphasised that the question is always whether the defendant was under a duty to avoid or prevent the kind of damage which the plaintiff in fact suffered; (b) that Lord Oliver underlined the same point where, having referred to the Shire of Sutherland case and to the Caparo case, he continued, at p. 486:

> "The essential question which has to be asked in every case, given that damage which is the essential ingredient of the action has occurred, is whether the relationship between the plaintiff and the defendant is such - or, to use the favoured expression, whether it is of sufficient 'proximity' - that it imposes upon the latter a duty to take care to avoid or prevent that loss which has in fact been sustained."

I have not found this to be an easy case. Having looked at length at the documents and the transcripts of the evidence, I have been driven to the conclusion that, as the law stands at present, McNaughton have not been able to establish the existence of a duty of care owed to them by Mr. Pritchard or H.A. at any material time. I would allow the appeal.

4.4 Disclaimers

In some instances, the defendants may have taken steps against assuming responsibility for their statement or advice, in which case the validity of such steps must be considered. In *Hedley Byrne v Heller,* the credit reference was issued with a disclaimer excluding liability *'without responsibility'.* The defendants were not liable because of the disclaimer.

This decision was made before the implementation of Unfair Contract Terms Act 1977. Any attempt to rely upon a disclaimer will now be subject to this statute. Exclusions or restrictions for death or personal injury are invalid, and in relation to other negligently caused damage, the exclusion must satisfy the test of reasonableness. What is reasonable in accordance with s 11 and Sch 2 will depend on the particular circumstances of the case. In *Smith v Eric S. Bush* [1989] 2 WLR 790, surveyors attempted to rely upon a disclaimer, but it was found that the disclaimer fell foul of the Unfair Contract Terms Act 1977 and therefore could not be relied upon.

4.5 Negligent Misstatements Relied upon by Third Parties

In *Hedley Bryne,* the plaintiff was the recipient of a negligent statement, the credit reference. A duty of care has also been recognised when the subject, rather than the recipient of a statement, has suffered as a result of statements being given without due care as can be demonstrated in the following case.

Spring Appellant v Guardian Assurance Plc. and Others Respondents [1995] 2 AC 296

Panel: Lord Keith of Kinkel, Lord Goff of Chieveley, Lord Lowry, Lord Slynn of Hadley and Lord Woolf

Facts: The defendants wrote a disparaging (and inaccurate) job reference about the plaintiff. The plaintiff was unable to obtain other employment within the life-assurance industry and brought a claim against the defendant for negligence. The question was whether a duty of care was owed to the subject of the reference in addition to the person that had requested it. At trial it was found that a duty of care was owed to the subject of the reference, as well as the recipient of the reference. The House of Lords agreed that this duty was owed and had been breached.

LORD KEITH OF KINKEL

...In my opinion the same grounds of public policy are applicable where the claim is based not on defamation as such but on negligence associated with the making or publication of an untrue statement, where the occasion on which that was done was a privileged one in the sense in which that expression is used in the context of defamation law. If liability in negligence were to follow from a reference prepared without reasonable care, the same adverse consequences would flow as those sought to be guarded against by the defence of qualified privilege. Those asked to give a reference would be inhibited from speaking frankly lest it should be found that they were liable in damages through not taking sufficient care in its preparation. They might well prefer, if under no legal duty to give a reference, to refrain from doing so at all. Any reference given might be bland and unhelpful and information which it would be in the interest of those seeking the reference to receive might be withheld.

...In general, precisely the same grounds of public policy which make the defence of qualified privilege available in an action for defamation strongly favour the exclusion of an action for damages for negligence in similar situations. If it were to be held that such an action was to be available in relation to the giving of references in the employment field, there would be pressure to extend the principle to cover all situations where the defence of qualified privilege would be available if the action were one for defamation, and such extension could not logically be resisted. Thus the whole rationale of the defence of qualified privilege would be overthrown. While giving Mr. Spring a right of action in negligence would operate favourably in his interest and in those of other individuals who might find themselves in a like position, the adverse consequences from the point of view of public interest which would flow from doing so in my opinion militate strongly against it.

My Lords, for these reasons I would affirm the decision of the Court of Appeal on the issue of negligence.

Lord Goff based his reasoning on the concept of assumption of responsibility. By giving a reference, the person providing it assumed responsibility to the claimant to give a careful reference. It is difficult to get a job without a reference and an action in defamation may not always prove satisfactory. This concept of assumption of responsibility is of particular importance when faced with novel situations, where the loss incurred is pure economic loss.

Further Reading

Mark Lunney and Ken Olliphant, *Tort Law Text and Materials: A Fundamental Restatement*, (3rd edition) Oxford University Press 2008, Chapter 8

5

Breach of Duty

Topic List

Introduction

Having established the existence of a duty of care, it is next necessary to consider whether that duty has been breached by the defendant. Whether or not there has been a breach depends on two things: what the *standard* of care owed under the duty is; and whether that standard has or has not been met by the defendant.

The general standard of care is that of the reasonable person. The 'reasonable person', or 'reasonable man' as the courts would once have said, is a hypothetical person. What is to be expected of a reasonable person is something that the courts will judge objectively.

The courts will rarely impose a lower standard. The simple fact that a particular defendant lacks the skill or experience necessary to act as a hypothetical reasonable person would have in the circumstances does not mean that they will be held to a lower standard. This is a concept well illustrated by our first case.

Nettleship v Weston [1971] 2 QB 691

Panel: Lord Denning MR, Salmon and Megaw LJJ

Facts: The claimant was injured when a car being driven by a learner driver, whom he was instructing, collided with a street lamp. The accident was caused by the defendant, whose driving was not up to the standard of an experienced driver. The Court of Appeal held that a learner driver owes the same standard of care as an experienced driver – that of a reasonably competent driver. The fact that the driver is not experienced will not reduce the standard of care that is owed.

LORD DENNING MR

I take it to be clear that if a driver has a passenger in the car he owes a duty of care to him. But what is the standard of care required of the driver? Is it a lower standard than he or she owes towards a pedestrian on the pavement? I should have thought not. But, suppose that the driver has never driven a car before, or has taken too much to drink, or has poor eyesight or hearing: and, furthermore, that the passenger *knows* it and yet accepts a lift from him. Does that make any difference? Dixon J. thought it did. In *The Insurance Commissioner v. Joyce* (1948) 77 C.L.R. 39. 56, he said:

> "If a man accepts a lift from a car driver whom he *knows* to have lost a limb or an eye or to be deaf, he cannot complain if he does not exhibit the skill and competence of a driver who suffers from no defect. ... If he knowingly accepts the voluntary services of a driver affected by drink, he cannot complain of improper driving caused by his condition, because it involves no breach of duty."

That view of Dixon J. seems to have been followed in South Australia: see *Walker v. Turton-Sainsbury* [1952] S.A.S.R. 159; but in the Supreme Court of Canada Rand J. did not agree with it: see *Car and General Insurance Co. v. Seymour and Maloney* (1956) 2 D.L.R. (2d) 369, 375.

We have all the greatest respect for Sir Owen Dixon, but for once I cannot agree with him. The driver owes a duty of care to every passenger in the car, just as he does to every pedestrian on the road: and he must attain the same standard of care in respect of each. If the driver were to be excused according to the knowledge of the passenger, it would result in endless confusion and injustice. One of the passengers may know that the learner driver is a mere novice. Another passenger may believe him to be entirely competent. One of the passengers may believe the driver to have had only two drinks. Another passenger may know that he has had a dozen. Is the one passenger to recover and the other not? Rather than embark on such inquiries, the law holds that the driver must attain the same standard of care for passengers as for pedestrians. The knowledge of the passenger may go to show that he was guilty of contributory negligence in ever accepting the lift - and thus reduce his damages - but it does not take away the duty of care, nor does it diminish the standard of care which the law requires of the driver: see *Dann v. Hamilton* [1939] 1 K.B. 509 and *Slater v. Clay Cross Co. Ltd.* [1956] 2 Q.B. 264, 270.

Alert

I would only add this: If the knowledge of the passenger were held to take away the duty of care, it would mean that we would once again be applying the maxim: 'Scienti non fit injuria." That maxim was decisively rejected by the House of Lords in cases between employer and workmen; see *Smith v. Baker & Sons* [1891] A.C. 325: and by Parliament in cases between occupier and visitor: see section 2 (4) of the Occupiers' Liability Act 1957, overruling *London Graving Dock Co. Ltd. v. Horton* [1951] A.C. 737. We should not allow it to be introduced today in motor car cases even though it was backed by Sir Owen Dixon. But that was in 1948. He might think differently today.

The Responsibility of a Learner Driver towards his Instructor

The special factor in this case is that Mr. Nettleship was not a mere passenger in the car. He was an instructor teaching Mrs. Weston to drive.

Seeing that the law lays down, for all drivers of motor cars, a standard of care to which all must conform, I think that even a learner driver, so long as he is the sole driver, must attain the same standard towards all passengers in the car, including an instructor. But the instructor may be debarred from claiming for a reason peculiar to himself. He may be debarred because he has voluntarily agreed to waive any claim for any injury that may befall him. Otherwise he is not debarred. He may, of course, be guilty of contributory negligence and have his damages reduced on that account. He may, for instance, have let the learner take control too soon, he may not have been quick enough to correct his errors, or he may have participated in the negligent act himself: see *Stapley v. Gypsum Mines Ltd.* [1953] A.C. 663 But, apart from contributory negligence, he is not excluded unless it be that he has voluntarily agreed to incur the risk.

Alert

This brings me to the defence of volenti non fit injuria. Does it apply to the instructor? In former times this defence was used almost as an alternative defence to contributory negligence. Either defence defeated the action. Now that contributory negligence is not a complete defence, but only a ground for reducing the damages, the defence of volenti non fit injuria has been closely considered, and, in consequence, it has been severely limited. Knowledge of the risk of injury is not enough. Nor is a willingness to take the risk of injury. Nothing will suffice short of an agreement to waive any claim for negligence. The plaintiff must agree, expressly or impliedly, to waive any claim for any injury that may befall him due to the lack of reasonable care by the defendant: or, more accurately, due to the failure of the defendant to measure up to the standard of care that the law requires of him. That is shown in England by *Dann v. Hamilton* [1939] 1 K.B. 509 and *Slater v. Clay Cross Co. Ltd.* [1956] 2 Q.B. 264; and in Canada by *Lehnert v. Stein* (1962) 36 D.L.R. (2d) 159; and in New Zealand by *Morrison v. Union Steamship Co. Ltd. of New Zealand* [1964] N.Z.L.R. 468. The doctrine has been so severely curtailed that in the view of Diplock L.J.:

> "the maxim in the absence of expressed contract has no application to negligence simpliciter where the duty of care is based solely upon proximity or 'neighbourship' in the Atkinian sense": see *Wooldridge v. Sumner* [1963] 2 Q.B. 43, 69.

Applying the doctrine in this case, it is clear that Mr. Nettleship did not agree to waive any claim for injury that might befall him. Quite the contrary. He inquired about the insurance policy so as to make sure that he was covered. If and in so far as Mrs. Weston fell short of the standard of care which the law required of her, he has a cause of action. But his claim may be reduced in so far as he was at fault himself - as in letting her take control too soon or in not being quick enough to correct her error.

I do not say that the professional instructor - who agrees to teach for reward - can likewise sue. There may well be implied in the contract an agreement by him to waive any claim for injury. He ought to insure himself, and may do so, for aught I know. But the instructor who is just a friend helping to teach never does insure himself. He should, therefore, be allowed to sue.

Conclusion thus far

In all that I have said, I have treated Mrs. Weston as the driver who was herself in control of the car. On that footing, she is plainly liable for the damage done to the lamp post. She is equally liable for the injury done to Mr. Nettleship. She owed a duty of care to each. The standard of care is the same in either case. It is measured objectively by the care to be expected of an experienced, skilled and careful driver. Mr. Nettleship is not defeated by the maxim volenti non fit injuria. He did not agree, expressly or impliedly, to waive any claim for damages owing to her failure to measure up to the standard. But his damages may fall to be reduced owing to his failure to correct her error quick enough. Although the judge dismissed the claim, he did (in case he was wrong) apportion responsibility. He thought it would be just and equitable to regard them as equally to blame. I would accept this apportionment.

LORD JUSTICE SALMON

I need not recite the facts which have been so lucidly stated by Lord Denning M.R. I entirely agree with all he says about the responsibility of a learner driver in criminal law. I also agree that a learner driver is responsible and owes a duty in civil law towards persons on or near the highway to drive with the same degree of skill and care as that of the reasonably competent and experienced driver. The duty in civil law springs from the relationship which the driver, by driving on the highway, has created between himself and persons likely to suffer damage by his bad driving. This is not a special relationship. Nor, in my respectful view, is it affected by whether or not the driver is insured. On grounds of public policy, neither the criminal nor civil responsibility is affected by the fact that the driver in question may be a learner, infirm or drunk. The onus, of course, lies on anyone claiming damages to establish a breach of duty and that it has caused the damage which he claims.

Any driver normally owes exactly the same duty to a passenger in his car as he does to the general public, namely, to drive with reasonable care and skill in all the relevant circumstances. As a rule, the driver's personal idiosyncrasy is not a relevant circumstance. In the absence of a special relationship what is reasonable care and skill is measured by the standard of competence usually achieved by the ordinary driver. In my judgment, however, there may be special facts creating a special relationship which displaces this standard or even negatives any duty, although the onus would certainly be upon the driver to establish such facts. With minor reservations I respectfully agree with and adopt the reasoning and conclusions of Sir Owen Dixon in his judgment in *The Insurance Commissioner v. Joyce* (1948) 77 C.L.R. 39. I do not agree that the mere fact that the driver has, to the knowledge of his passenger, lost a limb or an eye or is deaf can affect the duty which he owes the passenger to drive safely. It is well known that many drivers suffering from such disabilities drive with no less skill and competence than the ordinary man. The position, however, is totally different when, to the knowledge of the passenger, the driver is so drunk as to be incapable of driving safely. Quite apart from being negligent, a passenger who accepts a lift in such circumstances clearly cannot expect the driver to drive other than dangerously.

The driver of the vehicle lacked the necessary experience to avoid causing the accident. However, a reasonably competent driver would have been able to avoid the accident and that was the standard that was imposed. It is worth considering the rationale behind this.

It can be said that the courts adopt a claimant-centred approach to the question of duty. The courts focus not on what could fairly be expected of a particular defendant, but rather on what a potential claimant is reasonably entitled to expect. Passengers in cars, along with all road users, are entitled to expect that those driving vehicles in public are reasonably competent drivers.

The courts seek to keep the test as objective as possible. While this may initially seem harsh on particular defendants, it is a potential unfairness that may be counteracted by the second part of the breach test – whether the standard of care owed has actually been met in the circumstances. We will come on to consider that issue later in this chapter.

There are, however, certain instances where the courts do impose a different standard of care from that of the reasonable person. First, we shall consider the lower standard imposed for children. Then we shall look at the higher standard imposed on professionals.

5.1 Children

In deciding the standard of care that will be owed by a child, the courts will take into account the child's age. Thus the standard of care imposed will not be that of a reasonable person, but rather that of a reasonable child of X years of age. This is undoubtedly a lower standard, as illustrated by the decision in *Mullin v Richards* [1998] 1 WLR 1304.

Mullin v Richards [1998] 1 WLR 1304

Panel: Butler-Sloss and Hutchison LJJ and Sir John Vinelott

Facts: The claimant and the defendant were both schoolgirls aged 15 who were having a play sword-fight using plastic rulers. One of the rulers broke, and a fragment of plastic from it went into the claimant's eye, causing her to lose all sight in that eye. The Court of Appeal held that in setting the standard of care owed by a child in negligence, the courts would take account of the age of the child concerned, and set the standard according to what could reasonably be expected of a reasonable child of that age. In the event, a reasonable 15 year old could not have foreseen the risk of injury, and so there was no breach of duty.

LORD JUSTICE HUTCHINSON

...The question for the judge is not whether the actions of the defendant were such as an ordinarily prudent and reasonable adult in the defendant's situation would have realised gave rise to a risk of injury, it is whether an ordinarily prudent and reasonable 15-year-old schoolgirl in the defendant's situation would have realised as much. ...

Applying those principles to the facts of the present case the central question to which this appeal gives rise is whether on the facts found by the judge and in the light of the evidence before him he was entitled to conclude that an ordinary, reasonable 15-year-old schoolgirl in the first defendant's position would have appreciated that by participating to the extent that she did in a play fight, involving the use of plastic rulers as though they were swords, gave rise to a risk of injury to the plaintiff of the same general kind as she sustained. ...

This was in truth nothing more than a schoolgirl's game such as on the evidence was commonplace in this school and there was, I would hold, no justification for attributing to the participants the foresight of any significant risk of the likelihood of injury. They had seen it done elsewhere with some frequency. They had not heard it prohibited or received any warning about it. They had not been told of any injuries occasioned by it. They were not in any sense behaving culpably. So far as foresight goes, had they paused to think they might, I suppose, have said: "It is conceivable that some unlucky injury might happen," but if asked if there was any likelihood of it or any real possibility of it, they would, I am sure, have said that they did not foresee any such possibility. Taking the view therefore that the judge — who, as I have said, readily and almost without question accepted that on his findings of fact there was negligence on the part of both these young ladies — was wrong in his view and there was no evidence on which he could come to it, I would allow the appeal and direct that judgment be entered for the first defendant. I have to say that I appreciate that this result will be disappointing to the plaintiff for whom one can have nothing but sympathy, because she has suffered a grave injury through no fault of her own. But unfortunately she has failed to establish in my view that anyone was legally responsible for that injury and, accordingly, her claim should have failed.

In holding that a reasonable 15-year old child would not appreciate the risks of playing with a ruler that subsequently shattered and caused injury to the claimant, the court clearly imposed a lesser standard than that of the hypothetical reasonable adult. It is also worth noting that, similar to the concept of the reasonable person, the reasonable child of X years is not expected to be especially bright nor unusually lacking in intelligence. The courts do not, in this jurisdiction, take into account any subjective aspects of the child's personality. The only allowance made for the child is that their age will be taken into account, and they will be held to the standard that could reasonably be expected of an average, hypothetical child of that age.

5.2 Professionals

When assessing the duty of care owed by professionals exercising their professional skill the courts generally impose a higher standard than that of the reasonable person. For example, a doctor carrying out a medical procedure will be held to owe the standard of a reasonably competent doctor, not simply that of a reasonable person. A reasonable person will not be expected to carry out a medical procedure properly. A reasonably competent doctor may well be.

Bolam v Friern Hospital Management Committee [1957] 1 WLR 582

Panel: McNair J and a jury

Facts: A doctor administered a form of electro-convulsive (electric shock) therapy to the claimant without administering a relaxant drug, providing any form of manual restraint and without warning the claimant of the slight risks associated with the treatment. The claimant suffered fractures after a muscle spasm resulting from the treatment, and claimed damages against the hospital. The court held that the standard of care to be expected in such a case was that of a reasonably competent doctor, but also that where a substantial body of medical opinion would have acted in the same manner as the defendant, there would be no breach of duty.

MR JUSTICE McNAIR

In the ordinary case which does not involve any special skill, negligence in law means a failure to do some act which a reasonable man in the circumstances would do, or the doing of some act which a reasonable man in the circumstances would not do; and if that failure or the doing of that act results in injury, then there is a cause of action. How do you test whether this act or failure is negligent? In an ordinary case it is generally said you judge it by the action of the man in the street. He is the ordinary man. In one case it has been said you judge it by the conduct of the man on the top of a Clapham omnibus. He is the ordinary man. But where you get a situation which involves the use of some special skill or competence, then the test as to whether there has been negligence or not is not the test of the man on the top of a Clapham omnibus, because he has not got this special skill. The test is the standard of the ordinary skilled man exercising and professing to have that special skill. A man need not possess the highest expert skill; it is well established law that it is sufficient if he exercises the ordinary skill of an ordinary competent man exercising that particular art. I do not think that I quarrel much with any of the submissions in law which have been put before you by counsel. Mr. Fox-Andrews put it in this way, that in the case of a medical man, negligence means failure to act in accordance with the standards of reasonably competent medical men at the time. That is a perfectly accurate statement, as long as it is remembered that there may be one or more perfectly proper standards; and if he conforms with one of those proper standards, then he is not negligent.

This case makes clear that the standard expected of a doctor is that of a reasonably competent doctor. This is a professional standard, and is higher than that of a reasonable person. The case also makes clear that, like in *Nettleship*, no allowance will be made by the courts for a doctor's juniority. [This is common, and reflects the courts' refusal to allow the test for the standard of care owed to become anything other than objective.] A junior or trainee doctor will be held to the standard of a reasonably competent, fully qualified doctor. Again, this is evidence of a claimant-centred approach by the courts, focussing not on the abilities of the particular defendant, but on the level of care that a claimant is entitled to expect.

Link
See also *Wilsher v Essex AHA* [1988] AC 1074

5.3 Which Standard to Apply?

In many cases, it will be easy to see which standard the courts will apply. In others, however, it will be less clear. What happens if a professional is exercising his professional skill but in a private capacity? The cases that we have on this point largely indicate that the courts will look to the act being done, rather than the actor. In other words, it is the nature of the act being performed that dictates the standard of care that will be owed, whereas the qualifications of the individual play a secondary role.

Wells v Cooper [1958] 2 QB 265

Panel: Jenkins, Parker and Pearce LJJ

Facts: The claimant was visiting the defendant's house when he was injured after falling about four feet from an unprotected platform. He had pulled the handle of a door with some force, but the handle had not been properly fixed, and it came off in his hand. As a result, the claimant fell backwards and sustained his injuries. The Court of Appeal held that irrespective of the defendant's substantial DIY experience the standard of care owed by the defendant in relation to his carrying out DIY in his own home was that of the reasonable non-professional carpenter (the reasonable person).

LORD JUSTICE JENKINS

We think that if the defendant had envisaged the possibility of the handle coming off in the hand of a person pulling on it, he could hardly have failed to appreciate the likelihood of untoward consequences such as did in fact occur; and accordingly Mr. Fletcher's second issue appears to us to be the substantial issue in the case. It involves consideration of the standard of care to be demanded of the defendant in relation to the fixing of the handle.

As above related, the defendant did the work himself. We do not think the mere fact that he did it himself instead of employing a professional carpenter to do it constituted a breach of his duty of care. No doubt some kinds of work involve such highly specialized skill and knowledge, and create such serious dangers if not properly done, that an ordinary occupier owing a duty of care to others in regard to the safety of premises would fail in that duty if he undertook such work himself instead of employing experts to do it for him. See *Haseldine v. C. A. Daw & Son Ltd.*, per Scott L.J. But the work here in question was not of that order. It was a trifling domestic replacement well within the competence of a householder accustomed to doing small carpentering jobs about his home, and of a kind which must be done every day by hundreds of householders up and down the country. Accordingly, we think that the defendant did nothing unreasonable in undertaking the work himself. But it behoved him, if he was to discharge his duty of care to persons such as the plaintiff, to do the work with reasonable care and skill, and we think the degree of care and skill required of him must be measured not by reference to the degree of competence in such matters which he personally happened to possess, but by reference to the degree of care and skill which a reasonably competent carpenter might be expected to apply to the work in question. Otherwise, the extent of the protection that an invitee could claim in relation to work done by the invitor himself would vary according to the capacity of the invitor, who could free himself from liability merely by showing that he had done the best of which he was capable, however good, bad or indifferent that best might be.

Accordingly, we think the standard of care and skill to be demanded of the defendant in order to discharge his duty of care to the plaintiff in the fixing of the new handle in the present case must be the degree of care and skill to be expected of a reasonably competent carpenter doing the work in question. This does not mean that the degree of care and skill required is to be measured by reference to the contractual obligations as to the quality of his work assumed by a professional carpenter working for reward, which would, in our view, set the standard too high. The question is simply what steps would a reasonably competent carpenter wishing to fix a handle such as this securely to a door such as this have taken with a view to achieving that object.

Philips v William Whiteley [1938] 1 All ER 566

Panel: Goddard J

Facts: The defendants organised, at the claimant's request, for a jeweller to pierce the claimant's ears so that she could wear earrings. The claimant subsequently developed an infection from the hole in her ear, and alleged that this was due to the piercing procedure having been performed negligently by the jeweller. The court held that the standard of care owed in such circumstances was that of a reasonable jeweller, not that of a reasonable doctor or surgeon.

MR JUSTICE GODDARD

In this case, the first thing that I have to consider is the standard of care demanded from Mr Couzens – or, I should say, from Whiteleys, because Whiteleys were the people who undertook to do this piercing. It is not easy in any case to lay down a particular canon or standard by which the care can be judged, but, while it is admitted here, and admitted on all hands, that Mr Couzens did not use the same precautions of procuring an aseptic condition of his instruments as a doctor or a surgeon would use, I do not think that he could be called upon to use that degree of care. Whiteleys have to see that whoever they employ for the operation uses the standard of care and skill that may be expected from a jeweller, and, of course, if the operation is negligently performed – if, for instance, a wholly unsuitable instrument were used so that the ear was badly torn, or something of that sort happened – undoubtedly they would be liable. So, too, if they did not take that degree of care to see that the instruments were clean which one would expect a person of the training and the standing of a jeweller to use. To say, however, that a jeweller warrants or undertakes that he will use instruments which have the degree of surgical cleanliness that a surgeon brings about when he is going to perform a serious operation, or indeed any operation, is, I think, putting the matter too high. The doctors all seem to agree in this case that, if a lady went to a surgeon for the piercing of her ears, he would render his instruments sterile. After all, however, aseptic surgery is a thing of very modern growth. As anybody who has read the life of Lord Lister or the history of medicine in the last fifty or sixty years knows, it is not so many years ago that the best surgeon in the land knew nothing about even antiseptic surgery. Then antiseptic surgery was introduced, and that was followed by aseptic surgery. I do not think that a jeweller holds himself out as a surgeon or professes that he is going to conduct the operation of piercing a lady's ears by means of aseptic surgery, about which it is not to be supposed that he knows anything.

If a person wants to ensure that the operation of piercing her ears is going to be carried out with that proportion of skill and so forth that a Fellow of the Royal College of Surgeons would use, she must go to a surgeon. If she goes to a jeweller, she must expect that he will carry it out in the way that one would expect a jeweller to carry it out. One would expect that he would wash his instruments. One would expect that he would take some means of disinfecting his instrument, just in the same way as one knows that the ordinary layman, when he is going to use a needle to prick a blister or prick a little gathering on a finger, generally takes the precaution to put the needle in a flame, as I think Mr Couzens did. I accept the evidence of Mr Couzens as to what he says he did on this occasion – how he put his instrument in a flame before he left his shop, and how he washed his hands, and so forth. I think that he did. I see no reason to suppose that he is not telling me the absolute truth when he says what he did, and, as Dr Pritchard, who holds the very high qualification of a Fellow of the Royal College of Physicians, said, for all practical purposes that is enough. That is to say, for the ordinary every-day matters that would be regarded as enough. It is not a degree of surgical cleanliness, which is a very different thing from ordinary cleanliness. It is not the cleanliness which a doctor would insist upon, because, as I say, Mr Couzens is not a doctor. He was known not to be a doctor. One does not go to a jeweller to get one's ears attended to if one requires to have a doctor in attendance to do it. If one wants a doctor in attendance, one goes to his consulting room or one has him come to see one. I do not see any ground here for holding that Mr Couzens was negligent in the way in which he performed this operation. It might be better, and I think that it probably would, if he boiled his instrument beforehand at his place, or if he took a spirit lamp with him and boiled his instrument at the time, but in view of the medical evidence, the evidence of Dr Pritchard, which I accept, I see no ground for holding that Mr Couzens departed from the standard of care which you would expect that a man of his position and his training, being what he held himself out to be, was required to possess. Therefore, the charge of negligence fails.

In some instances, the courts have indicated that if a person takes undertakes a task for which he knows he is not adequately qualified, this can in itself be evidence of negligence.

Greaves & Co. (Contractors) Ltd. v Baynham Meikle & Partners [1975] 1 W.L.R. 1095

Panel: Lord Denning MR, Browne and Geoffrey Lane LJJ

Facts: The claimants were contractors who had built a building to the defendants' design and who had been held liable for the defects in it. They brought an action against the defendants, who were consultant engineers, alleging negligence in the designing of the building, and seeking a contribution towards the damages they themselves had been liable for. The court held that the defendants, holding themselves out as experts, owed the standard of reasonably competent professional engineers, and that they had breached that duty.

LORD DENNING MR

It seems to me that in the ordinary employment of a professional man, whether it is a medical man, a lawyer, or an accountant, an architect or an engineer, his duty is to use reasonable care and skill in the course of his employment. The extent of this duty was described by McNair J. *in Bolam v. Friern Hospital Management Committee* [1957] 1 W.L.R. *582*, 586, approved by the Privy Council in *Chin Keow v. Government of Malaysia* [1967] 1 W.L.R. 813, 816:

> " ... where you get a situation which involves the use of some special skill or competence, then the test as to whether there has been negligence or not is not the test of the man on the top of a Clapham omnibus, because he has not got this special skill. The test is the standard of the ordinary skilled man exercising and professing to have that special skill. A man need not possess the highest expert skill; it is well established law that it is sufficient if he exercises the ordinary skill of an ordinary competent man exercising that particular art."

In applying that test, it must be remembered that the measures to be taken by a professional man depend on the circumstances of the case. Although the judge talked about a " higher duty," I feel sure that what he meant was that in the circumstances of this case special steps were necessary in order to fulfil the duty of care: see *Readhead v. Midland Railway Co.* (1869) L.R. 4 Q.B. 379 , 393. In this case a new mode of construction was to be employed. The Council of the British Standards Institution had issued a circular [*Composite Construction in Structural Steel and Concrete. Part 1: Simply-supported Beams in Building*] which contained this note:

> "The designer should satisfy himself that no undesirable vibrations can be caused by the imposed loading. Serious vibrations may result when dynamic forces are applied at a frequency near to one of the natural frequencies of the members."

Mr. Baynham was aware of that note but he read it as a warning against resonances, that is, rhythmic impulses, and not as a warning against vibrations in general. So he did not take measures to deal with the random impulses of stacker trucks. There was evidence, too, that other competent designers might have done the same as Mr. Baynham. On that ground the judge seems to have thought that Mr. Baynham had not failed in the ordinary duty of care. But that does not excuse him. Other designers might have fallen short too. It is for the judge to set the standard of what a competent designer could do. And the judge in the next breath used words which seem to me to be a finding that Mr. Baynham did fail. It is a key passage [1974] 1 W.L.R. 1261 , 1269:

> "I do, however, find that he knew, or ought to have known, that the purpose of the floor was safely to carry heavily laden trucks and that he was warned about the dangers of vibration and did not take these matters sufficiently into account. The design was inadequate for the purpose."

It seems to me that that means that Mr. Baynham did not take the matters sufficiently into account which he ought to have done. That amounts to a finding of breach of the duty to use reasonable care and skill. On each of the grounds, therefore, I think the plaintiffs are entitled to succeed. They are entitled to a declaration of liability and indemnity. I would, accordingly, dismiss the appeal.

5.4 Has the Standard been Met?

Having decided what standard of care is owed by the defendant in a particular set of circumstances, the next part of our breach test is to decide whether the defendant has met that standard. If the defendant has not met the standard owed then there has been a breach of duty. It is at this point in the test that the courts can and do take into account subjective aspects of the defendant's personality, and in so doing the courts can counteract some of the potential unfairness of the objective first part of the test.

In deciding whether the standard has been met, the courts can take several things into account. Firstly, the courts can take into account all of the circumstances of the incident in question. The courts can also look at any/all relevant personal attributes of the defendant, and can also take into account policy considerations in what we can identify as a cost/benefit analysis.

In the following cases we shall see examples of considerations that the courts take into account when deciding whether the standard of care owed has been met.

The first consideration we shall look at is that which has become known as 'common practice'.

Bolam v Friern Hospital Management Committee [1957] 1 WLR 582

Panel: McNair J and a jury

Facts: for the facts of this case, see page 84

MR JUSTICE McNAIR

But the emphasis which is laid by the defence is on this aspect of negligence, that the real question you have to make up your minds about on each of the three major topics is whether the defendants, in acting in the way they did, were acting in accordance with a practice of competent respected professional opinion. Mr. Stirling submitted that if you are satisfied that they were acting in accordance with a practice of a competent body of professional opinion, then it would be wrong for you to hold that negligence was established...

...I myself would prefer to put it this way, that he is not guilty of negligence if he has acted in accordance with a practice accepted as proper by a responsible body of medical men skilled in that particular art. I do not think there is much difference in sense. It is just a different way of expressing the same thought. Putting it the other way round, a man is not negligent, if he is acting in accordance with such a practice, merely because there is a body of opinion who would take a contrary view. At the same time, that does not mean that a medical man can obstinately and pig-headedly carry on with some old technique if it has been proved to be contrary to what is really substantially the whole of informed medical opinion.

The *Bolam* test is essentially something to be used by the defendant to show that he has not breached his duty. If he can point to a reasonable body of opinion within his profession – not necessarily a majority opinion – that would have acted in the same manner, then he will not be held to have breached his duty. In the next case, we will see this test applied again in the medical profession, but it should be noted that the *Bolam* standard can be and has been applied to any profession where a substantial body of opinion exists that supports the action taken by the defendant.

Maynard v West Midlands Regional Health Authority [1984] 1 WLR 634

Panel: Lord Fraser of Tullybelton, Lord Elwyn-Jones, Lord Scarman, Lord Roskill and Lord Templeman

Facts: Both a consultant surgeon and a consultant physician examined the claimant, a patient in their care, and concluded that while the most likely diagnosis for the claimant's illness was tuberculosis, there were other possibilities, one of which was Hodgkin's disease. Since Hodgkin's disease was potentially fatal if not treated immediately, both consultants decided to perform an operation on the claimant immediately, rather than wait for the results of tests which could have confirmed the diagnosis but which would have taken several weeks. The procedure concerned was inherently risky, and although it was performed correctly the claimant was injured as a result of it. The House of Lords held that negligence could not be established simply by identifying a substantial body of medical opinion that thought the treatment had been incorrect, if there was an equally substantial body of opinion that supported the action taken by the consultants. Thus, in this case, there had been no breach of duty.

LORD SCARMAN

A case which is based on an allegation that a fully considered decision of two consultants in the field of their special skill was negligent clearly presents certain difficulties of proof. It is not enough to show that there is a body of competent professional opinion which considers that theirs was a wrong decision, if there also exists a body of professional opinion, equally competent, which supports the decision as reasonable in the circumstances. It is not enough to show that subsequent events show that the operation need never have been performed, if at the time the decision to operate was taken it was reasonable in the sense that a responsible body of medical opinion would have accepted it as proper. I do not think that the words of Lord President Clyde in *Hunter v. Hanley*, 1955 S.L.T. 213, 217 can be bettered:

"In the realm of diagnosis and treatment there is ample scope for genuine difference of opinion and one man clearly is not negligent merely because his conclusion differs from that of other professional men ... The true test for establishing negligence in diagnosis or treatment on the part of a doctor is whether he has been proved to be guilty of such failure as no doctor of ordinary skill would be guilty of if acting with ordinary care ..."

I would only add that a doctor who professes to exercise a special skill must exercise the ordinary skill of his speciality. Differences of opinion and practice exist, and will always exist, in the medical as in other professions. There is seldom any one answer exclusive of all others to problems of professional judgment. A court may prefer one body of opinion to the other: but that is no basis for a conclusion of negligence.

The courts also do not require professionals to guard against risks that were not known of at the time the tort was committed. In this sense, it can be said that the courts will only ever require a defendant to be knowledgeable up to the 'state of the art' in his profession.

Roe v Minister of Health and Another [1954] 2 QB 66

Panel: Somervell, Denning and Morris LJJ

Facts: The claimant had been anaesthetised for an operation by a specialist anaesthetist, using the drug nupercaine, which was injected into the spine. Unknown to the anaesthetist, the drug had been kept in ampoules (containers) that contained invisible cracks and/or flaws at the molecular level, and the drug itself had become contaminated with phenol, which, when injected into the claimant's spine, caused permanent paralysis from the waist down. The Court of Appeal held that since there was no way at the time of the incident that the medical staff could have known or foreseen that the ampoules would be defective, and that the contamination of the nupercaine would result, they could not be said to have breached their duty of care.

LORD JUSTICE DENNING

If the anaesthetists had foreseen that the ampoules might get cracked with cracks that could not be detected on inspection they would no doubt have dyed the phenol a deep blue; and this would have exposed the contamination. But I do not think that their failure to foresee this was negligence. It is so easy to be wise after the event and to condemn as negligence that which was only a misadventure. We ought always to be on our guard against it, especially in cases against hospitals and doctors. Medical science has conferred great benefits on mankind, but these benefits are attended by considerable risks. Every surgical operation is attended by risks. We cannot take the benefits without taking the risks. Every advance in technique is also attended by risks. Doctors, like the rest of us, have to learn by experience; and experience often teaches in a hard way. Something goes wrong and shows up a weakness, and then it is put right. That is just what happened here. Dr. Graham sought to escape the danger of infection by disinfecting the ampoule. In escaping that known danger he unfortunately ran into another danger. He did not know that there could be un-detectable cracks, but it was not negligent for him not to know it at that time. We must not look at the 1947 accident with 1954 spectacles. The judge acquitted Dr. Graham of negligence and we should uphold his decision.

This case demonstrates that where an activity is common practice within a profession or industry at the time of the alleged tort, the duty of care owed will generally not have been breached. This can be thought of as a policy-reasoned approach, in that the courts do not want to unduly burden professional defendants who are acting in a manner which is accepted by their profession or industry. However, there may be instances – as in our next case – where the common practice is in itself negligent, and where the court holds, therefore, that there has been a breach of duty.

Stokes v Guest, Keen and Nettlefold (Bolts and Nuts) Ltd [1968] 1 WLR 1776

Panel: Swanick J

Facts: The claimant claimed damages for the death of her husband, who had died of an unusual cancer. The most likely cause of the cancer was oil that the deceased had been exposed to over the 15 years of his employment by the defendants. The defendants had employed, since 1941 – nine years before the deceased started work at their factory – a medical specialist to whom they delegated all medical matters including general safety in the factory, and who had special knowledge of occupational diseases and industrial hygiene. Since 1941, various medical scientists had warned of the risks of cancer and had recommended generally that workers be periodically tested for signs of the disease and made aware of the risks. The medical specialist employed by the defendants took a different view on the level of risk involved, and neither tested the employees nor made them aware of the risks of the disease. The claimant argued that the defendants had been negligent in failing to be aware of the risk of cancer, and failing to make the deceased aware of the risks. The court held that where an employer did not fall below the standard of a generally recognised practice, there would be no breach of duty. However, liability was imposed vicariously for the negligence of the medical specialist, who, as a qualified doctor, owed a higher standard of care and should have known of the risks and taken action to avoid them.

MR JUSTICE SWANICK

I deduce the principles, that the overall test is still the conduct of the reasonable and prudent employer, taking positive thought for the safety of his workers in the light of what he knows or ought to know; where there is a recognised and general practice which has been followed for a substantial period in similar circumstances without mishap, he is entitled to follow it, unless in the light of common sense or newer knowledge it is clearly bad; but, where there is developing knowledge, he must keep reasonably abreast of it and not be too slow to apply it; and where he has in fact greater than average knowledge of the risks, he may be thereby obliged to take more than the average or standard precautions. He must weigh up the risk in terms of the likelihood of injury occurring and the potential consequences if it does; and he must balance against this the probably effectiveness of the precautions that can be taken to meet it and the expense and inconvenience they involve. If he is found to have fallen below the standard to be properly expected of a reasonable and prudent employer in these respects, he is negligent.

 Alert

There is, however, an additional complication in this case, not directly covered by authority so far as I am aware. For in this case the negligence alleged against the defendants lies largely in the sphere of vicarious responsibility for the actions or inaction of Dr. Lloyd, who was in their full-time employment as factory doctor and was thus their servant. It is of course plain that, if an employer delegates to a servant the performance of any part of his duty towards his workmen, he is responsible for the servant's negligence, however skilled the task; and I myself would take the view that, where the task requires a special skill or art, the servant must be judged by the standards pertaining to that skill or art, in so far as he is possessed of and exercising it.

The courts will also take into account, when deciding whether a defendant has met the standard of care that he owes, the seriousness of the injury that the claimant suffers. Remember that the law of negligence remains essentially claimant-focussed, so the courts will look to compensate for negligently caused injury if possible.

Watson v British Boxing Board of Control Ltd and Another [2001] QB 1134

Panel: Lord Phillips of Worth Matravers MR, May and Laws LJJ

Facts: The claimant was a professional boxer who sustained head injuries during a professional fight that was regulated by the defendants. He was treated by doctors beside the ring, but was not resuscitated until half an hour after the fight had ended, when he arrived in hospital. By the time he underwent surgery, he had suffered permanent brain damage. The claimant brought an action claiming that the defendants had been negligent in failing to provide resuscitation equipment ringside, for use if, as happened, a boxer required that kind of emergency treatment. The trial judge held that there had been a breach of duty, and the Court of Appeal upheld that decision.

LORD PHILLIPS OF WORTH MATRAVERS MR

Serious brain damage such as that suffered by Mr Watson, though happily an uncommon consequence of a boxing injury, represented the most serious risk posed by the sport and one that required to be addressed. …

I have already indicated that I do not accept the basis of the [defendant's] challenge [to] the [trial] judge's finding that the protocol in place ought to have included a requirement for a doctor to attend immediately where a fight was stopped because a boxer could no longer defend himself. Even absent such an express requirement, it seems to me that, if the protocol had been in place, the doctors present should have been aware of the desirability of examining Mr Watson's condition in the circumstances that had occurred, whether or not the rules expressly required this. It seems to me that this is almost implicit in [defence counsel] Mr Walker's argument that to issue such a requirement expressly was to instruct a doctor as to how to perform his duty.

A defendant seeking to disturb the findings of fact of a trial judge in relation to causation undertakes a hard task. I consider that the judge was entitled to find on the evidence that, had the Hamlyn protocol been in place, the outcome of Mr Watson's injuries would have been significantly better. On the law relied upon by the judge, this was all that Mr Watson needed to succeed.

The final consideration that we need to look at is the balancing exercise the courts endeavour to undertake where there is some potential benefit to the risky exercise that was undertaken and that resulted in the claimant's harm. This is essentially policy-based, as it is thought that in some circumstances the potential benefit from the activity outweighed the risk of the harm that was caused, and therefore should not be regarded as being in breach of duty. The courts are generally open to the idea that defendants should not be discouraged from taking some risks when the potential benefits are substantial.

Watt v Hertfordshire County Council [1954] 1 WLR 835

Panel: Singleton, Denning and Morris LJJ

Facts: A fireman who was travelling with heavy-lifting equipment in a lorry that had not been outfitted for carrying such equipment was injured when, while the lorry was rushing to the scene of an emergency, the heavy equipment came unsecured and caught his ankle. The Court of Appeal held that the risk of injury was relatively minor compared with the potential benefit to be gained from arriving quickly at the scene of the emergency, where a woman was trapped, and that there had thus been no breach of duty.

LORD JUSTICE DENNING

It is well settled that in measuring due care you must balance the risk against the measures necessary to eliminate the risk. To that proposition there ought to be added this: you must balance the risk against the end to be achieved. If this accident had occurred in a commercial enterprise without any emergency there could be no doubt that the servant would succeed. But the commercial end to make profit is very different from the human end to save life or limb. The saving of life or limb justifies taking considerable risk, and I am glad to say that there have never been wanting in this country men of courage ready to take those risks, notably in the fire service.

In this case the risk involved in sending out the lorry was not so great as to prohibit the attempt to save life. I quite agree that fire engines, ambulances and doctors' cars should not shoot past the traffic lights when they show a red light. That is because the risk is too great to warrant the incurring of the danger. It is always a question of balancing the risk against the end.

LORD JUSTICE MORRIS

I also agree. The accident in this case came about as a result of a somewhat unusual concatenation of circumstances. There had for a very long time been no call for the use of the jack. Any such call, according to the evidence, was extremely rare. It so happened that a call came at a time when the Austin vehicle which would normally have carried the jack was otherwise engaged. I do not think it can be said to have been unreasonable to have had the Austin vehicle for use in the way that was arranged. Had the station been a larger station, had there been unlimited resources, unlimited space and an unlimited number of vehicles, it might be that another fitted vehicle would have been available; but that was not reasonably practicable or possible. What happened was that when the call for the jack came the sub-officer had to decide what to do, and I do not think that it would have been in accordance with the traditions of the wonderful service with which we are concerned if he had said that he could do nothing other than call on St. Albans. What he decided to do was in accordance with the practice of the fire service.

In this case the risk of injury to the firefighter was minimal, and the potential benefits to be gained by rushing to the scene of the accident were held by the court to be high enough that it was a risk worth taking. Thus, in the circumstances, the court held that there had been no breach of the duty. This can be contrasted with an earlier case.

Ward v London County Council [1938] 2 All ER 341

Panel: Charles J

Facts: The claimant brought an action for damages sustained by himself, his wife and their two children, all of whom were in the claimant's car when it was struck at a crossroads by a fire engine that went through a red light in an attempt to get to the scene of an emergency more quickly. The court held that the risks taken by the driver of the fire engine were not outweighed by the potential benefits of arriving more quickly at the emergency scene, and there had thus been a breach of duty.

MR JUSTICE CHARLES

According to the driver's own story, that is precisely what he did. He saw this car coming across fast, at a moment when with the greatest ease he could have stopped and given the road to the car, which was proceeding in accordance with the signal indications. No emergency would justify the driver of a fire engine in taking the risk of colliding with such a vehicle. In my judgment, the driver was taking his chance, and rushing over that crossing at a high speed, endangering other vehicles that might be in the vicinity, approaching, or designing to cross, those crossroads with the lights in their favour.

It is said that, because he was driving a fire engine, he was in a certain privileged position. That is not so. He was not in a privileged position at all. It is perfectly true that, when the bell is clanged, people generally draw aside, but, if they do not draw aside, the driver of a fire engine has no business to charge into them. He must use reasonable care, and get to the scene of the fire as quickly as possible. Indeed, the traffic regulations of the London County Council make it perfectly clear that that is the position which is recognised by them. The fire brigade must get there as quickly as possible, and they add, and I have no doubt rightly, that stopping at the red signal in practice is found not to hamper the proper conduct of the fire brigade in the carrying out of its duty.

In this case the risks of driving a fire engine at high speed through a red light were too high to be acceptable. The court made clear that there is no benefit to be gained from risking life and limb in order to get to the scene of an emergency more quickly. In essence, the court was stating that it is not worth risking one life to save another – no one person is worth more than anyone else. Thus in this case, the defendants had breached their duty.

5.5 Proving the Breach

The last thing we need to look at is the practical aspect of proving a breach of duty. There are two things which, in addition to proving the breach on the facts, can help a claimant demonstrate a breach.

First, claimants are aided by the Civil Evidence Act 1968 s 11. This provides for the use of criminal convictions as evidence of a breach of duty in civil proceedings. So, if a defendant is convicted of dangerous driving, a claimant can use the fact that the defendant was convicted of that offence to prove that the defendant breached his duty to drive with the skill of a reasonably competent driver when that incident occurred. Note that the conviction must arise from the same circumstances as the tort – a conviction for dangerous driving from one incident is not admissible as proof of negligence for a different incident. In other words, a conviction cannot be used as proof of a driver's predilection for driving unsafely, only as evidence of unsafe driving in the circumstances in question.

The second thing that can aid claimants is the doctrine of *res ipsa loquitur* – literally: 'the facts speak for themselves'. This is a doctrine that, if used, makes it much easier for the claimant to demonstrate that the defendant has breached his duty of care, by requiring the defendant to prove that he was not negligent.

Mahon v Osborne [1939] 2 KB 14

Panel: Scott, Mackinnon and Goddard LJJ

Facts: A patient died three months after undergoing an operation in hospital. During the operation, a number of surgical swabs had been used, and one of these had been left inside the patient's body after the surgery. It was this swab that caused the death of the patient. The patient's mother brought an action alleging negligence on the part of the surgeon, and sought to rely on the maxim *res ipsa loquitur* to require the defendant to prove that he had not been negligent. The majority of the Court of Appeal (Scott LJ dissenting) held that *res ipsa loquitur* could apply in this case.

LORD JUSTICE GODDARD

I now turn to the evidence in the case. The plaintiff, beyond proving facts necessary to establish damage and putting in answers to interrogatories, called no further evidence. She proved by the interrogatories that the swab had been left in at the operation performed by the defendant, and that was enough to call upon him for an explanation. And here, as I understand the Court is not unanimous on the point, I think it right to say that in my opinion the doctrine of res ipsa loquitur does apply in such a case as this, at least to the extent I mention below.

The surgeon is in command of the operation, it is for him to decide what instruments, swabs and the like are to be used, and it is he who uses them. The patient, or, if he dies, his representatives, can know nothing about this matter. There can be no possible question but that neither swabs nor instruments are ordinarily left in the patient's body, and no one would venture to say that it is proper, although in particular circumstances it may be excusable, so to leave them. If, therefore, a swab is left in the patient's body, it seems to me clear that the surgeon is called on for an explanation, that is, he is called on to show not necessarily why he missed it but that he exercised due care to prevent it being left there. It is no disparagement of the devoted and frequently gratuitous service which the profession of surgery renders to mankind to say that its members may on occasion fall short of the standard of care which they themselves, no less than the law, require, and, if a patient on whom had befallen such a misfortune as we are now considering were not entitled to call on the surgeon for an explanation, I cannot but feel that an unwarranted protection would be given to carelessness, such as I do not believe the profession itself would either expect or desire.

Further Reading

Mark Lunney and Ken Olliphant, *Tort Law Text and Materials: A Fundamental Restatement,* (3rd edition) Oxford University Press 2008, Chapter 4

6

Causation

Topic List

Introduction

Causation is an essential element of a negligence claim. It is divided into two parts. First, the claimant must prove factual causation, i.e. that the defendant's breach was the factual cause of their damage. This is not difficult where there is only one possible cause of the claimant's damage. It can be satisfied by application of what is known as the 'but for' test. This asks the question: 'but for the defendant's breach, would the injury to the claimant have occurred, at that time and in that way?' If the answer is no, factual causation is satisfied. However, factual causation is more difficult to resolve where, for example, there is more than one possible cause of the claimant's damage, or where there is insufficient evidence as to precisely what, in fact, caused the damage. It is in these circumstances that the courts have sometimes been more innovative in terms of the causation tests they have adopted, largely for policy reasons that will be examined in this chapter.

Provided factual causation has been satisfied, the claimant must also prove that the defendant should be legally liable for the damage (known as 'legal causation'). This will involve consideration of whether there have been intervening acts occurring between the original defendant's breach and the claimant's damage. These acts may have been committed by a third party, by the claimant himself, or they may be natural acts ('Acts of God') for example, flash floods or bolts of lightning. Only acts which are deemed unreasonable and/or unforeseeable will break the chain, extinguishing the defendant's liability at that point.

Questions as to the *extent* of any liability on the defendant's part, while considered by some academics as part of legal causation, will not be looked at in this way here.

Link
See Chapter 7 on Remoteness for discussion as to the extent of a defendant's legal liability to a claimant.

6.1 Factual Causation

6.1.1 The 'But For' Test

The 'but for' test should be the starting point when considering factual causation. The term 'but for' is widely held to have been coined by Denning LJ in the case of *Cork v Kirby Maclean Ltd* [1952] 2 All ER 402, where he said '...If you can say that the damage would not have happened but for a particular fault, then that fault is in fact a cause of the damage; but if you can say that the damage would have happened just the same, fault or no fault, then the fault is not a cause of the damage'.

The application of the 'but for' test is clearly illustrated, (although the phrase 'but for' is not actually used) in the following case.

Barnett v Chelsea and Kensington Hospital Management Committee [1969] 1 QB 428

Panel: Nield J

Facts: Three night-watchmen attended the casualty department of a hospital run by the defendants, complaining of vomiting after drinking tea. The nurse who saw them telephoned the duty medical casualty officer, who advised her to tell the men to go home and to see their own doctors. As a result, the men left. About five hours later one of the men died from arsenic poisoning, the arsenic having been introduced into the tea. Medical evidence suggested that the man would probably have died in any event, even if he had been admitted to hospital five hours earlier. The issue for the court was whether, in law, the plaintiff, (the deceased man's wife) could satisfy factual causation. The action was dismissed.

MR JUSTICE NIELD

It remains to consider whether it is shown that the deceased's death was caused by that negligence or whether, as the defendants have said, the deceased must have died in any event. In his concluding submission Mr. Pain submitted that the casualty officer should have examined the deceased and had he done so he would have caused tests to be made which would have indicated the treatment required and that, since the defendants were at fault in these respects, therefore the onus of proof passed to the defendants to show that the appropriate treatment would have failed, and authorities were cited to me. I find myself unable to accept that argument, and I am of the view that the onus of proof remains upon the plaintiff, and I have in mind (without quoting it) the decision cited by Mr. Wilmers in *Bonnington Castings Ltd. v. Wardlaw*. However, were it otherwise and the onus did pass to the defendants, then I would find that they have discharged it, as I would proceed to show. ...

Without going in detail into the considerable volume of technical evidence which has been put before me, it seems to me to be the case that when death results from arsenical poisoning it is brought about by two conditions; on the one hand dehydration and on the other disturbance of the enzyme processes. If the principal condition is one of enzyme disturbance - as I am of the view it was here - then the only method of treatment which is likely to succeed is the use of the specific antidote which is commonly called B.A.L. Dr. Goulding said in the course of his evidence:

"The only way to deal with this is to use the specific B.A.L. I see no reasonable prospect of the deceased being given B.A.L. before the time at which he died" - and at a later point in his evidence - "I feel that even if fluid loss had been discovered death would have been caused by the enzyme disturbance. Death might have occurred later."

I regard that evidence as very moderate, and it might be a true assessment of the situation to say that there was no chance of B.A.L. being administered before the death of the deceased.

For those reasons, I find that the plaintiff has failed to establish, on the balance of probabilities, that the defendants' negligence caused the death of the deceased.

Although the medical casualty officer had breached his duty to the deceased, by failing to see and examine him (the defendants being vicariously in breach), the plaintiff had failed to establish that the defendant's breach caused the death. In other words, 'but for' the breach, the deceased would have died anyway, so factual causation was not satisfied.

6.1.2 Problems with the 'But For' Test

As mentioned in the introduction to this chapter, the 'but for' test is useful for relatively simple situations, concerning one possible cause of damage. However, where there may be more than one cause, or where there is insufficient evidence to establish causation, the 'but for' test is inadequate, leaving open the potential for a claimant to have no remedy against defendants, even where there have been obvious breaches which have, on any reading, caused loss to the claimant. This situation arose in the next case (which pre-dates *Barnett*) and was dealt with by the court in a way that has had far-reaching consequences for the law of causation in tort.

Bonnington Castings Ltd v Wardlaw [1956] AC 613

Panel: Viscount Simonds, Lord Reid, Lord Tucker, Lord Keith of Avonholm and Lord Somervell of Harrow

Facts: The plaintiff (respondent) was a steel dresser, who, through the course of his employment with the defendants, was exposed to silica dust emanating from both the pneumatic hammer with which he worked and from swing grinders. The defendants had acted reasonably in protecting the plaintiff from dust from the hammer – no extraction method was known or practicable in respect of this, but the defendants breached their statutory duties in respect of the swing grinders which should have been kept free from obstruction. The plaintiff contracted pneumoconiosis caused by his exposure to the silica dust and sued the defendants for damages.

The problem for the plaintiff was that, by the nature of the way in which the damage was inflicted, it was not possible for him to prove, even to the civil standard of proof, that it was the dust from the swing grinders (present as a result of the defendant's breach) as opposed to the dust from the hammer (non-tortious) that had caused his injury.

LORD REID

...It is admitted for the appellants that they were in breach of this regulation in that for considerable periods dust from the swing grinders escaped into the shop where the respondent was working owing to the appliances for its interception and removal being choked and therefore inadequate. The question is whether this breach of the regulation caused the respondent's disease. If his disease resulted from his having inhaled part of the noxious dust from the swing grinders which should have been intercepted and removed, then the appellants are liable to him in damages: but if it did not result from that, then they are not liable. ...

It would seem obvious in principle that a pursuer or plaintiff must prove not only negligence or breach of duty but also that such fault caused or materially contributed to his injury, and there is ample authority for that proposition both in Scotland and in England. I can find neither reason nor authority for the rule being different where there is breach of a statutory duty. The fact that Parliament imposes a duty for the protection of employees has been held to entitle an employee to sue if he is injured as a result of a breach of that duty, but it would be going a great deal farther to hold that it can be inferred from the enactment of a duty that Parliament intended that any employee suffering injury can sue his employer merely because there was a breach of duty and it is shown to be possible that his injury may have been caused by it. In my judgment, the employee must in all cases prove his case by the ordinary standard of proof in civil actions: he must make it appear at least that on a balance of probabilities the breach of duty caused or materially contributed to his injury. ...

The medical evidence was that pneumoconiosis is caused by a gradual accumulation in the lungs of minute particles of silica inhaled over a period of years. That means, I think, that the disease is caused by the whole of the noxious material inhaled and, if that material comes from two sources, it cannot be wholly attributed to material from one source or the other. I am in agreement with much of the Lord President's opinion in this case, but I cannot agree that the question is: which was the most probable source of the respondent's disease, the dust from the pneumatic hammers or the dust from the swing grinders? It appears to me that the source of his disease was the dust from both sources, and the real question is whether the dust from the swing grinders materially contributed to the disease. What is a material contribution must be a question of degree. A contribution which comes within the exception de minimis non curat lex is not material, but I think that any contribution which does not fall within that exception must be material. I do not see how there can be something too large to come within the de minimis principle but yet too small to be material. ...

...In my opinion, it is proved not only that the swing grinders may well have contributed but that they did in fact contribute a quota of silica dust which was not negligible to the pursuer's lungs and therefore did help to produce the disease.That is sufficient to establish liability against the appellants, and I am therefore of opinion that this appeal should be dismissed.

The defendant's appeal was dismissed. The onus lay on the plaintiff to show only that, on the balance of probabilities, the breach caused *or materially contributed to the injury*, and that on the facts, the dust from the swing grinders *did* materially contribute to the plaintiff's injury.

This case concerned cumulative exposure to a noxious substance, only some of which was caused by the defendant's breach. Had the House of Lords adopted a strict interpretation of the 'but for' test, the claimant would have lost. The precedent was set. But how would it be applied in subsequent cases? The next case, with similar facts to *Bonnington*, arguably took factual causation even further, making it easier still for the claimant to satisfy this part of their claim.

McGhee v National Coal Board [1973] 1 WLR 1

Panel: Lord Reid, Lord Wilberforce, Lord Simon of Glaisdale, Lord Kilbrandon and Lord Salmon

Facts: The plaintiff worked in brick kilns owned by the defendant. He was sent to empty brick kilns where the working conditions were hotter and more dusty than usual, and shortly afterwards, having experienced skin irritation, was found to have contracted dermatitis. He sued his employers who admitted that the dermatitis was attributable to working in the brick kilns, and that they had breached their common law duty in failing to provide adequate washing facilities for their employees. This was important because medical evidence showed that dermatitis was caused by tiny abrasions to the outer layer of skin, followed by injury to the cells under the skin. Profuse sweating softened the outer layer of skin. When that skin was then exposed to brick dust, large quantities of the dust would adhere to the skin, exposing the cells underneath to injury, and dermatitis would result. Washing immediately was the only way to remove the dust, and so a failure to provide adequate washing facilities resulted in prolonged exposure to dust on the skin, until the plaintiff had cycled home and could wash there. While admitting a breach in this respect, the defendant employers argued that their breach had not caused, nor materially contributed, to the plaintiff's disease.

In allowing the appeal, it was held that in the absence of comprehensive medical knowledge as to all the material factors leading to dermatitis, the appellant was entitled to recover damages from his employers. There was no substantial difference between materially increasing the *risk* of injury and materially contributing to the injury, and as such, the employers had created the risk by virtue of their breach and should be liable.

LORD REID

It has always been the law that a pursuer succeeds if he can show that fault of the defender caused or materially contributed to his injury. There may have been two separate causes but it is enough if one of the causes arose from fault of the defender. The pursuer does not have to prove that this cause would of itself have been enough to cause him injury. That is well illustrated by the decision of this House *in Bonnington Castings Ltd. v. Wardlaw [1956] AC 613*. There the pursuer's disease was caused by an accumulation of noxious dust in his lungs. The dust which he had inhaled over a period came from two sources. The defenders were not responsible for one source but they could and ought to have prevented the other. The dust from the latter source was not in itself sufficient to cause the disease but the pursuer succeeded because it made a material contribution to his injury.

The respondents seek to distinguish *Wardlaw*'s [*Bonnington*'s] case by arguing that then it was proved that every particle of dust inhaled played its part in causing the onset of the disease whereas in this case it is not proved that every minor abrasion played its part.

In the present case the evidence does not show — perhaps no one knows — just how dermatitis of this type begins. It suggests to me that there are two possible ways. It may be that an accumulation of minor abrasions of the horny layer of the skin is a necessary precondition for the onset of the disease. Or it may be that the disease starts at one particular abrasion and then spreads, so that multiplication of abrasions merely increases the number of places where the disease can start and in that way increases the risk of its occurrence.

I am inclined to think that the evidence points to the former view. But in a field where so little appears to be known with certainty I could not say that that is proved. If it were, then this case would be indistinguishable from *Wardlaw*'s case. But I think that in cases like this we must take a broader view of causation. The medical evidence is to the effect that the fact that the man had to cycle home caked with grime and sweat added materially to the risk that this disease might develop. It does not and could not explain just why that is so. But experience shows that it is so. Plainly that must be because what happens while the man remains unwashed can have a causative effect, though just how the cause operates is uncertain. I cannot accept the view expressed in the Inner House that once the man left the brick kiln he left behind the causes which made him liable to develop dermatitis. That seems to me quite inconsistent with a proper interpretation of the medical evidence. Nor can I accept the distinction drawn by the Lord Ordinary between materially increasing the risk that the disease will occur and making a material contribution to its occurrence.

There may be some logical ground for such a distinction where our knowledge of all the material factors is complete. But it has often been said that the legal concept of causation is not based on logic or philosophy. It is based on the practical way in which the ordinary man's mind works in the everyday affairs of life. From a broad and practical viewpoint I can see no substantial difference between saying that what the defender did materially increased the risk of injury to the pursuer and saying that what the defender did made a material contribution to his injury.

I would therefore allow this appeal.

LORD WILBERFORCE

...But the question remains whether a pursuer must necessarily fail if, after he has shown a breach of duty, involving an increase of risk of disease, he cannot positively prove that this increase of risk caused or materially contributed to the disease while his employers cannot positively prove the contrary. In this intermediate case there is an appearance of logic in the view that the pursuer, on whom the onus lies, should fail — a logic which dictated the judgments below. The question is whether we should be satisfied, in factual situations like the present, with this logical approach. In my opinion, there are further considerations of importance. First, it is a sound principle that where a person has, by breach of a duty of care, created a risk, and injury occurs within the area of that risk, the loss should be borne by him unless he shows that it had some other cause. Secondly, from the evidential point of view, one may ask, why should a man who is able to show that his employer should have taken certain precautions, because without them there is a risk, or an added risk, of injury or disease, and who in fact sustains exactly that injury or disease, have to assume the burden of proving more: namely, that it was the addition to the risk, caused by the breach of duty, which caused or materially contributed to the injury? In many cases, of which the present is typical, this is impossible to prove, just because honest medical opinion cannot segregate the causes of an illness between compound causes. And if one asks which of the parties, the workman or the employers, should suffer from this inherent evidential difficulty, the answer as a matter of policy or justice should be that it is the creator of the risk who, ex hypothesi must be taken to have foreseen the possibility of damage, who should bear its consequences. ...

 Alert

The next important case in this area concerned medical negligence, and the question was whether the court would be prepared to accept the *McGhee* approach to causation in these circumstances. The answer was no.

Wilsher v Essex Area Health Authority [1988] AC 1074

Panel: Lord Bridge of Harwich, Lord Fraser of Tullybelton, Lord Lowry, Lord Griffiths and Lord Ackner

Facts: The plaintiff was born prematurely and required oxygen. The hospital staff inserted a catheter into his vein rather than his artery, causing too much oxygen to be administered. The plaintiff subsequently suffered from an incurable condition of the eye ('RLF'), causing total blindness in one eye, and almost total blindness in the other. Medical evidence was inconclusive as to the precise cause of the eye condition.

The condition could have been caused by the excess oxygen, but it could equally have been caused by any one of four other (non-tortious) risks, to which the plaintiff had also been exposed. At first instance, affirmed by the Court of Appeal (Sir Nicholas Browne-Wilkinson V-C dissenting) the plaintiff succeeded, relying on *McGhee* causation principles. The appeal was allowed and the dissenting judgment of Sir Nicholas Browne-Wilkinson V-C was approved.

LORD BRIDGE OF HARWICH

...A distinction is, of course, apparent between the facts of *Bonnington Castings Ltd. v. Wardlaw*, where the "innocent" and "guilty" silica dust particles which together caused the pursuer's lung disease were inhaled concurrently and the facts of *McGhee v. National Coal Board* [1973] 1 WLR 1 where the "innocent" and "guilty" brick dust was present on the pursuer's body for consecutive periods. In the one case the concurrent inhalation of "innocent" and "guilty" dust must both have contributed to the cause of the disease. In the other case the consecutive periods when "innocent" and "guilty" brick dust was present on the pursuer's body may both have contributed to the cause of the disease or, theoretically at least, one or other may have been the sole cause. But where the layman is told by the doctors that the longer the brick dust remains on the body, the greater the risk of dermatitis, although the doctors cannot identify the process of causation scientifically, there seems to be nothing irrational in drawing the inference, as a matter of common sense, that the consecutive periods when brick dust remained on the body probably contributed cumulatively to the causation of the dermatitis. I believe that a process of inferential reasoning on these general lines underlies the decision of the majority in *McGhee's* case. ...

The conclusion I draw from these passages is that *McGhee v. National Coal Board* [1973] 1 WLR 1 laid down no new principle of law whatever. On the contrary, it affirmed the principle that the onus of proving causation lies on the pursuer or plaintiff. Adopting a robust and pragmatic approach to the undisputed primary facts of the case, the majority concluded that it was a legitimate inference of fact that the defenders' negligence had materially contributed to the pursuer's injury. The decision, in my opinion, is of no greater significance than that and to attempt to extract from it some esoteric principle which in some way modifies, as a matter of law, the nature of the burden of proof of causation which a plaintiff or pursuer must discharge once he has established a relevant breach of duty is a fruitless one.

In the Court of Appeal in the instant case Sir Nicholas Browne-Wilkinson V-C, being in a minority, expressed his view on causation with understandable caution. But I am quite unable to find any fault with the following passage in his dissenting judgment [1987] QB730, 779:

[Quoting from Sir Nicholas Browne-Wilkinson V-C in the Court of Appeal]

"To apply the principle in McGhee v. National Coal Board [1973] 1 WLR 1 the present case would constitute an extension of that principle. In the McGhee case there was no doubt that the pursuer's dermatitis was physically caused by brick dust: the only question was whether the continued presence of such brick dust on the pursuer's skin after the time when he should have been provided with a shower caused or materially contributed to the dermatitis which he contracted. There was only one possible agent which could have caused the dermatitis, viz., brick dust, and there was no doubt that the dermatitis from which he suffered was caused by that brick dust.

In the present case the question is different. There are a number of different agents which could have caused the RLF. Excess oxygen was one of them. The defendants failed to take reasonable precautions to prevent one of the possible causative agents (e.g. excess oxygen) from causing RLF. But no one can tell in this case whether excess oxygen did or did not cause or contribute to the RLF suffered by the plaintiff. The plaintiff's RLF may have been caused by some completely different agent or agents, e.g. hypercarbia, intraventricular haemorrhage, apnoea or patent ductus arteriosus. In addition to oxygen, each of those conditions has been implicated as a possible cause of RLF. This baby suffered from each of those conditions at various times in the first two months of his life. There is no satisfactory evidence that excess oxygen is more likely than any of those other four candidates to have caused RLF in this baby. To my mind, the occurrence of RLF following a failure to take a necessary precaution to prevent excess oxygen causing RLF provides no evidence and raises no presumption that it was excess oxygen rather than one or more of the four other possible agents which caused or contributed to RLF in this case.

The position, to my mind, is wholly different from that in [McGhee] where there was only one candidate (brick dust) which could have caused the dermatitis, and the failure to take a precaution against brick dust causing dermatitis was followed by dermatitis caused by brick dust. In such a case, I can see the common sense, if not the logic, of holding that, in the absence of any other evidence, the failure to take the precaution caused or contributed to the dermatitis. To the extent that certain members of the House of Lords decided the question on inferences from evidence or presumptions, I do not consider that the present case falls within their reasoning. A failure to take preventative measures against one out of five possible causes is no evidence as to which of those five caused the injury."

Note that Lord Bridge described the decision in McGhee as no more than a 'robust and pragmatic' approach to the undisputed facts of that case, and an application of ordinary principles of causation already accepted in *Bonnington*. This interpretation of *McGhee* was heavily criticised (although the decision in *Wilsher* accepted as correct) by the House of Lords in the case of *Fairchild v Glenhaven Funeral services Ltd* [2003] 1 AC 32 (see below). On a simplistic level, *Wilsher* can be viewed simply as a rejection of the *McGhee* approach in favour of the orthodox 'but for' test of factual causation.

There is undoubtedly strength in the argument that *Bonnington* and *McGhee* on the one hand, and *Wilsher* on the other, were so fundamentally different, as to render heavy-handed any attempt to force the same factual causation test on both. Both *Bonnington* and *McGhee* concerned one agent causing damage – dust (silica and brick dust respectively). However, in *Wilsher*, there were five independent possible causes, any one of which could have been responsible for the damage. In that case, the independent causes did not act cumulatively to produce the damage in the plaintiff, whereas in *Bonnington* and *McGhee*, that is exactly what happened, the dust in each case coming from both 'innocent' and 'guilty' sources. These different approaches to factual causation, governed by the nature of the circumstances in question, was one of the live issues discussed in the next case.

6.1.3 Which approach to Factual Causation is correct?

Fairchild v Glenhaven Funeral Services Ltd [2003] 1 AC 32

Panel: Lord Bingham of Cornhill, Lord Nicholls of Birkenhead, Lord Hoffmann, Lord Hutton and Lord Rodger of Earlsferry

Facts: Three appeals were heard together and concerned three claimants, each of whom had developed mesothelioma (a form of cancer) from exposure to asbestos dust or fibres while at work, having worked for several different employers over a period of time. Each claimant sought damages from the defendant employers who had breached their duty to protect the employees from the risk of contracting the disease by exposing them to inhalation of the dust/fibres. While it was accepted that the greater the exposure to asbestos, the greater the likelihood of contracting mesothelioma, the specific way in which asbestos caused the disease was not known at that time. In particular, there was no evidence as to whether the disease could be caused by exposure to a single asbestos fibre or only by exposure to several fibres.

The Court of Appeal rejected all three claims, holding that the claimants had been unable to establish, on the balance of probabilities, which period of exposure had caused their damage (having decided that the disease was triggered on a single occasion which should be identifiable). In other words, the claims failed at the factual causation stage. The claimants appealed to the House of Lords.

LORD BINGHAM OF CORNHILL

...The issue in these appeals does not concern the general validity and applicability of [the 'but for' test for factual causation] which is not in question, but is whether in special circumstances such as those in these cases there should be any variation or relaxation of it. The overall object of tort law is to define cases in which the law may justly hold one party liable to compensate another. Are these such cases? A and B owed C a duty to protect C against a risk of a particular and very serious kind. They failed to perform that duty. As a result the risk eventuated and C suffered the very harm against which it was the duty of A and B to protect him. Had there been only one tortfeasor, C would have been entitled to recover, but because the duty owed to him was broken by two tortfeasors and not only one, he is held to be entitled to recover against neither, because of his inability to prove what is scientifically unprovable. If the mechanical application of generally accepted rules leads to such a result, there must be room to question the appropriateness of such an approach in such a case. ...

Thus there was a risk [in this case] that the defendant might be held liable for acts for which he should not be held legally liable but no risk that he would be held liable for damage which (whether legally liable or not) he had not caused. The crux of cases such as the present, if the appellants' argument is upheld, is that an employer may be held liable for damage he has not caused. The risk is the greater where all the employers potentially liable are not before the court. This is so on the facts of each of the three appeals before the House, and is always likely to be so given the long latency of this condition and the likelihood that some employers potentially liable will have gone out of business or disappeared during that period. It can properly be said to be unjust to impose liability on a party who has not been shown, even on a balance of probabilities, to have caused the damage complained of. On the other hand, there is a strong policy argument in favour of compensating those who have suffered grave harm, at the expense of their employers who owed them a duty to protect them against that very harm and failed to do so, when the harm can only have been caused by breach of that duty and when science does not permit the victim accurately to attribute, as between several employers, the precise responsibility for the harm he has suffered. I am of opinion that such injustice as may be involved in imposing liability on a duty-breaking employer in these circumstances is heavily outweighed by the injustice of denying redress to a victim. Were the law otherwise, an employer exposing his employee to asbestos dust could obtain complete immunity against mesothelioma (but not asbestosis) claims by employing only those who had previously been exposed to excessive quantities of asbestos dust. Such a result would reflect no credit on the law. ...

 Alert

LORD NICHOLLS OF BIRKENHEAD

The present appeals are another example of such circumstances, where good policy reasons exist for departing from the usual threshold "but for" test of causal connection. Inhalation of asbestos dust carries a risk of mesothelioma. That is one of the very risks from which an employer's duty of care is intended to protect employees. ... There must be good reason for departing from the normal threshold "but for" test. The reason must be sufficiently weighty to justify depriving the defendant of the protection this test normally and rightly affords him, and it must be plain and obvious that this is so. Policy questions will loom large when a court has to decide whether the difficulties of proof confronting the plaintiff justify taking this exceptional course. It is impossible to be more specific…

[W]hen applying the principle described above [material increase in risk from *McGhee*] the court is not, by a process of inference, concluding that the ordinary "but for" standard of causation is satisfied. Instead, the court is applying a different and less stringent test. It were best if this were recognised openly.

LORD HOFFMANN

…What are the significant features of the present case? First, we are dealing with a duty specifically intended to protect employees against being unnecessarily exposed to the risk of (among other things) a particular disease. Secondly, the duty is one intended to create a civil right to compensation for injury relevantly connected with its breach. Thirdly, it is established that the greater the exposure to asbestos, the greater the risk of contracting that disease. Fourthly, except in the case in which there has been only one significant exposure to asbestos, medical science cannot prove whose asbestos is more likely than not to have produced the cell mutation which caused the disease. Fifthly, the employee has contracted the disease against which he should have been protected.

In these circumstances, a rule requiring proof of a link between the defendant's asbestos and the claimant's disease would, with the arbitrary exception of single-employer cases, empty the duty of content. If liability depends upon proof that the conduct of the defendant was a necessary condition of the injury, it cannot effectively exist. It is however open to your Lordships to formulate a different causal requirement in this class of case. The Court of Appeal was in my opinion wrong to say that in the absence of a proven link between the defendant's asbestos and the disease, there was no "causative relationship" whatever between the defendant's conduct and the disease. It depends entirely upon the level at which the causal relationship is described. To say, for example, that the cause of Mr Matthews's cancer was his significant exposure to asbestos during two employments over a period of eight years, without being able to identify the day upon which he inhaled the fatal fibre, is a meaningful causal statement. The medical evidence shows that it is the only kind of causal statement about the disease which, in the present state of knowledge, a scientist would regard as possible. There is no a priori reason, no rule of logic, which prevents the law from treating it as sufficient to satisfy the causal requirements of the law of negligence. The question is whether your Lordships think such a rule would be just and reasonable and whether the class of cases to which it applies can be sufficiently clearly defined.

So the question of principle is this: in cases which exhibit the five features I have mentioned, which rule would be more in accordance with justice and the policy of common law and statute to protect employees against the risk of contracting asbestos-related diseases? One which makes an employer in breach of his duty liable for the employee's injury because he created a significant risk to his health, despite the fact that the physical cause of the injury *may* have been created by someone else? Or a rule which means that unless he was subjected to risk by the breach of duty of a single employer, the employee can never have a remedy? My Lords, as between the employer in breach of duty and the employee who has lost his life in consequence of a period of exposure to risk to which that employer has contributed, I think it would be both inconsistent with the policy of the law imposing the duty and morally wrong for your Lordships to impose causal requirements which exclude liability.

I therefore regard *McGhee* as a powerful support for saying that when the five factors I have mentioned are present, the law should treat a material increase in risk as sufficient to satisfy the causal requirements for liability. The only difficulty lies in the way *McGhee* was explained in *Wilsher v Essex Area Health Authority* [1988] AC 1074. The latter was not a case in which the five factors were present. It was an action for clinical negligence in which it was alleged that giving a premature baby excessive oxygen had caused retrolental fibroplasia, resulting in blindness. The evidence was that the fibroplasia could have been caused in a number of different ways including excessive oxygen but the judge had made no finding that the oxygen was more likely than not to have been the cause. The Court of Appeal ... held that the health authority was nevertheless liable because even if the excessive oxygen could not be shown to have caused the injury, it materially increased the risk of the injury happening.

The Court of Appeal reached this conclusion by treating the causal requirement rule applied in *McGhee* as being of general application. Mustill LJ said, at pp 771-772:

"If it is an established fact that conduct of a particular kind creates a risk that injury will be caused to another or increases an existing risk that injury will ensue; and if the two parties stand in such a relationship that the one party owes a duty not to conduct himself in that way; and if the first party does conduct himself in that way; and if the other party does suffer injury of the kind to which the risk related; then the first party is taken to have caused the injury by his breach of duty, even though the existence and extent of the contribution made by the breach cannot be ascertained."

The House of Lords, in a speech by Lord Bridge of Harwich with which all other noble Lords concurred, rejected this broad principle. I would respectfully agree. The principle in *McGhee*'s case is far narrower and I have tried to indicate what its limits are likely to be. It is true that actions for clinical negligence notoriously give rise to difficult questions of causation. But it cannot possibly be said that the duty to take reasonable care in treating patients would be virtually drained of content unless the creation of a material risk of injury were accepted as sufficient to satisfy the causal requirements for liability. And the political and economic arguments involved in the massive increase in the liability of the National Health Service which would have been a consequence of the broad rule favoured by the Court of Appeal in *Wilsher*'s case are far more complicated than the reasons given by Lord Wilberforce for imposing liability upon an employer who has failed to take simple precautions...

In allowing the appeals, it was held that in situations such as this, where employees had been exposed to asbestos fibres, by different defendants over different periods of employment, causing mesothelioma, (and where the disease could not conclusively be linked to any particular occasion or cumulative exposure), then a *modified approach to causation was justified*, (the *McGhee* approach!) In other words, it was enough for the claimants to prove that each defendant's breach had materially increased the risk of contracting the disease. Factual causation was satisfied. (*McGhee* was applied; *Wilsher* distinguished.)

6.1.4 Recent Cases Dealing with Factual Causation

There have been a number of recent cases where the issue of factual causation has been scrutinised, but we will concentrate here on just two of these, where the *Fairchild* approach was applied (and the *McGhee* test used). The first is *Karen Sienkiewicz (Administratrix of the Estate of Enid Costello Deceased) v Greif (UK) Ltd* [2009] EWCA Civ 1159. This concerned a woman who contracted mesothelioma while at work, as a result of breaches by the defendant. She later died. The discussion in the Court of Appeal was wide-ranging (and much of it outside the scope of this chapter). It focused on the appropriate test in cases of this kind. The Court allowed the appeal by the estate of the deceased woman, and held that the correct test, applying *Fairchild*, was the material increase in risk approach used in *McGhee*.

Perhaps more surprisingly, in the second case, *Bailey v Ministry of Defence and Another* [2009] 1 WLR 1052, the *Fairchild* approach to factual causation was applied again, even though the context was clinical, rather than work-related.

Bailey v Ministry of Defence and Another [2009] 1 WLR 1052

Panel: Waller, Sedley and Smith LJJ

Facts: Here, the claimant was admitted to the hospital of the first defendant with a gall stone. After surgery, the claimant developed pancreatitis and was monitored in the intensive care unit of the hospital. She was subsequently moved to a second hospital where she suffered a cardiac arrest leading to brain damage. The judge at first instance found that the cardiac arrest, resulting from her overall weakness, had two cumulative causes – the first defendant's negligent lack of care at the first hospital (a tort) and the pancreatitis (non-tortious). He held that factual causation was established because the claimant had successfully proved that the defendant's lack of care had *materially contributed* to the claimant's overall weakness. The defendant's appeal was dismissed.

LOED JUSTICE WALLER

...Are there any cases in the medical negligence context which cast any doubt on applying *Wardlaw's* case [i.e. the material increase approach] in that context? Certainly in *Wilsher's case* [1988] AC 1074 the House of Lords applied strictly the "but for" test and rejected the Court of Appeal's interpretation of *McGhee's case* [1973] 1 WLR 1 but it was not a case of causes cumulatively causing injury but a case where there were different distinct causes which operated in a different way and might have caused the injury and where the claimant could not establish which cause either "caused or contributed" to his injury. It was the inadequacies of medical science that put the claimant in the position of not being able to establish the probability of one cause as against the other but the House of Lords were not prepared to place the case in an exceptional category.

Hotson's case [1987] AC 750 was a case where the House of Lords held that the cause of the injury was the non-negligent falling out of the tree and that that injury would, on the balance of probabilities, have occurred anyway without the negligent delay in treatment; thus the negligent conduct made no contribution to causing that injury. *Gregg v Scott* [2005] 2 AC 176 was again a medical negligence case but was not concerned with whether the negligence made a material contribution to the damage.

In my view one cannot draw a distinction between medical negligence cases and others. I would summarise the position in relation to cumulative cause cases as follows. If the evidence demonstrates on a balance of probabilities that the injury would have occurred as a result of the non-tortious cause or causes in any event, the claimant will have failed to establish that the tortious cause contributed. *Hotson*'s case exemplifies such a situation. If the evidence demonstrates that "but for" the contribution of the tortious cause the injury would probably not have occurred, the claimant will (obviously) have discharged the burden. In a case where medical science cannot establish the probability that "but for" an act of negligence the injury would not have happened but can establish that the contribution of the negligent cause was more than negligible, the "but for" test is modified, and the claimant will succeed.

The instant case involved cumulative causes acting so as to create a weakness and thus the judge in my view applied the right test, and was entitled to reach the conclusion he did...

 Alert

6.2 Successive Injuries and Factual Causation

This addresses the question of how the court should proceed where the claimant suffers loss due to the first defendant's negligence, but, before the trial, an unrelated event causes further or different damage to the claimant. (This overlaps with the issue of quantifying damages which is outside the scope of the GDL.) Each defendant satisfies the 'but for' test, and is the factual cause of the claimant's damage. Should the first defendant be held in law to have caused all the damage, or only some of it? We will look at the three most important cases.

Performance Cars Ltd v Abraham [1962] 1 QB 33

Panel: Lord Evershed MR, Harman and Donovan LJJ

Facts: The plaintiff's Rolls Royce motorcar was damaged when the defendant negligently collided with it. The plaintiff sued the defendant for the cost of a respray. However, prior to this incident, the same Rolls Royce had been involved in another collision, caused by a different negligent driver, also necessitating a respray. The plaintiff had obtained judgment against that first driver but it had never been satisfied, so the Rolls Royce already required a respray before it was damaged by the defendant. The judge at first instance found the defendant liable for the cost of the respray, but on appeal to the Court of Appeal, it was held that the defendant was not liable, because his action was not the factual cause of the damage. Accordingly, the plaintiff had suffered no extra loss as a result of the defendant's action.

LORD EVERSHED MR

In my judgment in the present case the defendant should be taken to have injured a motor-car that was already in certain respects (that is, in respect of the need for respraying) injured; with the result that to the extent of that need or injury the damage claimed did not flow from the defendant's wrongdoing. It may no doubt be unfortunate for the plaintiffs that the collisions took place in the order in which they did. Had the first collision been that brought about by the defendant and had they recovered the £75 now in question from him, they could not clearly have recovered the same sum again from the other wrongdoer. It is, however, in my view irrelevant (if unfortunate for the plaintiffs) that the judgment obtained against the other wrongdoer has turned out to be worthless.

For the reasons which I have stated I would allow the appeal.

Baker v Willoughby [1970] AC 467

Panel: Lord Reid, Lord Guest , Viscount Dilhorne , Lord Donovan and Lord Pearson

Facts: The claimant was hit by the defendant's car while crossing the road, sustaining injuries to his leg which prevented him from continuing in his employment. He therefore found alternative employment in a scrap metal yard, but before the trial, he was shot and injured in the same leg by robbers trying to steal scrap metal. The claimant's leg was later amputated.

The issue for the House of Lords was whether the first defendant's liability stopped at the point of the shooting, or whether he would still, in law, be held to be the factual cause of all the damage, including the amputation.

LORD PEARSON

There is a plausible argument for the defendant on the following lines. The original accident, for which the defendant is liable, inflicted on the plaintiff a permanently injured left ankle, which caused pain from time to time, diminished his mobility and so reduced his earning capacity, and was likely to lead to severe arthritis. The proper figure of damages for those consequences of the accident, as assessed by the judge before making his apportionment, was £1,600. That was the proper figure for those consequences if they were likely to endure for a normal period and run a normal course. But the supervening event, when the robbers shot the plaintiff in his left leg, necessitated an amputation of the left leg above the knee. The consequences of the original accident therefore have ceased. He no longer suffers pain in his left ankle, because there no longer is a left ankle. He will never have the arthritis. There is no longer any loss of mobility through stiffness or weakness of the left ankle, because it is no longer there. The injury to the left ankle, resulting from the original accident, is not still operating as one of two concurrent causes both producing discomfort and disability. It is not operating at all nor causing anything. The present state of disablement, with the stump and the artificial leg on the left side, was caused wholly by the supervening event and not at all by the original accident. Thus the consequences of the original accident have been submerged and obliterated by the greater consequences of the supervening event.

That is the argument, and it is formidable. But it must not be allowed to succeed, because it produces manifest injustice. The supervening event has not made the plaintiff less lame nor less disabled nor less deprived of amenities. It has not shortened the period over which he will be suffering. It has made him more lame, more disabled, more deprived of amenities. He should not have less damages through being worse off than might have been expected.

The nature of the injustice becomes apparent if the supervening event is treated as a tort (as indeed it was) and if one envisages the plaintiff suing the robbers who shot him. They would be entitled, as the saying is, to "take the plaintiff as they find him." (*Performance Cars Ltd. v. Abraham* [1962] 1 QB 33) They have not injured and disabled a previously fit and able-bodied man. They have only made an already lame and disabled man more lame and more disabled. Take, for example, the reduction of earnings. The original accident reduced his earnings from £x per week to £y per week, and the supervening event further reduced them from £y per week to £z per week. If the defendant's argument is correct, there is, as Mr. Griffiths has pointed out, a gap. The plaintiff recovers from the defendant the £x-y not for the whole period of the remainder of his working life, but only for the short period up to the date of the supervening event. The robbers are liable only for the £y-z from the date of the supervening event onwards. In the Court of Appeal an ingenious attempt was made to fill the gap by holding that the damages recoverable from the later tortfeasors (the robbers) would include a novel head of damage, viz., the diminution of the plaintiff's damages recoverable from the original tortfeasor (the defendant). I doubt whether that would be an admissible head of damage: it looks too remote. In any case it would not help the plaintiff, if the later tortfeasors could not be found or were indigent and uninsured. These later tortfeasors cannot have been insured in respect of the robbery which they committed.

I think a solution of the theoretical problem can be found in cases such as this by taking a comprehensive and unitary view of the damage caused by the original accident. Itemisation of the damages by dividing them into heads and sub-heads is often convenient, but is not essential. In the end judgment is given for a single lump sum of damages and not for a total of items set out under heads and sub-heads. The original accident caused what may be called a "devaluation" of the plaintiff, in the sense that it produced a general reduction of his capacity to do things, to earn money and to enjoy life. For that devaluation the original tortfeasor should be and remain responsible to the full extent, unless before the assessment of the damages something has happened which either diminishes the devaluation (e.g. if there is an unexpected recovery from some of the adverse effects of the accident) or by shortening the expectation of life diminishes the period over which the plaintiff will suffer from the devaluation. If the supervening event is a tort, the second tortfeasor should be responsible for the additional devaluation caused by him.

 Alert

A crude but effective mechanism for determining factual causation and the extent of liability in such cases appears to be this: where a tort follows a tort, the first defendant's liability does not stop at the point of the second tort (although the second defendant – where he can be found – will be responsible for the additional damage he has caused). Where a non-tort follows a tort, the defendant's liability *does* stop at the point of the second event, it being something for which the defendant cannot be held responsible. This can be seen from *Jobling v United Dairies Ltd* [1982] AC 794. The claimant suffered injury to his back at work, reducing his earning capacity, caused by the breach of his employer's statutory duty. Before the trial against his employer, the claimant suffered a spinal disease (myelopathy), unrelated to the first injury, rendering him incapable of working at all. The claimant relied on *Baker,* arguing that the House of Lords should hold the defendant liable beyond the point of the second injury, but his argument was rejected. The defendant was held to be liable only up until the second event, it being one of the vicissitudes of life for which it would not be fair to hold a defendant responsible.

6.3 Legal Causation

There are some situations where a new act occurs after the first defendant's act, which adds to the damage sustained by the claimant. This situation differs from the position regarding successive injuries that we looked at above, because here, the acts all contribute to the *same* injury suffered by the claimant. So the claimant's damage is the result of the defendant's act *plus* some other event. The court has to determine whether or not the intervening act, the *novus actus interveniens*, breaks the factual chain of causation, effectively halting the first defendant's liability at that point. The question is whether the first defendant ought legally to be held liable for the damage: this is known as legal causation. It is heavily steered by policy.

There are only three types of act that can potentially break the chain of causation: acts of third parties, of the claimant and of God (natural events).

6.3.1 Acts of Third Parties

Where the subsequent act is the act of a third party, the courts have held that it will only break the chain if it is unreasonable and/or unforeseeable.

The Oropesa [1943] P 32

Panel: Lord Wright, Scott and Mackinnon LJJ

Facts: Two ships, *The Manchester Regiment* and *The Oropesa*, collided at sea due to the negligent navigation of the crew of *The Oropesa*. The captain of *The Manchester Regiment* thought that his ship, although badly damaged, could be saved. At first he sent fifty of his crew in two life boats to *The Oropesa*, and about an hour and a half later, he himself decided to get into a lifeboat, with sixteen crew members, with the aim of getting on board *The Oropesa* to discuss what to do next. However, the rough weather got suddenly worse, and the lifeboat capsized before it reached *The Oropesa*, killing nine of the men on board, including an engineer, whose family were the plaintiffs in this action. *The Manchester Regiment* later sank.

The issue for the Court of Appeal was whether the captain, (a third party), by his actions, acted as a *novus actus interveniens*, breaking the chain of causation initiated by the defendant's negligence. It was held that the captain's act did not break the chain of causation because he had acted reasonably in the emergency situation. The death was directly caused by the collision.

LORD WRIGHT

...Certain well-known formulæ are invoked, such as that the chain of causation was broken and that there was a novus actus interveniens. These phrases, sanctified as they are by standing authority, only mean that there was not such a direct relationship between the act of negligence and the injury that the one can be treated as flowing directly from the other. Cases have been cited which show great difference of opinion on the true answer in the various circumstances to the question whether the damage was direct or too remote. I find it very difficult to formulate any precise and all-embracing rule. I do not think that the authorities which have been cited succeed in settling that difficulty. It may be said that in dealing with the law of negligence it is possible to state general propositions, but when you come to apply those principles to determine whether there has been actionable negligence in any particular case, you must deal with the case on its facts. ...

The question is not whether there was new negligence, but whether there was a new cause. ... To break the chain of causation it must be shown that there is something which I will call ultroneous, something unwarrantable, a new cause which disturbs the sequence of events, something which can be described as either unreasonable or extraneous. or extrinsic. (sic) I doubt whether the law can be stated more precisely than that. ...

LORD JUSTICE SCOTT

...I am satisfied that the action taken by the master to save the lives of those for whom he was responsible was reasonable, and, therefore, that there was no break in the chain of causation. ...

An example of where the act of a third party did break the chain can be found in *Knightley v Johns* [1982] 1 WLR 349. Here, the first defendant caused a serious road accident at the end of a one-way tunnel. The claimant was a police officer on the scene, ordered by the officer in charge to ride down the tunnel on his motorcycle, against the flow of traffic and close it. In doing this, the claimant was hit by an oncoming car. The Court of Appeal held that the commanding officer's actions (the act of a third party) were so unreasonable and unforeseeable in these circumstances that they broke the causal link between the first defendant's negligence and the claimant's injury. The court was careful to stress that such situations as this would be judged on a case by case basis.

6.3.2 Acts of the Claimant

Sometimes, the claimant's own actions will break the chain of causation, again where they are deemed to be unreasonable and/or unforeseeable. (Note, however, that since the Law Reform (Contributory Negligence) Act 1945 came into force, the court now has the power to reduce the claimant's damages to the extent they consider just and equitable, where the claimant has in some way contributed by their actions to their injury. This approach provides the defendant with a partial defence, and is used much more frequently than the all-or-nothing approach to legal causation.)

 **Link**
Contributory Negligence is examined fully in Chapter 8, General Defences

McKew v Holland and Hannen and Cubitts (Scotland) Ltd [1969] 3 All ER 1621

Panel: Lord Reid, Lord Hodson, Lord Guest, Viscount Dilhorne and Lord Upjohn

Facts: The claimant damaged his leg in the course of employment for which the defendant was responsible. As a result, the claimant's left leg collapsed beneath him from time to time. He should have recovered within two weeks had it not been for a subsequent accident to the leg, caused when the claimant's leg collapsed beneath him as he descended a steep staircase with no handrail. The claimant was with his daughter at the time, so he pushed her aside to try to prevent injury to her, and then fell down the stairs. He suffered a fractured ankle. It was held that the defendants were not responsible for the second injury, because the claimant's action in descending a steep staircase with no handrail and without assistance was unreasonable.

> LORD REID
>
> ...So in my view the question here is whether the second accident was caused by the appellant doing something unreasonable. It was argued that the wrongdoer must take his victim as he finds him and that that applies not only to a thin skull but also to his intelligence. But I shall not deal with that argument because there is nothing in the evidence to suggest that the appellant is abnormally stupid. This case can be dealt with equally well by asking whether the appellant did something which a moment's reflection would have shown him was an unreasonable thing to do. ...

This case can be contrasted with *Wieland v Cyril Lord Carpets* [1969] 3 All ER 1006, reported in the same year, in which the claimant's actions were held to be *reasonable*, with the result that the defendant was liable for her second injury as well as her first. (The claimant's act did not constitute a *novus actus interveniens*.) Here, the claimant was forced to wear a neck brace as a result of the defendant's negligence. This limited her ability to use her bifocal glasses, with the result that she fell down the stairs of the hospital in which she had been treated, despite having (reasonably) asked her son to help her.

6.3.3 'Acts of God' or Natural Acts

Such acts will only break the chain of causation where they are unconnected with the defendant's negligence and therefore unforeseeable. It is rare for a natural act to break the chain. An example of a natural event that did *not* break the chain of causation can be seen in *Humber Oil Trustee Ltd v Sivand* [1998] CLC 751, in which the Court of Appeal found that the defendants should have foreseen the collapse of the sea bed (the natural event) which necessitated further expense to repair the harbour installations (which had initially been damaged as a result of the defendant's negligence).

Further Reading

Stephen O'Doherty, *Personal Injury: Causation: a floating concept* (June 2009) 159 *NLJ* 809 5

Mark Lunney & Ken Oliphant, *Tort Law, Text and Materials*, (3rd edition) Oxford University Press 2008

Sarah Green, 'A Game of Doctors and Purses': Coherence of Medical Negligence Cases (March 2006) *MLR* 2006 14 1

J. Stapleton, Lords a'leaping evidentiary gaps (2002) 10 *Torts LJ* 276

7

Remoteness of Damage

Topic List

1   Judicial Approaches to Remoteness

Introduction

Once the issue of causation has been determined by the court, consideration will be given as to whether the damage suffered by the claimant is too remote from the defendant's breach. The concept of remoteness involves the law drawing a line as to the consequences, suffered by the claimant, that the defendant is liable for as a result of their breach. Not to have some limitation on such consequences could result in the defendant being liable for unusual or unlikely events; effectively 'crushing' the defendant disproportionately to the wrong they have done ('crushing liability').

You should note that a number of academics and authorities believe that the issue of remoteness concerns the presence of a *novus actus interveniens* breaking the chain of causation between the defendant's acts and the claimant's damage. This casebook regards *novus actus* as part of causation in law.

Link
See Chapter 6 on Causation

7.1 Judicial Approaches to Remoteness

In determining the extent of the defendant's liability for the claimant's damage, judicial opinion originally favoured the concept of directness; the defendant was responsible for all the direct consequences suffered by the claimant, regardless of whether such exigencies were foreseeable or not. Providing the chain of consequences remained direct, the defendant would be liable for all the resulting damage they caused (even if such damage could not be regarded as foreseeable). This approach can be traced back to the Court of Appeal decision in *Re Polemis and Furness, Withy & Co Ltd* [1921] 3 KB 560.

Re Polemis and Furness, Withy & Co Ltd [1921] 3 KB 560

Panel: Bankes, Warrington and Scrutton LJJ

Facts: Whilst unloading a ship in Casablanca, one of the defendant employees negligently dropped a wooden plank into the hold. The plank caused a spark which ignited benzene (petrol) vapour contained in the pit of the ship's hold. The resulting fire completely destroyed the ship. Despite the fire not being a foreseeable consequence (one that could not have been anticipated by a reasonable person from the dropping of the plank into the hold) the Court of Appeal found the defendant charterers liable for all the damage caused. The Court of Appeal dismissed the defendant's argument that they should only be liable for damage to the ship that was anticipated as likely to happen, for example, a dent or scratch to the side of the ship from the plank falling. It was held that the charterers were liable for all the direct consequences from the negligence of their employees even though such consequences could not reasonably have been contemplated.

LORD JUSTICE WARRINGTON

The presence or absence of reasonable anticipation of damage determines the legal quality of the act as negligent or innocent. If it be thus determined to be negligent, then the question whether particular damages are recoverable depends only on the answer to the question whether they are the direct consequence of the act. ...

In the present case it is clear that the act causing the plank to fall was in law a negligent act, because some damage to the ship might reasonably be anticipated. If this is so then the appellants are liable for the actual loss, that being on the findings of the arbitrators the direct result of the falling board.

LORD JUSTICE SCRUTTON

...In this case, however, the problem is simpler. To determine whether an act is negligent, it is relevant to determine whether any reasonable person would foresee that the act would cause damage; if he would not, the act is not negligent. But if the act would or might probably cause damage, the fact that the damage it in fact causes is not the exact kind of damage one would expect is immaterial, so long as the damage is in fact directly traceable to the negligent act, and not due to the operation of independent causes having no connection with the negligent act, except that they could not avoid its results. Once the act is negligent, the fact that its exact operation was not foreseen is immaterial. This is the distinction laid down by the majority of the Exchequer Chamber in *Smith v London and South Western Ry. Co*, and by the majority of the Court in *Banc in Rigby v. Hewitt and Greenland v. Chaplin*, and approved recently by Lord Sumner in *Weld-Blundell v. Stephens* and Sir Samuel Evans in *H.M.S. London*. In the present case it was negligent in discharging cargo to knock down the planks of the temporary staging, for they might easily cause some damage either to workmen, or cargo, or the ship. The fact that they did directly produce an unexpected result, a spark in an atmosphere of petrol vapour which caused a fire, does not relieve the person who was negligent from the damage which his negligent act directly caused.

For these reasons the experienced arbitrators and the judge appealed from came, in my opinion, to a correct decision, and the appeal must be dismissed with costs.

It is frequently commented that the Court of Appeal's decision in *Re Polemis* is open to a number of interpretations. One possible view from the judgment is based on the notion that because some damage of a relevant type is reasonably foreseeable then the defendant should be liable for all the damage of that type, for example, if damage to property is reasonably foreseeable, the defendant is liable for all the damage of the same type (such as that caused by fire and by a falling plank). The defendant was liable in *Re Polemis* for the fire damage because damage to property, howsoever caused, was reasonably foreseeable. An alternative interpretation (and the view subsequently adopted by the Privy Council in the case below) states that, as long as some damage, of whatever type, is foreseeable from the defendant's act, they are liable for all the damage as a direct consequence of the defendant's behaviour. This includes being liable for any type of damage suffered by the claimant, including personal injury, property damage, economic loss, etc.

The theory that a defendant is liable for all the direct consequences from their breach did not find universal support amongst the judiciary. It was felt that such a simplistic test could result in a defendant being liable for a degree of damage suffered by the claimant beyond that regarded as equitable. It is at this juncture that we arrive at the seminal authority in this area, namely *Overseas Tankship (UK) Ltd v Morts Dock and Engineering Ltd, The Wagon Mound (No 1)* [1961] AC 388.

Overseas Tankship (UK) Ltd v Morts Dock and Engineering Ltd, The Wagon Mound (No 1) [1961] AC 388

Panel: Viscount Simonds, Lord Reid, Lord Radcliffe, Lord Tucker and Lord Morris of Borth-Y-Gest

Facts: The plaintiffs, ship repairers, claimed for fire damage to their wharf in Sydney Harbour, Australia. The defendants had chartered a ship in the harbour which had been spilling oil for a number of days. This oil slick floated on the water towards the plaintiff's wharf. Welders, employed by the plaintiff, noticed the oil and sought expert advice on the advisability of continuing with their welding operations. They were assured that there was no risk given the type of oil involved (i.e. furnace oil) which required an extremely high ignition point to catch alight. In the event, the welding did ignite the oil having initially set alight some jetsam and flotsam in the harbour. The resulting fire destroyed the plaintiff's wharf. The plaintiff argued, following *Re Polemis*, that the defendant should be liable for all the damage caused as a direct result of their breach, i.e. the spillage of oil. This case was appealed to the Judicial Committee of the Privy Council who decided to depart from the earlier Court of Appeal decision in *Re Polemis*. It was held that the defendant would only be liable for damage that was reasonably foreseeable from their breach. With reference to the specific damage caused by the *Wagon Mound's* spillage, the fire was held not to be reasonably foreseeable given that the defendants had sought and obtained reliable expert advice that such damage was extremely unlikely. However, the pollution damaged caused by the oil, was foreseeable and, therefore, recoverable.

VISCOUNT SIMONDS

...This concept applied to the slowly developing law of negligence has led to a great variety of expressions which can, as it appears to their Lordships, be harmonised with little difficulty with the single exception of the so-called rule in *Polemis*. For, if it is asked why a man should be responsible for the natural or necessary or probable consequences of his act (or any other similar description of them) the answer is that it is not because they are natural or necessary or probable, but because, since they have this quality, it is judged by the standard of the reasonable man that he ought to have foreseen them. Thus it is that over and over again it has happened that in different judgments in the same case, and sometimes in a single judgment, liability for a consequence has been imposed on the ground that it was reasonably foreseeable or, alternatively, on the ground that it was natural or necessary or probable. The two grounds have been treated as coterminous, and so they largely are.

But, where they are not, the question arises to which the wrong answer was given in *Polemis*. For, if some limitation must be imposed upon the consequences for which the negligent actor is to be held responsible - and all are agreed that some limitation there must be - why should that test (reasonable foreseeability) be rejected which, since he is judged by what the reasonable man ought to foresee, corresponds with the common conscience of mankind, and a test (the "direct" consequence) be substituted which leads to no-where but the never-ending and insoluble problems of causation. "The lawyer," said Sir Frederick Pollock, "cannot afford to adventure himself with philosophers in the logical and metaphysical controversies that beset the idea of cause." Yet this is just what he has most unfortunately done and must continue to do if the rule in *Polemis* is to prevail. A conspicuous example occurs when the actor seeks to escape liability on the ground that the "chain of causation" is broken by a "nova causa" or "novus actus interveniens."…

It is not the act but the consequences on which tortious liability is founded. Just as (as it has been said) there is no such thing as negligence in the air, so there is no such thing as liability in the air. Suppose an action brought by A for damage caused by the carelessness (a neutral word) of B, for example, a fire caused by the careless spillage of oil. It may, of course, become relevant to know what duty B owed to A, but the only liability that is in question is the liability for damage by fire. It is vain to isolate the liability from its context and to say that B is or is not liable, and then to ask for what damage he is liable. For his liability is in respect of that damage and no other. If, as admittedly it is, B's liability (culpability) depends on the reasonable foreseeability of the consequent damage, how is that to be determined except by the foreseeability of the damage which in fact happened - the damage in suit? And, if that damage is unforeseeable so as to displace liability at large, how can the liability be restored so as to make compensation payable?

But, it is said, a different position arises if B's careless act has been shown to be negligent and has caused some foreseeable damage to A. Their Lordships have already observed that to hold B liable for consequences however unforeseeable of a careless act, if, but only if, he is at the same time liable for some other damage however trivial, appears to be neither logical nor just. This becomes more clear if it is supposed that similar unforeseeable damage is suffered by A and C but other foreseeable damage, for which B is liable, by A only. A system of law which would hold B liable to A but not to C for the similar damage suffered by each of them could not easily be defended. Fortunately, the attempt is not necessary. For the same fallacy is at the root of the proposition. It is irrelevant to the question whether B is liable for unforeseeable damage that he is liable for foreseeable damage, as irrelevant as would the fact that he had trespassed on Whiteacre be to the question whether he has trespassed on Blackacre. Again, suppose a claim by A for damage by fire by the careless act of B. Of what relevance is it to that claim that he has another claim arising out of the same careless act? It would surely not prejudice his claim if that other claim failed: it cannot assist it if it succeeds. Each of them rests on its own bottom, and will fail if it can be established that the damage could not reasonably be foreseen. We have come back to the plain common sense stated by Lord Russell of Killowen in *Bourhill v Young*. As Denning LJ said in *King v Phillips*: "there can be no doubt since *Bourhill v Young* that the test of liability for shock is foreseeability of injury by shock." Their Lordships substitute the word "fire" for "shock" and endorse this statement of the law.

Clearly the Privy Council was influenced by the concept of foreseeability as utilised in *Donoghue v Stevenson* [1932] AC 562 and subsequent cases. Likewise, the equitable notion that a person should only be liable for damage that can be objectively determined as likely to occur from the defendant's breach would appear to prevail.

Link
See Chapter 4 on Duty of Care

It should be noted that *The Wagon Mound,* as a Privy Council decision, was only of persuasive precedent. The courts were free to depart from this authority had they wished to do so. In fact, both the test of directness, as advocated in *Re Polemis,* and the test of reasonable foreseeability, as cited in *The Wagon Mound,* remain valid law. Subsequent cases, however, have clearly demonstrated a judicial preference for the latter approach as being the correct test in determining the remoteness of damage.

7.1.1 The type of damage

An ambiguity arising from *The Wagon Mound* decision concerns the precise type or kind of damage that has to be foreseeable. The Privy Council appeared to distinguish between some types of damage as being foreseeable and, therefore, recoverable (i.e. pollution) and others not (i.e. the fire damage). Numerous cases have vied as to whether a wide or narrow approach should be adopted in considering this issue. For example, note the generous interpretation adopted by Rees J below.

Bradford v Robinson Rentals Ltd. [1967] 1 WLR 337

Panel: Rees J

Facts: The plaintiff, a mobile television repair engineer, suffered frostbite to both his hands and feet having been required by his employer, the defendants, to travel in a faulty van in extremely cold weather. The fan heater in the van was not working (a fact about which the defendants were aware) requiring the plaintiff to keep the window open in order to prevent his breath icing up the windscreen. Both the extreme coldness and his fatigue (at being required to drive in such a stressful situation for 20 hours resulted, the plaintiff argued, in him suffering frostbite. He commenced an action against the defendants for damages based on employers' liability.

MR JUSTICE REES

...It was strongly argued on behalf of the defendants that injury to his health suffered by the plaintiff in this case by "frost-bite" or cold injury was not reasonably foreseeable. There was no evidence that before the plaintiff started the journey either the plaintiff himself or the defendants' servants, the Exeter branch manager or the senior engineer, actually contemplated that the plaintiff might suffer from "frost-bite" if he were required to carry out the journey. I am, however, satisfied that any reasonable employer in possession of all the facts known to the branch manager and senior engineer on January 8 would have realised — and they must have realised — that if the plaintiff was required to carry out the journey he would certainly be subjected to a real risk of some injury to his health arising from prolonged exposure to an exceptional degree of cold.

No doubt the kinds of injury to health due to prolonged exposure to an exceptional degree of cold are commonly thought to include, for example, that the victim might suffer from a common cold or in a severe case from pneumonia, or that he might suffer from chilblains on his hands and feet. The question I have to consider is whether the plaintiff has established that the injury to his health by "frost-bite" (and I use the lay term for convenience), which is admittedly unusual in this country, is nevertheless of the type and kind of injury which was reasonably foreseeable. …

In all these circumstances I hold that the defendants did, by sending the plaintiff out on this journey, expose him to a reasonably foreseeable risk of injury arising from exposure to severe cold and fatigue. That breach of duty caused the plaintiff to suffer from "frost-bite" or cold injury with serious consequences. Even if there had been — and there is not — evidence that the plaintiff was abnormally susceptible to "frost-bite" as opposed to the more common sequels of prolonged exposure to severe cold and fatigue, he would be entitled to succeed on the footing that a tortfeasor must take his victim as he finds him (see *Smith v Leech Brain & Co. Ltd*).

Not all members of the judiciary have been so flexible in their attitude towards such unusual or unexpected damage. There have been a number of authorities that have adopted a more conservative approach in determining the exact scope of damage that must be foreseeable.

Tremain v Pike and Another [1969] 1 WLR 1556

Panel: Payne J

Facts: The plaintiff contracted Weil's disease (leptospirosis) while employed as a herdsman by the defendant farmer. There are several causes of this disease including prolonged exposure to rats' urine. The court noted that the incidence of Weil's disease on the farm was very rare and there was no evidence that the farming community knew, or ought reasonably to have known, that such a disease existed or that a person may get this disease by merely handling matter contaminated by rats' urine, for example, straw bales.

The plaintiff alleged that he became infected by using or washing in contaminated water or by handling bales of hay, the contamination arising from an infestation of rats on the farm. He argued that he contracted the disease as a result of the defendant's negligence in failing to take adequate steps to keep the farm free of vermin.

MR JUSTICE PAYNE

...It is quite impossible to find on the balance of probabilities when or where the plaintiff became infected. To say that the haystack is more probable than the milking parlour does not mean that the stack can be accepted as the probable source. I feel able on the evidence to find that on the balance of probabilities the plaintiff became infected on the farm, but any greater precision would not be justified.

The employer's duty to his servants is to take reasonable care for their safety, and this safety extends to the safety of the premises and the plant, and to the method and conduct of the work, but is not restricted to those matters. Put in slightly different words, their duty is to take reasonable steps to avoid exposing the plaintiff to a reasonably foreseeable risk of injury. It follows from the contents of this judgment that in my opinion the defendants were not in breach of any duty of care to the plaintiff, nor was his disease attributable to any such breach. If, contrary to my view, it should be held that the defendants were in breach of duty in that they ought to have known of the extent of the infestation in March, 1967, and ought to have foreseen that the plaintiff was or might be exposed to some general hazard involving personal injury, illness or disease in consequence of the infestation, the defendants, as I think, are still immune from liability on the grounds that Weil's disease was at best a remote possibility which they could not reasonably foresee, and that the damage suffered by the plaintiff was, therefore, unforeseeable and too remote to be recoverable.

Link
See Chapters 9 and 10 on Employer's Liability

I do not accept Mr. Wien's contention that it is sufficient to show that the plaintiff was exposed generally to the risk of disease because of the possible contamination of animal feed or of milk at the farm or the possibility of the plaintiff being bitten, itself, in my view, an unlikely event. Weil's disease is not comparable to the other human disabilities which may flow from an infestation of rats. One must not overlook the fact that, if the defendants had to take effective precautions against Weil's disease, it would not be sufficient merely to keep the rat population in check by poisoning, trapping, hunting and so forth. A rat population of varying size would still remain on the farm as it does on all farms. It would be necessary to introduce protective clothing for the hands and arms, some check upon cuts and abrasions and a system of washing facilities and hygiene which, in my view, would be out of all proportion in cost and effort to the risk which had to be countered.

There is ample authority for the principles of law applied in this judgment. In *Hughes v Lord Advocate* [1963] AC 837, Lord Reid said, at p. 845:

"But a defender is liable, although the damage may be a good deal greater in extent than was foreseeable. He can only escape liability if the damage can be regarded as differing in kind from what was foreseeable."...

The kind of damage suffered here was a disease contracted by contact with rats' urine. This, in my view, was entirely different in kind from the effect of a rat bite, or food poisoning by the consumption of food or drink contaminated by rats. I do not accept that all illness or infection arising from an infestation of rats should be regarded as of the same kind. One cannot say in this case as was said by Lord Reid in *Hughes case*

[1963] AC 837 at p. 845 "if they [the defendants] had done as they ought to have done this accident would not have happened."...

For these reasons the plaintiff's claim fails, and there will be judgment for the defendants with costs.

The current approach of the courts would appear to favour the more liberal interpretation as utilised in *Bradford*. This is particularly so for claims involving personal injury as opposed to actions for property damage or economic loss. The next case provides a typical example of the prevailing attitude of the court.

Margereson And Another v J W Roberts Limited [1996] PIQR P358

Panel: Russell, Saville and Otton LJJ

Facts: The plaintiff claimed personal injury (the lung disease mesothelioma) from having, as a child, suffered prolonged contact with asbestos dust which had come from the defendant's factory. The plaintiff had frequent 'snowball' fights with the asbestos in the immediate vicinity of the defendant's factory. The plaintiff claimed that their mesothelioma had been caused through the defendant negligently allowing the dust to escape from their industrial premises.

LORD JUSTICE RUSSELL

We turn now to what we regard as the only legal issue in the appeals. What was the duty owed to Mr Margereson and to Mrs Hancock? The answer is to be found almost entirely in the speech of Lord Lloyd in *Page v Smith* [1996] 1 AC at 190 when he said:

"The test in every case ought to be whether the defendant can reasonably foresee that his conduct will expose the plaintiff to the risk of personal injury. If so, then he comes under a duty of care to that plaintiff. If a working definition of "Personal Injury" is needed, it can be found in section 38(1) of the Limitation Act 1980. 'Personal Injuries' includes any disease and any impairment of a person's physical or mental condition."...

We add only that in the context of this case we take the view that liability only attaches to these defendants if the evidence demonstrated that they should reasonably have foreseen a risk of some pulmonary injury, not necessarily mesothelioma. ...

Link
See Chapter 3 on Psychiatric Injury ('Nervous Shock')

7.1.2 The way in which the damage occurs

Despite the clarity in *The Wagon Mound (No 1)* as to the type of damage recoverable, there was still a lacuna as to whether the method by which the damage occurred had to be reasonably foreseeable. *Hughes v Lord Advocate* [1963] AC 837 settled this issue. There is no need to foresee exactly *how* the damage has occurred, so long as that damage is reasonably foreseeable as a consequence of the defendant's breach.

Hughes v Lord Advocate [1963] AC 837

Panel: Lord Reid, Lord Jenkins, Lord Morris of Borth-Y-Gest, Lord Guest and Lord Pearce

Facts: The defendant post office employees, while working on the highway, had left a man-hole uncovered. The nine year old plaintiff decided to climb into it, to explore. To assist him in the dark, the plaintiff picked up a paraffin safety lamp which had been placed near the entrance of the hole. Though the evidence is not entirely clear, it would appear that the plaintiff accidentally dropped the lamp into the void, causing some background petrol vapour to ignite. The plaintiff was badly burnt in the subsequent explosion. At first instance, the plaintiff was unsuccessful, the way in which his injury occurred being held to be unforeseeable.

LORD GUEST

...In dismissing the appellant's claim the Lord Ordinary and the majority of the judges of the First Division reached the conclusion that the accident which happened was not reasonably foreseeable. In order to establish a coherent chain of causation it is not necessary that the precise details leading up to the accident should have been reasonably foreseeable: it is sufficient if the accident which occurred is of a type which should have been foreseeable by a reasonably careful person (*Miller v South of Scotland Electricity Board*, Lord Keith of Avonholm; *Harvey v Singer Manufacturing Co Ltd*, Lord Patrick) or as Lord Mackintosh expressed it in the *Harvey* case, the precise concatenation of circumstances need not be envisaged. Concentration has been placed in the courts below on the explosion which, it was said, could not have been foreseen because it was caused in a unique fashion by the paraffin forming into vapour and being ignited by the naked flame of the wick. But this, in my Opinion, is to concentrate on what is really a non-essential element in the dangerous situation created by the allurement. The test might better be put thus: Was the igniting of paraffin outside the lamp by the flame a foreseeable consequence of the breach of duty? In the circumstances, there was a combination of potentially dangerous circumstances against which the Post Office had to protect the appellant. If these formed an allurement to children it might have been foreseen that they would play with the lamp, that it might tip over, that it might be broken, and that when broken the paraffin might spill and be ignited by the flame. All these steps in the chain of causation seem to have been accepted by all the judges in the courts below as foreseeable. But because the explosion was the agent which caused the burning and was unforeseeable, therefore the accident, according to them, was not reasonably foreseeable. In my opinion, this reasoning is fallacious. An explosion is only one way in which burning can be caused. Burning can also be caused by the contact between liquid paraffin and a naked flame. In the one case paraffin vapour and in the other case liquid paraffin is ignited by fire. I cannot see that these are two different types of accident. They are both burning accidents and in both cases the injuries would be burning injuries. Upon this view the explosion was an immaterial event in the chain of causation. It was simply one way in which burning might be caused by the potentially dangerous paraffin lamp. I adopt, with respect, Lord Carmont's observation in the present case: "The defender cannot, I think, escape liability by contending that he did not foresee all the possibilities of the

> manner in which allurements - the manhole and the lantern - would act upon the childish mind."...
>
> I have therefore reached the conclusion that the accident which occurred and which caused burning injuries to the appellant was one which ought reasonably to have been foreseen by the Post Office employees and that they were at fault in failing to provide a protection against the appellant entering the shelter and going down the manhole.

Unfortunately, despite the clarity of decision in *Hughes,* the Court of Appeal muddied the issue again in *Doughty v Turner Manufacturing Co* [1964] 1 QB 518.

Doughty v Turner Manufacturing Co. [1964] 1 QB 518

Panel: Lord Pearce, Harman and Diplock LJJ

Facts: Employees for the defendant negligently allowed an asbestos cauldron lid cover to slide into a vat of molten liquid. As a result of the (unknown) chemical reaction between the high temperature of the liquid in the vat and the asbestos lid, there was an explosion which severely injured the plaintiff. The Court of Appeal, distinguishing *Hughes*, found the defendant not liable. In *Doughty,* the risk involved (i.e. moving an asbestos lid) was fundamentally different, in terms of foreseeability, from the risks presented in *Hughes*.

> LORD JUSTICE HARMAN
>
> The plaintiff's argument most persuasively urged by Mr. James rested, as I understood it, on admissions made that, if this lid had been dropped into the cauldron with sufficient force to cause the molten material to splash over the edge, that would have been an act of negligence or carelessness for which the defendants might be vicariously responsible. Reliance was put upon *Hughes v. Lord Advocate*, where the exact consequences of the lamp overturning were not foreseen, but it was foreseeable that, if the manhole were left unguarded, boys would enter and tamper with the lamp, and it was not unlikely that serious burns might ensue for the boys. Their Lordships' House distinguished *The Wagon Mound* case on the ground that the damage which ensued, though differing in degree, was the same in kind as that which was foreseeable. So it is said here that a splash causing burns was foreseeable and that this explosion was really only a magnified splash which also caused burns and that, therefore, we ought to follow *Hughes v Lord Advocate* and hold the defendants liable. I cannot accept this. In my opinion, the damage here was of an entirely different kind from the foreseeable splash. Indeed, the evidence showed that any disturbance of the material resulting from the immersion of the hard-board was past an appreciable time before the explosion happened. This latter was caused by the disintegration of the hard-board under the great heat to which it was subjected and the consequent release of the moisture enclosed within it. This had nothing to do with the agitation caused by the dropping of the board into the cyanide. I am of opinion that it would be wrong on these facts to make another inroad on the doctrine of foreseeability which seems to me to be a satisfactory solvent of this type of difficulty.

7.1.3 The extent of the damage

Another issue the courts have had to contend with is the extent of damage for which the defendant is liable. For example, though personal injury is foreseeable from a defendant driving into the claimant's car, what if the claimant has an underlying condition, such as haemophilia, which exacerbates his injuries? In such circumstances, the policy would appear to be that once the type of damage is foreseeable, the defendant is liable for the full extent of the damage, even if this is not foreseeable. Several cases support this approach, for example *Hughes v Lord Advocate* (see above).

7.1.4 The Thin Skull rule

This rule, often typified with the maxim the defendant must 'take their victim as they find them', effectively imposes liability on the defendant, for all the personal injury suffered by the claimant, notwithstanding any particular susceptibility, weakness or pre-disposition that claimant may have. If a victim with haemophilia suffers lacerations due to the defendant's negligence and subsequently dies, the defendant will be held responsible for the fatality and cannot forward the argument that an 'average' man would not have possessed such underlying weakness.

There was a short period post *Wagon Mound (No 1)* in which some doubted the validity of the rule. It was argued that any weaknesses, susceptibilities, etc, possessed by the claimant could not be regarded as reasonably foreseeable. This issue was quickly laid to rest in the next Court of Appeal case.

Smith v Leech Brain & Co Ltd and Another [1962] 2 QB 405

Panel: Lord Parker CJ

Facts: The plaintiff's husband, a galvaniser employed by the defendants, suffered a burnt lip having been splashed by molten metal while at work. Unknown to him, he had a form of pre-malignant cancer; the burn acting as a catalyst for him to develop the full disease. He died three years later. Lord Parker CJ stated that the Privy Council in *The Wagon Mound (No1)* had not imposed foreseeability as to the extent of the damage but simply that the type or kind of damage had to be foreseen. Therefore, the thin skull rule was not to be regarded as negated by that decision. The question for the court was whether the damage by burning was of the same kind or type as damage in the form of cancer. The court held that it was and the defendant was found liable.

LORD PARKER CJ

There are really three rival views with which I am confronted. The first one is that this cancer may have been caused by the burn itself without there being any pre-malignant condition; it was admitted that that would be highly unusual, although reasons were given for suggesting that that may have occurred here.

The second, and other extreme view, is that not merely a pre-malignant condition but malignancy itself must have existed long before the accident.

The third view is that as a result of working in gasworks, as the plaintiff's husband did for nine years from 1926 to 1935, he was suffering from pre-malignant changes, and that the burn was the promoting agency which made the cancer develop.

I am satisfied that on the balance of probabilities the third view is the correct one. I find that there was no visible sign of anything wrong with his lip before the accident.

Accordingly, I find that the burn was the promoting agency of cancer in tissues which already had a pre-malignant condition. In those circumstances, it is clear that the plaintiff's husband, but for the burn, would not necessarily ever have developed cancer. On the other hand, having regard to the number of matters which can be promoting agencies, there was a strong likelihood that at some stage in his life he would develop cancer. But that the burn did contribute to, or cause in part, at any rate, the cancer and the death, I have no doubt.

The third question is damages. Here I am confronted with the recent decision of the Privy Council in *Overseas Tankship (UK) Limited v. Morts Dock and Engineering Co. Ltd. (The Wagon Mound*. But for that case, it seems to me perfectly clear that, assuming negligence proved, and assuming that the burn caused in whole or in part the cancer and the death, the plaintiff would be entitled to recover. It is said on the one side by Mr. May that although I am not strictly bound by the *Wagon Mound* since it is a decision of the Privy Council, I should treat myself as free, using the arguments to be derived from that case, to say that other cases in these courts - other cases in the Court of Appeal - have been wrongly decided.

For my part, I am quite satisfied that the Judicial Committee in the *Wagon Mound* case did not have what I may call, loosely, the thin skull cases in mind. It has always been the law of this country that a tortfeasor takes his victim as he finds him. It is unnecessary to do more than refer to the short passage in the decision of Kennedy J. in *Dulieu v White & Sons*, where he said: "If a man is negligently run over or otherwise negligently injured in his body, it is no answer to the sufferer's claim for damages that he would have suffered less injury, or no injury at all, if he had not had an unusually thin skull or an unusually weak heart."...

In those circumstances, it seems to me that this is plainly a case which comes within the old principle. The test is not whether these employers could reasonably have foreseen that a burn would cause cancer and that he would die. The question is whether these employers could reasonably foresee the type of injury he suffered, namely, the burn. What, in the particular case, is the amount of damage which he suffers as a result of that burn, depends upon the characteristics and constitution of the victim.

Numerous other authorities have confirmed that in dealing with the extent of personal injury, a claimant's underlying weaknesses and susceptibilities are subject to the thin skull rule.

7.1.5 The effect of the claimant's impecuniosity

We need to consider claims for other types of loss, for example, consequential economic loss, specifically those arising as a direct result of the claimant's impecuniosity (a lack of money). Specifically, the issue is whether the thin skull rule extends to finances: must the defendant take the claimant's finances as they find them? (This is known colloquially as the thin wallet rule.) The answer is now yes, but the law was not always clear.

Lagden v O'Connor [2004] 1 AC 1067

Panel: Lord Nicholls of Birkenhead, Lord Slynn of Hadley, Lord Hope of Craighead, Lord Scott of Foscote and Lord Walker of Gestingthorpe

Facts: As a result of the defendant's negligence, the claimant's ten year old car was damaged. Unfortunately, as a result of unemployment and ill health, the claimant had limited financial means and was unable to afford the cost of car hire. He did, however, take advantage of a credit hire agreement (an arrangement more expensive then other options but the only one he was eligible for). The House of Lords allowed the claim for the full financial costs involved in the claimant agreeing to the financial package. Effectively, the House of Lords accepted that the greater credit expenses incurred by the claimant were foreseeable as a direct result of the defendant's conduct.

LORD HOPE OF CRAIGHEAD

The Judicial Committee did not go so far in *Alcoa Minerals* as to say that *The Liesbosch* was wrongly decided. As it was a decision of the House of Lords, it was for the House and not the Board to decide whether the rule that was laid down in that case should now be departed from. The opportunity for the House to take that step has now come. It is not necessary for us to say that *The Liesbosch* was wrongly decided. But it is clear that the law has moved on, and that the correct test of remoteness today is whether the loss was reasonably foreseeable. The wrongdoer must take his victim as he finds him: talem qualem, as Lord Collins said in the *Clippens Oil case* [1907] AC 291, 303. This rule applies to the economic state of the victim in the same way as it applies to his physical and mental vulnerability. It requires the wrongdoer to bear the consequences if it was reasonably foreseeable that the injured party would have to borrow money or incur some other kind of expenditure to mitigate his damages.

Conclusion

Through pragmatism, and a certain degree of expediency, the courts have modified the test of reasonable foreseeability in order to ensure a degree of justice in each case. Furthermore, the judicial reasoning in some of the authorities seems to indicate a degree of backward reasoning in applying the test, i.e. the court deciding the eventual outcome and then trailing backwards to justify their decision. This may explain the lack of any uniform approach in this area of law.

Further Reading

Davies, M, The Road from Morocco: Polemis Through Donoghue to No-Fault (1992) 45 MLR 534 – 55, 534

Jansen, The Idea of a Lost Chance (1999) 19 OJLS 271

Lunney, M, What Price a Chance? (1995) 15 LS1

Stapleton, J, Cause-in-Fact and the Scope of Liability for Consequences (2003) 119 LQR 388

Stauch, M, Risk and Remoteness of Damage in Negligence (2001) 64 MLR 191

Williams, G, The Risk Principle (1961) 77 LQR 179 – 212, 179

8

General Defences

Topic List

Introduction

Even where the claimant can demonstrate that he is owed a duty of care by the defendant, and that the duty has been breached, causing loss to that claimant, the claimant may still not succeed in his claim. The defendant might plead one or more of a number of defences to reduce or eliminate liability. These are known as general defences.

General defences are not popular with the court. A successful general defence means that the defendant, because of his negligence, has damaged the claimant, but does not have to compensate the claimant. The court will not want to deprive a successful claimant of his rightful damages. However, there are sound policy reasons why a claimant should lose or have their damages reduced, such as when the claimant was acting in an illegal manner or had partly caused the damage himself. Indeed, all general defences in tort are heavily influenced by policy, as we will see.

The key common law general defences are known by Latin phrases – *volenti non fit injuria* and *ex turpi causa non oritur* action, but these are also often referred to in shorthand, as "consent" and "illegality".

Volenti non fit injuria

The Latin tag describes a simple principle - the claimant cannot claim where he has consented, (or is deemed to have consented) to run the risk of the injury, caused by the defendant, that he then sustains. This covers a number of areas, for example, a footballer cannot claim damages from another footballer for injuries he suffers from a legal tackle. By going onto the pitch, he consents to the risk of injury through fair play. A patient can consent to medical treatment that would otherwise be a battery.

There are three conditions for a defence of *volenti* to apply. First, the claimant must agree to the risk of injury; second, the claimant must have full knowledge of the nature of that risk; and third, the claimant's agreement to the risk must be voluntary.

8.1 Agreement

The first condition - agreement - can be express, but is more usually implied.

Imperial Chemical Industries Ltd v Shatwell [1965] AC 656

Panel: Lord Reid, Viscount Radcliffe, Lord Hodson, Lord Pearce and Lord Donovan

Facts: Mr Shatwell was a shot firer in a quarry owned by ICI. One of his jobs was to test detonators. This was self-evidently dangerous and ICI introduced a system where the testers should take cover in a shelter. Mr Shatwell and a fellow tester (his brother) decided, against both ICI instructions and statutory requirements, to test some detonators in the open. The testing went wrong and Mr Shatwell was seriously injured. He sued ICI on the basis that ICI was liable for the negligence of its employee, namely his own brother. The court held that the claim failed because Mr Shatwell agreed to the risk.

LORD REID

If the plaintiff invited or freely aided and abetted his fellow-servant's disobedience, then he was volens in the fullest sense. He cannot complain of the resulting injury either against the fellow-servant or against the master on the ground of his vicarious responsibility for his fellow-servant's conduct. ...

It was argued that in this case it has not been shown that [Mr Shatwell] had a full appreciation of the risk. In my view it must be held that he had. He knew that those better qualified than he was took the risk seriously. He knew that his employers had forbidden this practice and that it had then been prohibited by statutory regulation and he knew that his employers were taking strong measures to see that the order was obeyed. If he did not choose to believe what he was told I do not think that he could for that reason say that he did not fully appreciate the risk. He knew that the risk was that a charge would explode during testing, and no shot firer could be in any doubt about the possible consequences of that.

Nettleship v Weston [1971] 2 QB 691

Panel: Lord Denning MR, Salmon and Megaw LJJ

Facts: Mr Nettleship agreed to give Mrs Weston, the wife of a friend, some informal driving lessons. The third lesson went badly wrong. Mrs Weston froze at the wheel and crashed into a lamp-post, causing Mr Nettleship injury. The defence of *volenti* was raised. Mr Nettleship, however, had asked about insurance cover before giving lessons. This demonstrated that he had not consented to the risk of injury, as he wanted to ensure he was covered and could obtain compensation.

Link
This case is important in the context of both Duty of Care and Breach

LORD DENNING MR

This brings me to the defence of volenti non fit injuria. Does it apply to the instructor? In former times this defence was used almost as an alternative defence to contributory negligence. Either defence defeated the action. Now that contributory negligence is not a complete defence, but only a ground for reducing the damages, the defence of volenti non fit injuria has been closely considered, and, in consequence, it has been severely limited. Knowledge of the risk of injury is not enough. Nor is a willingness to take the risk of injury. Nothing will suffice short of an agreement to waive any claim for negligence. The plaintiff must agree, expressly or impliedly, to waive any claim for any injury that may befall him due to the lack of reasonable care by the defendant: or, more accurately, due to the failure of the defendant to measure up to the standard of care that the law requires of him. ...

Applying the doctrine in this case, it is clear that Mr. Nettleship did not agree to waive any claim for injury that might befall him. Quite the contrary. He inquired about the insurance policy so as to make sure that he was covered. If and in so far as Mrs. Weston fell short of the standard of care which the law required of her, he has a cause of action.

8.2 Full Knowledge of the Nature of the Risk

The second condition is that the claimant has full knowledge of the nature of the risk. This is often difficult to prove as two similar cases - both involving drunk controllers of vehicles – demonstrate. Despite their similar facts, they provided different results.

Dann v Hamilton **[1939] 1 KB 509**

Panel: Asquith J

Facts: Miss Dann and her mother went on a trip with Mr Hamilton. He drove them around London to see various sights and, on a couple of occasions, for a couple of beers. On their way back home, late at night, Mr Hamilton crashed; he was killed, Miss Dann injured. Miss Dann sued Mr Hamilton's estate.

MR JUSTICE ASQUITH

A complete knowledge of the danger is in any event necessary, but such knowledge does not necessarily import consent. It is evidence of consent, weak or strong according to circumstances. ...

I find it difficult to believe, although I know of no authority directly in point, that a person who voluntarily travels as a passenger in a vehicle driven by a driver who is known by the passenger to have driven negligently in the past is volens as to future negligent acts of such driver, even though he could have chosen some other form of transport if he had wished. Then, to take the last step, suppose that such a driver is likely to drive negligently on the material occasion, not because he is known to the plaintiff to have driven negligently in the past, but because he is known to the plaintiff to be under the influence of drink. That is the present case. Ought the result to be any different? After much debate I have come to the conclusion that it should not, and that the plaintiff, by embarking in the car, or re-entering it, with knowledge that through drink the driver had materially reduced his capacity for driving safely, did not impliedly consent to, or absolve the driver from liability for any subsequent negligence on his part whereby she might suffer harm. ...

There may be cases in which the drunkenness of the driver at the material time is so extreme and so glaring that to accept a lift from him is like engaging in an intrinsically and obviously dangerous occupation, intermeddling with an unexploded bomb or walking on the edge of an unfenced cliff. It is not necessary to decide whether in such a case the maxim "volenti non fit injuria" would apply, for in the present case I find as a fact that the driver's degree of intoxication fell short of this degree.

Morris v Murray and another **[1991] 2 QB 6**

Panel: Fox and Stocker LJJ and Sir George Waller

Facts: After a drinking binge (involving at least 17 whiskies each), Mr Murray offered to take Mr Morris for a pleasure flight in his aeroplane. The flight was unsuccessful – the plane crashed, Mr Murray was killed and Mr Morris injured. Mr Morris sued Mr Murray's estate in negligence.

LORD JUSTICE FOX

In my opinion, on the evidence [Mr Morris] knew that he was going on a flight; he knew that he was going to be piloted by Mr. Murray; and he knew that Mr. Murray had been drinking heavily that afternoon. [Mr Morris]'s actions that afternoon, from leaving the Blue Boar to the take off, suggest that he was capable of understanding what he was doing. There is no clear evidence to the contrary. I think he knew what he was doing and was capable of appreciating the risks. I do not overlook that [Mr Morris]'s evidence was that, if he had been sober, he would not have gone on the flight. That is no doubt so but it does not establish that he was in fact incapable of understanding what he was doing that afternoon. If he was capable of understanding what he was doing, then the fact is that he knowingly and willingly embarked on a flight with a drunken pilot. The flight served no useful purpose at all; there was no need or compulsion to join it. It was just entertainment. [Mr Morris] co-operated fully in the joint activity and did what he could to assist it. He agreed in evidence that he was anxious to start the engine and to fly. A clearer source of great danger could hardly be imagined. The sort of errors of judgment which an intoxicated pilot may make are likely to have a disastrous result. The high probability was that Mr. Murray was simply not fit to fly an aircraft. Nothing that happened on the flight itself suggests otherwise, from the take off downwind to the violence of the manoeuvres of the plane in flight.

The situation seems to me to come exactly within Asquith J's example of the case

Where "the drunkenness of the driver at the material time is so extreme and so glaring that to accept a lift from him is like engaging in an intrinsically and obviously dangerous occupation."

I think that in embarking upon the flight [Mr Morris] had implicitly waived his rights in the event of injury consequent on Mr. Murray's failure to fly with reasonable care... I would conclude, therefore, that [Mr Morris] accepted the risks and implicitly discharged Mr. Murray from liability for injury in relation to the flying of the plane.

 Alert

Provisions in the Road Traffic Act 1988 s 149, now prevent *volenti* being used in road accidents, but this does not affect the principle of *Dann*.

The claimant may consent to a *risk* of damage, but not to that damage occurring *recklessly* or deliberately. Participation in extreme sports, for example, is voluntary; a claimant will not automatically succeed if injured, but only if the defendant has been negligent *and* the harm is from a risk to which the claimant did not consent. Standing close to something dangerous may be sufficiently "*volens*" to bar the claimant from succeeding.

Wooldridge v Sumner and another [1963] 2 QB 43

Panel: Sellers, Danckwerts and Diplock LJJ

Facts: Mr Wooldridge was a photographer covering a horse show. To get the best action shots, he stood very close to a track being used by racehorses. One rider temporarily lost control and Mr Wooldridge tried to shepherd another spectator out of the way; in so doing he fell under the horse and was seriously injured. He sued the rider and the organiser of the show, who in turn raised the defence of *volenti*. The claim was unsuccessful.

LORD JUSTICE DANCKWERTS

...[I]n taking up his position in a place where spectators were not allowed in the afternoons and which must necessarily be in close proximity to horses proceeding at a gallop, in my opinion the plaintiff must be taken to accept the risk of something going wrong in the course of an event with resulting danger to persons so near to the line to be traversed by the competitors, even though he happened to be inexperienced in regard to competitions of this kind.

LORD JUSTICE DIPLOCK

The maxim in English law presupposes a tortious act by the defendant. The consent that is relevant is not consent to the risk of injury but consent to the lack of reasonable care that may produce that risk...and requires on the part of the plaintiff at the time at which he gives his consent full knowledge of the nature and extent of the risk that he ran.

However, consent to being involved in something potentially harmful does not of itself mean the claimant has consented to all risks. A footballer does not expect to be fouled on a football pitch to the extent that his career is over; there is no consent to serious foul play.

Condon v Basi [1985] 1 WLR 866

Panel: Sir John Donaldson MR, Stephen Brown LJ and Glidewell J

Facts: Sunday League football features players of differing abilities. Mr Basi was not a very good player. He fouled Mr Condon - a high, studs-first tackle for which he was sent off - and broke his opponent's leg. Mr Condon sued for damages. Mr Basi alleged that, as he was a poor amateur, allowances should be made for his inability to tackle. Mr Basi's defence failed.

SIR JOHN DONALDSON MR

It is not for me in this court to attempt to define exhaustively the duty of care between players in a soccer football game. Nor, in my judgment, is there any need because there was here such an obvious breach of the defendant's duty of care towards the plaintiff. He was clearly guilty, as I find the facts, of serious and dangerous foul play which showed a reckless disregard of the plaintiff's safety and which fell far below the standards which might reasonably be expected in anyone pursuing the game.

Mr Condon had not consented to such a tackle from Mr Basi; any defence of *volenti* was therefore bound to fail.

8.3 Agreement to Risk must be Voluntary

Finally, the claimant's consent must have been freely given, i.e. without coercion, be it physical or mental. This generally covers acts in the course of employment. An employee injured through doing something ordered by management cannot usually be said to have consented freely.

Bowater v Rowley Regis Corporation [1944] KB 476

Panel: Scott, Goddard and Du Parcq LJJ

Facts: Mr Bowater was a carter employed by Rowley Regis Corporation. He was asked to take a horse and cart out to collect litter. He objected, stating that the horse had a tendency to bolt, but was told to take it out regardless. The horse duly bolted and Mr Bowater was injured. Rowley Regis Corporation argued that Mr Bowater had consented to the risk. The defence failed.

LORD JUSTICE GODDARD

The maxim "volenti non fit injuria" is one which in the case of master and servant is to be applied with extreme caution. Indeed, I would say that it can hardly ever be applicable where the act to which the servant is said to be "volens" arises out of his ordinary duty, unless the work for which he is engaged is one in which danger is necessarily involved. Thus, a man in an explosives factory must take the risk of an explosion occurring in spite of the observance and provision of all statutory regulations and safeguards. A horse-breaker must take the risk of being thrown or injured by a restive or unbroken horse. It is an ordinary risk of his employment. [A] man, however, whose occupation is not one of a nature inherently dangerous but who is asked or required to undertake a risky operation is in a different position. To rely on this doctrine the master must show that the servant undertook that the risk should be on him. It is not enough that, whether under protest or not, he obeyed an order or complied with a request which he might have declined as one which he was not bound either to obey or to comply with. It must be shown that he agreed that what risk there was should lie on him.

Mr Bowater's job only required him to deal with tame horses, not horses which were, in the words of Du Parcq LJ, "mettlesome or intractable". Accordingly, the defence failed.

The principle can be extended to cover rescuers, on the basis that someone assisting in a rescue may feel that they *have* to do something to help. The moral or social duty effectively overrides free will. In *Haynes v Harwood* [1935] 1 KB 146, Mr Haynes was successful in his claim against Harwood, the owners of a horse-drawn van, when he was injured in stopping the horses from bolting; the defence of volenti did not succeed, even though Mr Haynes did not *have* to assist. Contrast the case of *Cutler v United Dairies Ltd* [1933] 2 KB 297; Mr Cutler did not succeed in his case, on similar facts, as the danger was over by the time he was injured by United Dairies' horse. He had consented to the risk of being knocked down because he approached the horse with no need to do so.

8.3.1 *Ex turpi causa non oritur actio*

Can the claimant succeed if they were injured while doing something illegal? On the face of it, the answer may seem obvious: it looks unfair for the claimant to benefit from their own wrong, and the defence ought to be successful. However, this can lead to greater unfairness to the claimant in some circumstances. If someone parks on a double yellow line, and is then run over by a drunk driver while crossing the road and seriously injured, should they lose their right to damages because of the comparatively minor "crime" of illegal parking? Almost certainly not: it is a question of degree, and there are two parts to this defence. First, the court will consider whether there has been an illegal act on the part of the claimant. Second, if there has been an illegal act, would the court consider it an affront to the public conscience to disallow that claim. Note the role of policy underpinning this defence.

Cases where *ex turpi causa* has succeeded are exceedingly rare. This can lead to results that are often considered surprising by the general public.

Revill v Newbery [1996] QB 567

Panel: Neill, Evans and Millett LJJ

Facts: Mr Revill was a burglar. He was told by a neighbour of Mr Newbery that Mr Newbery kept valuable items in a shed on an allotment. Mr Revill took advantage of this intelligence to try to break into the shed. However, Mr Newbery often slept in that shed, because of the risk of break-ins, and had a loaded shotgun handy to deal with intruders. When Mr Newbery heard the sound of Mr Revill at the door, he shot through a small hole and injured Mr Revill. Mr Revill sued in negligence, and was successful. The defence of *ex turpi* was not accepted.

LORD JUSTICE EVANS

This does not mean that the rule [of ex turpi causa] cannot apply, because the underlying principle is that there is a public interest which requires that the wrongdoer should not benefit from his crime or other offence. But it would mean, if it does apply in circumstances such as these, that the trespasser who was also a criminal was effectively an outlaw, who was debarred by the law from recovering compensation for any injury which he might sustain. This same consideration also prompts the thought that it is one thing to deny to a plaintiff any fruits from his illegal conduct, but different and more far-reaching to deprive him even of compensation for injury which he suffers and which otherwise he is entitled to recover at law.

LORD JUSTICE MILLETT

For centuries the common law has permitted reasonable force to be used in defence of the person or property. Violence may be returned with necessary violence. But the force used must not exceed the limits of what is reasonable in the circumstances. Changes in society and in social perceptions have meant that what might have been considered reasonable at one time would no longer be so regarded; but the principle remains the same. The assailant or intruder may be met with reasonable force but no more; the use of excessive violence against him is an actionable wrong.

It follows, in my opinion, that there is no place for the doctrine ex turpi causa non oritur actio in this context. If the doctrine applied, any claim by the assailant or trespasser would be barred no matter how excessive or unreasonable the force used against him.

The court did reduce Mr Revill's damages by 60 per cent because of his contributory negligence; the general public contributed the remainder following a newspaper campaign.

Therefore, if the injury is grossly beyond a moral punishment for the illegality, the defence will not work.

However, there are circumstances where the defence has succeeded.

Ashton v Turner and another [1981] QB 137

Panel: Ewbank J

Facts: Ashton and Turner robbed a radio store and were making their getaway in a car stolen from a third party. In trying to get around a taxi that blocked their path, Mr Turner lost control and crashed. Mr Ashton was seriously injured and he sued Mr Turner.

MR JUSTICE EWBANK

The conclusion I have come to is that the law of England may in certain circumstances not recognise the existence of a duty of care owed by one participant in a crime to another participant in the same crime, in relation to an act done in connection with the commission of that crime. That law is based on public policy, and the application of the law depends on a consideration of all the facts. Having regard to all the facts in this case I have come to the conclusion that a duty of care did not exist between the [Mr Turner and [Mr Ashton] during the course of the burglary and during the course of the subsequent flight in the get-away car.

In other words, the act of burglary was so serious the court could not recognise that a duty was owed between driver and passenger.

Vellino v Chief Constable of the Greater Manchester Police [2001] 1 EWCA Civ 1249, [2002] 1 WLR 218

Panel: Schiemann, Sedley LJJ and Sir Murray Stuart-Smith

Facts: The police visited Mr Vellino's flat with an arrest warrant. Mr Vellino had a record of trying to avoid arrest by jumping from his balcony. True to form, Mr Vellino tried the same escape route again. However, this time, his leap went wrong and he was seriously injured. He sued the police on the basis that, while he was under arrest, the police owed him a duty to stop him from harming himself. The claim failed for various reasons.

SIR MURRAY STUART-SMITH

... I derive the following propositions.

(1) The operation of the principle arises where the claimant's claim is founded upon his own criminal or immoral act. The facts which give rise to the claim must be inextricably linked with the criminal activity. It is not sufficient if the criminal activity merely gives occasion for tortious conduct of the defendant [for example, picking a burglar's pocket on the way to a burglary].

(2) The principle is one of public policy; it is not for the benefit of the defendant. Since if the principle applies, the cause of action does not arise, the defendant's conduct is irrelevant. There is no question of proportionality between the conduct of the claimant and defendant.

(3) In the case of criminal conduct this has to be sufficiently serious to merit the application of the principle. Generally speaking a crime punishable with imprisonment could be expected to qualify [note however that this is only a general point; compare *Revill*]. If the offence is criminal but relatively trivial, it is in any event difficult to see how it could be integral to the claim.

(4) The Law Reform (Contributory Negligence) Act 1945 is not applicable where the claimant's action amounts to a common law crime which does not give rise to liability in tort.

Applying these principles it is common ground that [Mr Vellino] has to rely on his criminal conduct in escaping lawful custody to found his claim. It is integral to the claim. The crime of escape is a serious one; it is a common law offence for which the penalty is at large. It is almost invariably punished by a sentence of imprisonment, although the length of the sentence is usually measured in months rather than years. In my judgment it is plainly a sufficiently serious offence for the purpose of the application of the maxim. ...

As stated above, the Road Traffic Act 1988 forbids a defence of *volenti* between a negligent driver and an injured passenger. However, this does not apply to a defence of *ex turpi causa*. Sometimes the court can hold that a passenger is complicit with a driver's illegal activity.

Pitts v Hunt [1991] 1 QB 24

Panel: Dillon, Balcombe and Beldam LJJ

Facts: Pitts and Hunt were friends who went out drinking together. Both were over the legal driving limit. Nevertheless they decided to return home on Hunt's motorcycle, (Hunt was driving). Hunt did not have a driving licence, which Pitts knew. Pitts encouraged Hunt into riding recklessly and frightening passers-by. Hunt lost control and was killed in the ensuing accident. Pitts was seriously injured. Pitts sued Hunt's estate. The claim failed because of Pitts' own wrongdoing.

LORD JUSTICE BELDAM

On the facts found by the judge in this case [Mr Pitts] was playing a full and active part in encouraging the young rider [Mr Hunt] to commit offences which, if a death other than that of the young rider himself had occurred, would have amounted to manslaughter, and not just manslaughter by gross negligence, on the judge's findings. It would have been manslaughter by the commission of a dangerous act either done with the intention of frightening other road users or when both [Mr Pitts] and the young rider were aware, or but for self-induced intoxication would have been aware, that it was likely to do so, and nevertheless they went on and did the act regardless of the consequences. Thus on the findings made by the judge in this case I would hold that [Mr Pitts] is precluded on grounds of public policy from recovering compensation for the injuries which he sustained in the course of the very serious offences in which he was participating.

LORD JUSTICE DILLON

I find a test that depends on what would or would not be an affront to the public conscience very difficult to apply, since the public conscience may well be affected by factors of an emotional nature, e.g., that these boys by their reckless and criminal behaviour happened to do no harm to anyone but themselves. Moreover if the public conscience happened to think that [Mr Pitts] should be compensated for his injuries it might equally think that the deceased driver of the motor cycle, had he survived and merely been injured, ought to be compensated, and that leads into the much-debated question whether there ought to be a universal scheme for compensation for the victims of accidents without regard to fault.

As can be seen from *Revill* above, the public conscience was not on Mr Revill's side, yet nevertheless he succeeded in his claim. Even though Mr Revill's behaviour was criminal, it was not sufficiently criminal to warrant his being denied a civil remedy.

8.4 Contributory Negligence

One problem with most general defences is that, at common law, they defeat the *entire* claim. The claimant can show that the defendant caused them damage, but does not recover a single penny from the defendant. This was particularly harsh where both the claimant and the defendant had contributed to the loss. Under common law, even if the vast majority of the damage had been caused by the defendant, the claimant would lose their right to damages, the logic seemingly being that the claimant would not have suffered any loss had they not been negligent.

The court developed various devices to soften this unfair result (for example, creating a doctrine whereby the *last* party to be negligent bore the full extent of the loss), but these were largely swept away by Parliament. The Law Reform (Contributory Negligence) Act 1945 states that, where both a claimant and defendant have contributed to a claimant's loss, the court can apportion losses between them as it sees fit. This is only a *partial* defence. The defendant cannot use contributory negligence to exonerate them from liability for all damage. Logically, if the claimant is 100 per cent liable for damage, the defendant will not have caused any damage and the claim would fail before considering defences.

The claimant will see a reduction for contributory negligence if he has contributed to his own loss; this can occur either when the claimant has caused the incident in the first place, or when the incident is entirely the defendant's fault, but the claimant's behaviour has made the damage worse than it would otherwise have been, (for example, by not wearing a seatbelt).

The availability of this partial defence has an impact on the complete defences. The court may be more willing to consider a case as one of contributory negligence rather than *volenti* or *ex turpi causa*, so that it can better do justice between the parties. Indeed, Sedley LJ in *Vellino*, in a dissenting judgment, stated that the Act was often more appropriate to use than "the blunt instrument of turpitude". It is important not to read too much into this; *ex turpi causa* provided a complete defence in *Vellino*. Nevertheless in practice, many judges may consider that allowing a complete defence in the case before them would be too harsh.

The Act gives judges a wide discretion and, as each case is decided on its own facts, precedent is of less use in working out a percentage figure for the claimant's contribution to the damage. However, some cases do help to set out where and how a claimant's negligence is sufficient to warrant a deduction.

Jones v Livox Quarries Ltd [1952] 2 QB 608

Panel: Singleton, Denning and Hodson LJJ

Facts: Mr Jones was working for Livox at a quarry. One of the regulations was that staff members were not allowed to ride on moving machinery. However, Mr Jones had jumped on a slow-moving vehicle called a traxcavator and was standing on its back. The traxcavator stopped, and a truck, unsighted, crushed Mr Jones. Mr Jones claimed against Livox. Livox defended on the basis that Mr Jones was contributorily negligent, as there was a risk of harm from travelling on the traxcavator. Mr Jones claimed that he was not contributorily negligent, as, although he should not have been riding on the traxcavator, it was not this act that had caused his injury, but the negligently-driven truck.

The court decided that Mr Jones was contributorily negligent by the mere fact of riding on the traxcavator and his damages were reduced by 20 per cent.

LORD JUSTICE SINGLETON

It was submitted to us that the prohibition against riding upon one of these vehicles was because of the danger of a man falling off, or the danger of his becoming trapped in some part of the machine. I think there is more than that to be considered. [Mr Jones], in riding on the traxcavator, was disobeying the orders of his employers. In so doing he was exposing himself to danger. It may well be that the chief danger was that he might fall off, or be thrown off, or that he might become entangled in some part of the machine on which he was riding; but those were not the only risks to which he subjected himself. He had put himself in a dangerous position which, in fact, exposed him to the particular danger which came upon him. He ought not to have been there.

The fact that he was in that particular position meant that he exposed himself, or some part of his body, to another risk, the risk that some driver following might not be able to pull up in time - it may be because that driver was certainly at fault. That is the view which the trial judge took of this case, and I do not see that that is a wrong view. It is not so much a question of "Was [Mr Jones]'s conduct the cause of the accident?" as "Did it contribute to the accident?", on the assumption that it was something of a kind which a reasonably careful man so placed would not have done. If he unreasonably, or improperly, exposed himself to this particular risk, I do not think that he ought to be allowed to say that it was not a cause operating to produce the damage, even though one may think that the prohibition against riding on the vehicle was not made with that particular risk in mind. Hallett J [who heard the case at first instance] felt great difficulty about this part of the case. So do I. My first impression was that the fact that [Mr Jones] was upon the traxcavator had nothing to do with the accident.

Alert

I think the real cause was the negligence of the driver of the dumper. The trial judge considered the relevant authorities, and in particular he considered what was said by this court in *Davies v Swan Motor Co. (Swansea) Ltd* [1949] 2 KB 291. I agree with him that the responsibility of the plaintiff for the accident was much less than that of the driver of the dumper. Still, when one has to consider the question of contributory negligence I do not see that it can be said that the judge was wrong in finding that [Mr Jones], who deliberately put himself into a position which exposed him to this danger, was to some extent responsible for that which happened; in other words, I do not think it would be right for this court on these findings to say that the judge was wrong in law; it is not argued before us that the proportion of liability ought to be altered if, in fact, there was contributory negligence on the part of [Mr Jones]. The submission, therefore, that [Mr Jones] ought not to have been found to blame at all fails.

LORD JUSTICE DENNING

In my opinion, however, foreseeability is not the decisive test of causation. It is often a relevant factor, but it is not decisive. Even though [Mr Jones] did not foresee the possibility of being crushed, nevertheless in the ordinary plain common sense of this business the injury suffered by the plaintiff was due in part to the fact that he chose to ride on the towbar to lunch instead of walking down on his feet. If he had been thrown off in the collision, Mr. Arthian Davies [Mr Jones' barrister] admits that his injury would be partly due to his own negligence in riding on the towbar; but he says that, because he was crushed, and not thrown off, his injury is in no way due to it. That is too fine a distinction for me. I cannot believe that that purely fortuitous circumstance can make all the difference to the case...The man's negligence here was so much mixed up with his injury that it cannot be dismissed as mere history. His dangerous position on the vehicle was one of the causes of his damage just as it was in *Davies*.

Alert

Therefore, if a claimant is acting in some way negligently, and suffers damage in some way related to that negligent behaviour, they are liable to some reduction in their claim. This can apply even if the claimant was acting in difficult circumstances. If the claimant is on the horns of a dilemma, they are still bound to act reasonably.

Sayers v Harlow Urban District Council [1958] 1 WLR 623

Panel: Lord Evershed MR, Morris and Ormerod LJJ

Facts: Mrs Sayers went to a public toilet in Harlow. The door on the cubicle jammed shut and she could not open it. There was nobody around to help, and after 10 to 15 minutes of calling for assistance she decided to climb out. Having tried and failed to fit through the gap between the door and ceiling, Mrs Sayers relied on the toilet roll holder to assist her descent, with disastrous results. She therefore sued the council which provided and maintained the toilet.

She succeeded in her claim, but damages were reduced by 25 per cent.

LORD EVERSHED MR

I think that in getting to the position where she could see, and did see, that escape via the top of the door was impossible, she acted without carelessness. But I think it true to say, and fair and right to say — though it is, of course, one of those matters when, no doubt, it is being wise after the event — that in getting back to terra firma again she should have appreciated that she could not properly and ought not to allow her balance to depend upon anything so unstable as a toilet roll and a fixture of a somewhat slender kind. It was not a grave error, and I think the consequences were unduly unfortunate in the circumstances; but I think it is impossible to acquit the plaintiff altogether from some carelessness.

In these matters the apportionment must be largely a question of, I will not say hazard, but at any rate of doing the best one can in fractions; and applying myself to it in that way, and not desiring to do more than indicate that [Mrs Sayers] was, as I think, in some degree careless and in some degree, therefore, blameworthy, I would apportion the matter as to three-fourths liability to the defendants, and one-fourth to her. In other words, I think [Mrs Sayers] ought to recover from the [council] 75 per cent. or three-fourths of whatever be the appropriate measure of damage suffered. If the claimant has not contributed to the causing of harm, but its conduct affects the level of damage, a reduction can still be applied.

 Alert

Froom v Butcher [1976] QB 286

Panel: Lord Denning MR, Lawton and Scarman LJJ

Facts: Mr Froom was driving perfectly competently down a road in Chigwell. The opposite side of the road was blocked with traffic. Mr Butcher was in that traffic. He pulled out to overtake and collided with Mr Froom. Mr Froom was injured. His injuries were exacerbated because he refused to wear a safety belt. At the time, wearing a safety belt was not compulsory. Mr Butcher claimed that Mr Froom had contributed to his loss by failing to take proper precautions and therefore damages should be reduced.

The Court held that a discount of 20 per cent should be applied.

LORD DENNING MR

It may well be asked: why should the injured plaintiff have his damages reduced? The accident was solely caused by the negligent driving of the defendant. Sometimes outrageously bad driving. It should not lie in his mouth to say: "You ought to have been wearing a seat belt."...I do not think that is the correct approach. The question is not what was the cause of the accident. It is rather what was the cause of the damage. In most accidents on the road the bad driving, which causes the accident, also causes the ensuing damage. But in seat belt cases the cause of the accident is one thing. The cause of the damage is another. The *accident* is caused by the bad driving. The *damage* is caused in part by the bad driving of the defendant, and in part by the failure of the plaintiff to wear a seat belt. If the plaintiff was to blame in not wearing a seat belt, the damage is in part the result of his own fault. He must bear some share in the responsibility for the damage: and his damages fall to be reduced to such extent as the court thinks just and equitable. ...

 Alert

Whenever there is an accident, the negligent driver must bear by far the greater share of responsibility. It was his negligence which caused the accident. It also was a prime cause of the whole of the damage. But in so far as the damage might have been avoided or lessened by wearing a seat belt, the injured person must bear some share. But how much should this be? Is it proper to inquire whether the driver was grossly negligent or only slightly negligent? or whether the failure to wear a seat belt was entirely inexcusable or almost forgivable?...Sometimes the evidence will show that the failure made no difference. The damage would have been the same, even if a seat belt had been worn. In such case the damages should not be reduced at all. At other times the evidence will show that the failure made all the difference. The damage would have been prevented altogether if a seat belt had been worn. In such cases I would suggest that the damages should be reduced by 25 per cent. But often enough the evidence will only show that the failure made a considerable difference. Some injuries to the head, for instance, would have been a good deal less severe if a seat belt had been worn, but there would still have been some injury to the head. In such case I would suggest that the damages attributable to the failure to wear a seat belt should be reduced by 15 per cent.

Despite Lord Denning MR's comments, the court applied a discount of 20 per cent, as that had been the finding of the original trial judge and was not the subject of appeal.

The court has a wide discretion in applying a discount for contributory negligence; for example, in *Revill* above, Mr Revill's damages were reduced by 60 per cent; in *Fitzgerald v Lane and another* [1987] QB 781, Mr Fitzgerald lost 50 per cent of his damages because he had dashed out into the road carelessly. In *Capps v Miller* [1989] 1 WLR 839 Mr Capps (who had been injured when knocked off his moped) lost 10 per cent of his damages because he had failed to fasten his crash helmet. In *Jebson v Ministry of Defence* [2000] 1 WLR 2055 Mr Jebson, who had drunkenly fallen off the back of an army vehicle following an army-supervised night out, lost 75 per cent of his damages.

8.5 Miscellaneous General Defences

There are a handful of other general defences that are only occasionally used. For example, a doctor who saves the life of an unconscious patient will have committed a trespass, because the patient would not have been able to consent to the treatment; however the doctor would have the defence of "necessity". Self-defence also amounts to a defence, as does an Act of God (e.g. extraordinary rainfall – *Nichols v Marsland* (1876-77) LR 2 Ex D 1). These are of minor importance only, and are used even less than *volenti* or *ex turpi causa*. There are other, specific defences, applicable only to certain torts. These will be dealt with in the chapters dealing with those torts.

Link

Link to Chapter 14 on Defamation and Chapter 15 on Nuisance

Further Reading

Murdie, Alan: 'Compensation for Criminals' SJ 2003, 147 (9), 252 – 253

O'Sullivan, Karen: 'Belt up?' NLJ 2010, 160 (7410), 454

9

Employers' Liability – Vicarious Liability

Topic List

Introduction

Vicarious liability is not a tort, but a doctrine which allows a claimant to bring an action against a third party who has responsibility for the tortfeasor. The defendant who has committed the tort will incur primary liability, whereas the second defendant who is vicariously liable will have secondary liability. The rationale behind this doctrine is that a claimant should be able to recover against an employer for the torts of the employee, because the employer has compulsory insurance to deal with such claims and should, in law, have responsibility for some of the actions of their employees. Without this device, many claimants would be left without compensation, where the tortfeasor has no money or insurance.

The most common situation where this occurs is in employer and employee relationships (although it can also arise in other situations such as principal and agent which is outside the scope of this chapter). For a claimant to succeed in a vicarious claim against a defendant, the claimant must prove three factors: (a) that a tort as been committed (by the tortfeasor), (b) that there is the requisite relationship of control between defendant and tortfeasor, in other words a relationship of employer/employee, and (c) that the tort was committed in the course of employment.

In this chapter we will look at (b) and (c) above. There is no need to look at factor (a) here, as this involves discussion of the tort itself (for example, negligence, defamation, etc) which is covered by other chapters. We will focus on key cases to establish the test to determine an employment relationship. We will then look at the cases to establish who is the employer where more than one possible employer exists. Finally, we will look at how the court would determine whether the tort was committed in the course of employment.

9.1 The Employment Relationship

A number of different tests have been used by the courts to determine whether the defendant is an employee. The courts will generally try to distinguish a contract of service (employment contract), from a contract for services (an independent contractor). These tests have generally focused on a factor such as the amount of control exercised over the worker, or examining whether the worker is fully integrated into the business. None of these single tests have proven satisfactory, however, and although no exhaustive list of factors has been compiled, the current approach is set out in the cases below.

Ready Mixed Concrete v Minister of Pensions [1968] 2 QB 497

Panel: Mackenna J

Facts: In this case the court examined whether a worker was an employee or an independent contractor. The worker drove a concrete mixer, painted in the company's colours and the contract stated that he was responsible for running the lorry. The lorry could not be used for any other business but the contract stated that the drivers were independent contractors and were to share in the profit and risk of loss. The court held that the driver was an independent contractor.

MR JUSTICE MACKENNA

I must now consider what is meant by a contract of service.

A contract of service exists if these three conditions are fulfilled. (i) The servant agrees that, in consideration of a wage or other remuneration, he will provide his own work and skill in the performance of some service for his master. (ii) He agrees, expressly or impliedly, that in the performance of that service he will be subject to the other's control in a sufficient degree to make that other master. (iii) The other provisions of the contract are consistent with its being a contract of service.

I need say little about (i) and (ii).

As to (i). There must be a wage or other remuneration. Otherwise there will be no consideration, and without consideration no contract of any kind. The servant must be obliged to provide his own work and skill. Freedom to do a job either by one's own hands or by another's is inconsistent with a contract of service, though a limited or occasional power of delegation may not be...

As to (ii). Control includes the power of deciding the thing to be done, the way in which it shall be done, the means to be employed in doing it, the time when and the place where it shall be done. All these aspects of control must be considered in deciding whether the right exists in a sufficient degree to make one party the master and the other his servant. The right need not be unrestricted. ...

The third and negative condition is for my purpose the important one ...

I can put the point which I am making in other words. An obligation to do work subject to the other party's control is a necessary, though not always a sufficient, condition of a contract of service. If the provisions of the contract as a whole are inconsistent with its being a contract of service, it will be some other kind of contract, and the person doing the work will not be a servant. The judge's task is to classify the contract (a task like that of distinguishing a contract of sale from one of work and labour). He may, in performing it, take into account other matters besides control. ...

Decipher
Remember that the control test used to be the sole method of deciding whether a contract of service existed, but was unsatisfactory (see *Cassidy v Ministry of Health* [1951] 2 KB 343).

Alert

Market Investigations Ltd. v Minister of Social Security [1969] 2 QB 173

Panel: Cooke J

Facts: The case concerned a part-time interviewer conducting market research for a company. The court had to decide whether she was engaged under a series of contracts for services or a contract of service. The company appealed from the decision that she was employed under a contract of service. The appeal was dismissed.

MR JUSTICE COOKE

...I begin by pointing out that the first condition which must be fulfilled in order that a contract may be classified as a contract of service is that stated by MacKenna J in the *Ready Mixed Concrete case* [1968] 2 QB 497, 515, namely, that A agrees that, in consideration of some form of remuneration, he will provide his own work and skill in the performance of some service for B. The fact that this condition is fulfilled is not, however, sufficient. Further tests must be applied to determine whether the nature and provisions of the contract as a whole are consistent or inconsistent with its being a contract of service.

I think it is fair to say that there was at one time a school of thought according to which the extent and degree of the control which B was entitled to exercise over A in the performance of the work would be a decisive factor. However, it has for long been apparent that an analysis of the extent and degree of such control is not in itself decisive. ...

If control is not a decisive test, what then are the other considerations which are relevant? ...

No exhaustive list has been compiled and perhaps no exhaustive list can be compiled of the considerations which are relevant in determining that question, nor can strict rules be laid down as to the relative weight which the various considerations should carry in particular cases. The most that can be said is that control will no doubt always have to be considered, although it can no longer be regarded as the sole determining factor; and that factors which may be of importance are such matters as whether the man performing the services provides his own equipment, whether he hires his own helpers, what degree of financial risk he takes, what degree of responsibility for investment and management he has, and whether and how far he has an opportunity of profiting from sound management in the performance of his task.

Decipher
Note how Cooke J does not attempt to produce a definitive test for determining the issue.

In the present case it is clear that on each occasion on which Mrs. Irving engaged herself to act as an interviewer for a particular survey she agreed with the company, in consideration of a fixed remuneration, to provide her own work and skill in the performance of a service for the company. I therefore proceed to ask myself two questions: First, whether the extent and degree of the control exercised by the company, if no other factors were taken into account, be consistent with her being employed under a contract of service. Second, whether when the contract is looked at as a whole, its nature and provisions are consistent or inconsistent with its being a contract of service, bearing in mind the general test I have adumbrated. ...

Note that Cooke J specified that the control test should not be used as the sole method of determining whether an employment relationship existed, and set out other factors that should also be considered. *Hall (Inspector of Taxes) v Lorimer* [1994] 1 All ER 250 provides a good example of how the courts have made use of Cooke J's test.

9.2 Lending Employees

We will now consider the situation where an employee is lent to someone else, for example another hirer. If the employee commits a tort while working for the hirer, the question arises as to whether the original employer or the hirer will then be vicariously liable. The following two cases provide some interesting guidance.

Mersey Docks and Harbour Board Appellants v Coggins & Griffith (Liverpool) Limited and Another Respondents [1947] AC 1

Panel: Viscount Simon, Lord Macmillan, Lord Porter, Lord Simonds and Lord Uthwatt

Facts: A harbour authority contracted with a firm of stevedores. The contract involved the harbour authority lending out a crane and a craneman to work the crane. The contract stipulated that the worker would be 'the servant of the hirers'. However, the harbour authority retained control over pay and also whether the worker could be dismissed. The craneman injured a third party through the negligent working of the crane and the question arose as to whether the harbour authority or the stevedores should be vicariously liable for the craneman's negligence.

The Court of Appeal held that the agreement between the stevedores and the harbour authority was irrelevant in determining liability and held that the harbour authority as the general permanent employers remained liable. The harbour authority appealed. Their appeal was dismissed.

LORD MACMILLAN

[Read by LORD PORTER] My Lords, the only question for your Lordships' determination is whether on the principle of respondeat superior, the responsibility for the negligence of the driver of the crane lies with the stevedores or with the appellant board, whom the plaintiff sued alternatively. The answer depends on whether the driver was acting as the servant of the stevedores or as the servant of the appellant board when he set the crane in motion. That the crane driver was in general the servant of the appellant board is indisputable. ... But it is always open to an employer to show, if he can, that he has for a particular purpose or on a particular occasion temporarily transferred the services of one of his general servants to another party so as to constitute him pro hac vice the servant of that other party with consequent liability for his negligent acts. The burden is on the general employer to establish that such a transference has been effected. Agreeing as I do with the trial judge and the Court of Appeal, I am of opinion that, on the facts of the present case, Newall was never so transferred from the service and control of the appellant board to the service and control of the stevedores as to render the stevedores answerable for the manner in which he carried on his work of driving the crane. The stevedores were entitled to tell him where to go, what parcels to lift and where to take them, that is to say, they could direct him as to what they wanted him to do; but they had no authority to tell him how he was to handle the crane in doing his work. In driving the crane, which was the appellant board's property confided to his charge, he was acting as the servant of the appellant board, not as the servant of the stevedores. ...

Alert

The case below illustrates an interesting decision reached by the Court of Appeal, in which they considered *Mersey Docks* and concluded that it assumed that dual liability could not arise, or at the very least, that it did not arise in that case. However, there was nothing to prevent the court from holding two parties to be vicariously liable for the negligence of the employee where the facts were appropriate.

Viasystems (Tyneside) Ltd v Thermal Transfer (Northern) Ltd and others [2006] QB 510

Panel: May and Rix LJJ

Facts: The first defendants in this case had been engaged to install air conditioning in the claimant's factory. The second defendants were then sub-contracted to do the ducting work. A workman was supplied by the third defendants to work on the ducting for the second defendants, on a labour-only basis. The workman, Darren Strang, negligently damaged the fire sprinkler system, resulting in flood damage to the factory. The issue arose as to whether more than one defendant could be vicariously liable for the negligence of the workman.

LORD JUSTICE MAY

The possibility of dual vicarious liability

The parties' cases and the judge's decision were predicated on an assumption that only one of the second or third defendants could in law be vicariously liable for Darren Strang's negligence, not both. Before we began hearing the appeal, counsel drew our attention to the discussion in Atiyah, Vicarious Liability in the Law of Torts (1967) in a chapter entitled "The Borrowed Servant", p 152, at p 156, where it is suggested that it is strange that the courts have never countenanced what might be an obvious solution in some cases, namely holding both the general and the temporary employer vicariously liable for an employee's negligence. We considered that this interesting possibility should be examined in this appeal. ...

...Vicarious liability is liability imposed by a policy of the law upon a party who is not personally at fault. So the core question on the facts of this case is who was entitled, and in theory, if they had had the opportunity, obliged, so to control Darren as to stop him crawling through the duct. In my judgment, the only sensible answer to that question in this case is that both Mr Megson and Mr Horsley were entitled, and in theory obliged, to stop Darren's foolishness. Mr Megson was the fitter in charge of Darren. Mr Horsley was the foreman on the spot. They were both entitled and obliged to control Darren's work, including the act which was his negligence. ...

In summary, therefore, there has been a long-standing assumption, technically unsupported by authority binding this court, that a finding of dual vicarious liability is not legally permissible. An assumption of such antiquity should not lightly be brushed aside, but the contrary has scarcely been argued and never considered in depth. This is not surprising, because in many, perhaps most, factual situations, a proper application of the Mersey Docks principles would not yield dual control, as it so plainly does in the present case. I am sceptical whether any of the cases from this jurisdiction which I have considered would, if they were re-examined, yield dual vicarious liability. ...

I conclude below in considering contribution that, if the relevant relationships yield dual control, it is highly likely at least that the measure of control will be equal. An equal measure of control will not often arise. Dual vicarious liability is most unlikely to be a

Decipher

Mr Megson was a fitter supplied by the third defendants and Mr Horsley was a foreman working for the second defendants.

Alert

possibility if one of the candidates for such liability is also personally at fault. It would be entirely redundant, if both were.

For these reasons I would allow the appeal in part and hold that each of the second and third defendants should be vicariously liable to the claimants. As between each other, there should be equal contribution.

Note that May LJ's approach seems to suggest that dual vicarious liability will rarely arise in subsequent cases.

9.3 Was the Tort committed in the Course of Employment?

The claimant will need to establish that the tort was committed in the course of employment in order for vicarious liability to arise, as the employer will not necessarily be held liable for every act the employee carries out. The definition of 'course of employment' has been described by Professor Winfield as being a wrongful act which is either expressly or impliedly authorised by the employer, or incidental to the carrying out of the employer's proper duties, or an unauthorised way of doing something authorised by the employer. The first two definitions are self-explanatory, the third requires some attention.

9.4 An Unauthorised way of doing something Authorised by the Employer

Century Insurance Company Limited, Appellants; v Northern Ireland Road Transport Board, Respondents [1942] AC 509

Panel: Viscount Simon LC, Lord Wright, Lord Romer and Lord Porter

Facts: In this case the driver of a petrol tanker threw a lit match onto the floor while simultaneously smoking a cigarette and transferring the petrol to a storage tank. This resulted in an explosion. The question which arose for the court was whether the careless act was done in the course of employment. The Court of Appeal held that this act *was* in the course of employment, being an unauthorised way (smoking and dropping the match) of doing something authorised (filling the tank with petrol)

LORD WRIGHT

...The act of a workman in lighting his pipe or cigarette is an act done for his own comfort and convenience and, at least generally speaking, not for his employer's benefit, but that last condition is no longer essential to fix liability on the employer ... Nor is such an act prima facie negligent. It is in itself both innocent and harmless. The negligence is to be found by considering the time when and the circumstances in which the match is struck and thrown down. The duty of the workman to his employer is so to conduct himself in doing his work as not negligently to cause damage either to the employer himself or his property or to third persons or their property, and thus to impose the same liability on the employer as if he had been doing the work himself and committed the negligent act. This may seem too obvious as a matter of common sense to require either argument or authority. I think what plausibility the contrary argument might seem to possess results from treating the act of lighting the cigarette in abstraction from the circumstances as a separate act. This was the line taken by the majority judgment in *Williams v. Jones*, but Mellor and Blackburn JJ. dissented, rightly as I think. I agree also with the decision of the Court of Appeal in *Jefferson v. Derbyshire Farmers, Ltd.* which is in substance on the facts indistinguishable from the present case. In my judgment the appeal should be dismissed.

Note that the above case extended the law to cover the possibility that acts done for the employee's benefit and not for the employer's benefit could also be deemed to be in the course of employment.

9.5 Acts Deemed Outside the Course of Employment

The following case provides an example of when the courts would *not* deem an act to be in the course of employment.

Daniels v Whetstone Entertainments, Ltd., and Allender [1962] 2 Lloyd's Rep 1

Panel: Davies, Buckley and Holroyd Pearce LJJ

Facts: The case concerned an employee who was employed as a 'bouncer' for a dance hall. He assaulted the plaintiff once while inside the dance hall, and then a further time when the plaintiff had already left the dance hall and presented no further threat of any affray. The question for the court to decide was whether the assaults were in the course of employment. It was held that the first assault was inside the course of employment, but the second was outside.

LORD JUSTICE DAVIES

...At the material time when the second Defendant struck the Plaintiff a blow outside the dance hall, was he doing the act which he was employed to do or the act which was so connected with the acts which he was expressly or impliedly authorised to do, so as to be a mode of doing those acts?

It is important for me to remind myself that at the time when these blows were struck the Plaintiff had already left the dance hall. Whether he had been ejected or not perhaps it is unnecessary for me to decide. He had already left and he was showing no intention whatsoever of returning and was doing no act or showing any intention to do any violence to the second Defendant.

...In those circumstances, I have come to the conclusion that the second Defendant at the time he struck the blow outside the dance hall, was not doing an act which he was employed to do; he was not doing an act which was of the type he was employed to do. He had completed all he was authorised to do; he had disobeyed the clear

 Alert

instructions of the manager to go back into the dance hall, and he was engaged on an act of private vengeance of his own. In those circumstances I find that he was not acting in the course of his employment. ...

Special Categories

9.6 Express Prohibition by the Employer

Rose v Plenty and Another [1976] 1 WLR 141

Panel: Lord Denning MR, Lawton and Scarman LJJ

Facts: The defendant, Mr Plenty, was a milkman. There were notices up at his depot expressly forbidding the milkmen to take children on their vehicles while making deliveries. Nevertheless, the practice continued. Mr Plenty was deemed to have been aware of the notices, but allowed a 13-year old boy, Leslie Rose, to assist him in his deliveries. On 21 June 1970, after delivering to a house, the boy jumped on to the milk float and then sat on it with one foot dangling down ready to jump off quickly. Mr Plenty carelessly drove too close to the kerb as he rounded a corner, and the wheel caught the boy's leg. The boy sustained a broken foot.

LORD DENNING MR

...In considering whether a prohibited act was within the course of the employment, it depends very much on the purpose for which it is done. If it is done for his employers' business, it is usually done in the course of his employment, even though it is a prohibited act. That is clear from *Limpus v. London General Omnibus Co.*, 1 H & C 526 ; *Young v. Edward Box & Co. Ltd.* [1951] 1 TLR 789 and *Ilkiw v. Samuels* [1963] 1 WLR 991. But if it is done for some purpose other than his masters' business, as, for instance, giving a lift to a hitchhiker, such an act, if prohibited, may not be within the course of his employment. Both *Twine v. Bean's Express Ltd.* (1946) 62 TLR 458 and *Conway v. George Wimpey & Co. Ltd.* (No. 2) [1951] 2 KB 266 are to be explained on their own facts as cases where a driver had given a lift to someone else, contrary to a prohibition and not for the purposes of the employers. ...

I would hold that the conduct of the roundsman was within the course of his employment and the masters are liable accordingly, and I would allow the appeal.

 Alert

Lord Justice Scarman came to the same conclusion, on the basis that the prohibited act (of enlisting the help of the boy) was an unauthorised way of doing something authorised. He asserted that there was no discrepancy between the authority of *Limpus v London General Omnibus Co.* 1 H & C 526 and Lord Denning MR's conclusion in this case and that the case law would be thoroughly reconcilable (even to a visitor from Mars!)

9.7 Deviations from an Authorised Route

The case below is the leading decision regarding employees who are paid to travel within working hours.

Smith, Respondent v Stages and Another, Appellants [1989] 2 WLR 529

Panel: Lord Keith of Kinkel, Lord Brandon of Oakbrook, Lord Griffiths, Lord Goff of Chieveley and Lord Lowry

Facts: This case involved two workers who had been sent to work in Pembroke and were paid for travelling time, although the method of transport had not been specified. There was an accident on the return journey which involved negligence on the part of the worker. The issue arose as to whether the accident occurred during the course of employment. The trial judge held that the accident did not occur during the course of employment. The Court of Appeal however held that the employers were vicariously liable and the employers appealed. The House of Lords held that the employees were in the course of employment and dismissed the appeal.

LORD LOWRY

...The paramount rule is that an employee travelling on the highway will be acting in the course of his employment if, and only if, he is at the material time going about his employer's business. One must not confuse the duty to turn up for one's work with the concept of already being "on duty" while travelling to it.

 Alert

It is impossible to provide for every eventuality and foolish, without the benefit of argument, to make the attempt, but some prima facie propositions may be stated with reasonable confidence.

1. An employee travelling from his ordinary residence to his regular place of work, whatever the means of transport and even if it is provided by the employer, is not on duty and is not acting in the course of his employment, but, if he is obliged by his contract of service to use the employer's transport, he will normally, in the absence of an express condition to the contrary, be regarded as acting in the course of his employment while doing so.

2. Travelling in the employer's time between workplaces (one of which may be the regular workplace) or in the course of a peripatetic occupation, whether accompanied by goods or tools or simply in order to reach a succession of workplaces (as an inspector of gas meters might do), will be in the course of the employment.

3. Receipt of wages (though not receipt of a travelling allowance) will indicate that the employee is travelling in the employer's time and for his benefit and is acting in the course of his employment, and in such a case the fact that the employee may have discretion as to the mode and time of travelling will not take the journey out of the course of his employment.

4. An employee travelling in the employer's time from his ordinary residence to a workplace other than his regular workplace or in the course of a peripatetic occupation

or to the scene of an emergency (such as a fire, an accident or a mechanical breakdown of plant) will be acting in the course of his employment.

5. A deviation from or interruption of a journey undertaken in the course of employment (unless the deviation or interruption is merely incidental to the journey) will for the time being (which may include an overnight interruption) take the employee out of the course of his employment.

6. Return journeys are to be treated on the same footing as outward journeys.

All the foregoing propositions are subject to any express arrangements between the employer and the employee or those representing his interests. They are not, I would add, intended to define the position of salaried employees, with regard to whom the touchstone of payment made in the employer's time is not generally significant. ...

9.8 Criminal Acts and Breach of Statutory Duty by the Employee

The general presumption in this area is that a criminal act takes the employee outside the sphere of their employment. This principle remains good law in principle. See, for example, *Warren v Henleys Ltd* [1948] 2 All ER 935. However, you will notice that after the case below, the test has been modified slightly, placing the emphasis on whether there is a 'close connection' between the criminal act and the sphere of work.

Lister and Others v Hesley Hall Ltd [2002] 1 AC 215

Panel: Lord Steyn, Lord Clyde, Lord Hutton, Lord Hobhouse of Woodborough and Lord Millett

Facts: The claimants in this case had been pupils at a boarding house which was attached to a school. They had been sexually abused over a number of years by the warden who was an employee of the defendants. The question for the court to decide was whether the warden had been acting in the course of employment when carrying out the sexual abuse, which was completely unknown to the defendants. The Court of Appeal held that the warden's acts could not be held to be an unauthorised way of carrying out an authorised act, and accordingly held the defendants not to be vicariously liable. Two of the claimants appealed to the House of Lords.

LORD STEYN

...For nearly a century English judges have adopted Salmond's statement of the applicable test as correct. Salmond said that a wrongful act is deemed to be done by a "servant" in the course of his employment if "it is either (a) a wrongful act authorised by the master, or (b) a wrongful and unauthorised mode of doing some act authorised by the master": Salmond, Law of Torts, 1st ed (1907) ...

It remains, however, to consider how vicarious liability for intentional wrongdoing fits in with Salmond's formulation. The answer is that it does not cope ideally with such cases. It must, however, be remembered that the great tort writer did not attempt to enunciate precise propositions of law on vicarious liability. At most he propounded a broad test which deems as within the course of employment "a wrongful and unauthorised mode of doing some act authorised by the master". And he emphasised the connection between the authorised acts and the "improper modes" of doing them. In reality it is simply a practical test serving as a dividing line between cases where it is or is not just to impose vicarious liability. The usefulness of the Salmond formulation is, however, crucially dependent on focusing on the right act of the employee. ...

If this approach to the nature of employment is adopted, it is not necessary to ask the simplistic question whether in the cases under consideration the acts of sexual abuse were modes of doing authorised acts. It becomes possible to consider the question of vicarious liability on the basis that the employer undertook to care for the boys through the services of the warden and that there is a very close connection between the torts of the warden and his employment. After all, they were committed in the time and on the premises of the employers while the warden was also busy caring for the children. ...

The application of the correct test

...The question is whether the warden's torts were so closely connected with his employment that it would be fair and just to hold the employers vicariously liable. On the facts of the case the answer is yes. After all, the sexual abuse was inextricably interwoven with the carrying out by the warden of his duties in Axeholme House. Matters of degree arise. But the present cases clearly fall on the side of vicarious liability.

 Alert

Note that in *Trotman v North Yorkshire County Council* [1999] LGR 584, the Court of Appeal held that a teacher who sexually abused a pupil was not acting in the course of employment as they were carrying out an act which was the very negation of the role in which they were employed. However, *Trotman* was overruled by *Lister,* in which it was held that the 'close connection' test should be used instead. The broader test in *Lister* makes it easier to establish vicarious liability in this area.

Further Reading

Brodie, Douglas J: 'Bouncers, beatings and vicarious liability' Rep B 2009, 89(Aug), 2-3

Kidner, R: 'Vicarious Liability: For Whom Should the "Employer" be Liable?' (1995) 15 LS 47

10

Employers' Liability – Primary Liability

Topic List

Introduction

Having already considered how, through vicarious liability, employers may be liable for torts committed by their employees, we now need to consider how employers might be liable in their own right. Employers' Primary Liability follows the same structure as a standard negligence action – its elements are the same. Employers' Primary Liability is a special type of negligence. Certain elements are based around the same authorities – for example, the causation element still uses the 'but for' test seen in the chapter on causation. However, other elements require knowledge of new cases, and it is these that will be considered in this chapter.

Link
to Chapter 6 on Causation

10.1 Duty of Care

The idea that employers owe a duty of care to their employees is a very old one. It was one of the pre-existing relationships where a duty was owed before the general duty found in *Donoghue v Stevenson* [1932] AC 562. Rather than use the three-stage test from *Caparo Industries v Dickman* [1990] 2 WLR 358, the duty of care owed by employers to employees can be located in *Wilsons and Clyde Coal v English* [1938] AC 57.

Wilsons and Clyde Coal v English [1938] AC 57

Panel: Lord Atkin, Lord Thankerton, Lord Macmillan, Lord Wright and Lord Maugham

Facts: The claimant, who was the respondent in this appeal, claimed damages for personal injury which he suffered travelling down a road connected to the defendant's mine, called the Mine Jigger Brae. The claimant was employed by the defendant and had been repairing an airway under the road. At the end of his shift, he proceeded down the road and was injured when he was crushed by haulage equipment that had been put in motion. The claimant claimed that there was an un-safe system of work at the mine, since the defendants knew that workers would be using the road at the end of the day shift to move from one part of the site to the other. The Court of Appeal held that the defendants owed the claimant a duty of care as employers which included three distinct parts: (a) an obligation to provide a safe place of work; (b) an obligation to provide competent fellow employees; and (c) an obligation to provide a safe system of work.

LORD THANKERTON

Counsel for the appellants admitted that primarily the master has a duty to take due care to provide and maintain a reasonably safe system of working in the mine, and he stated the question in the appeal as being whether a master, who has delegated the duty of taking due care in the provision of a reasonably safe system of working to a competent servant, is responsible for a defect in the system of which he had no knowledge; and he submitted the following general propositions in law:

First - If the master retains control, he has a duty to see that his servants do not suffer through his personal negligence, such as (1.) failure to provide proper and suitable plant, if he knows, or ought to have known, of such failure; (2.) failure to select fit and competent servants; (3.) failure to provide a proper and safe system of working; and (4.) failure to observe statutory regulations...

In my opinion the master cannot "delegate" his duty in this sense, though he may appoint some one, as his agent in the discharge of the duty, for whom he will remain responsible under the maxim respondeat superior. It therefore becomes necessary to examine the nature and limits of the doctrine of common employment.

While the duty which is owed is a single duty, not three separate ones, it is usually broken up into three constituent parts for ease of reference, and it is thus said that the employer is under a duty to provide: (a) a safe place of work and safe equipment; (b) competent fellow employees; and (c) a safe system of work. There is no clearer breakdown of the constituent parts of this duty than the one found in *Wilsons*, above. The case also establishes the principle that the employer cannot delegate his liability to an employee. While the employer may delegate the performance of the duty, he cannot delegate the liability that may attach to a breach of that duty. So, an employer might delegate health and safety matters to an employee branded 'Health and Safety Manager', but cannot avoid liability if that employee fails to manage health and safety matters properly.

The question of whether an employer can delegate liability to an employee was again considered, and the *Wilsons* approach affirmed, in *McDermid v Nash Dredging* [1987] AC 906.

McDermid v Nash Dredging & Reclamation Co Ltd [1987] AC 906

Panel: Lord Bridge of Harwich, Lord Hailsham of St Marylebone, Lord Brandon of Oakbrook, Lord Mackay of Clashfern and Lord Ackner

Facts: The claimant was a deckhand who worked on a tug-boat owned by the defendants and captained by an employee of the defendants. The system of work being operated was that the claimant would untie two ropes at either end of the tug from a dredger that the tug was used to pull. When both ropes were untied, the claimant would knock twice on the wheelhouse of the tug to signal the captain that it was safe to move the tug. The claimant was injured when, without waiting for the signal, the captain started the tug before one of the ropes was untied. The rope coiled around the claimant's leg and he was seriously injured. The House of Lords held that the defendants owed the claimant a duty of care which contained an obligation to both provide and operate a safe system of work, and that such a duty was non-delegable. The defendants could not delegate liability for breach of this duty to the captain of the tug.

LORD HAILSHAM OF ST MARYLEBONE

The plaintiff's claim in the proceedings was based on the allegation, inter alia, of a "non-delegable" duty resting on his employers to take reasonable care to provide a "safe system of work": cf. *Wilsons & Clyde Coal Co. Ltd. v. English* [1938] AC 57. The defendants did not, and could not, dispute the existence of such a duty of care, nor that it was "non-delegable" in the special sense in which the phrase is used in this connection. This special sense does not involve the proposition that the duty cannot be delegated in the sense that it is incapable of being the subject of delegation, but only that the employer cannot escape liability if the duty has been delegated and then not properly performed. Equally the defendants could not and did not attempt to dispute that it would be a central and crucial feature of any safe system on the instant facts that it would prevent so far as possible the occurrence of such an accident as actually happened, viz. injury to the plaintiff as the result of the use of the *Ina's* engine so as to move the *Ina* before both the ropes were clear of the dredger and stowed safely inboard and the plaintiff was in a position of safety.

Since such a system could easily have been designed and put in operation at the time of the accident in about half-a-dozen different ways, and since it is quite obvious that such a system would have prevented the accident had it been in operation, and since the duty to provide it was "non-delegable" in the sense that the defendants cannot escape liability by claiming to have delegated performance of their duty, it is a little difficult to see what possible defence there could ever have been to these proceedings. There was indeed a preposterous suggestion in the defendants' pleading that the plaintiff had caused or contributed to his own misfortune himself. There was never the smallest evidence of this, and, no doubt prudently, the defendants called no evidence, whether by Captain Sas or anyone else, to substantiate it. This frantic attempt to avoid or reduce liability had already died a natural death before the case left the court of trial. ...

In the event this appeal must be dismissed with costs. In my view it is, and always was, unarguable.

The next case considers whether the same approach should be taken when the claimant is not actually an employee of the defendant. Police officers are, for various historical reasons, not technically employees of the Chief Constable. However, as we can see from the case of *Mullaney v Chief Constable of West Midlands Police* [2001] EWCA Civ 700, [2001] Po LR 501 there is no difference in the approach taken by the courts.

Mullaney v Chief Constable of West Midlands Police [2001] EWCA Civ 700, [2001] Po LR 501

Panel: Potter and Clarke LJJ, and Bodey J

Facts: The claimant was a police officer employed by the defendants. Although police officers were, for historical reasons, not employed by the force in the traditional sense, they were quasi-employees. The claimant was injured when trying to arrest a suspect who attacked him in a public toilet. The claimant radioed for assistance from his colleagues, but they did not respond. The Court of Appeal held that the defendants owed a duty of care to the claimant notwithstanding that he was only a quasi-employee. Further, while the defendants had provided a safe system of work, they had failed to operate it since the claimant's call for assistance went unheeded.

LORD JUSTICE CLARKE

...Although the defendant as a chief constable was not the claimant's employer, because there was no employment relationship properly so called between them, he was in much the same position as an employer and as such owed the claimant the same duty as an employer would owe to his employees. Thus he owed a duty to take reasonable care for the safety of his officers including the claimant and that duty included a duty to take reasonable care to ensure that the system of work provided for them was a safe one. The provision of a safe system of work includes both the devising and operation of the system. The duty cannot be delegated. ...

The first question which arises under this head is whether there is any relevant distinction between the duty owed by an employer to his employees and the duty owed by a chief constable to the police officers in his charge. In my judgment ... there is not. ...

In all these circumstances, it is, in my judgment, now clear that the chief constable should be treated as owing to his officers the same duties as an employer owes to his employees, subject to such considerations of public policy as arise on the facts of a particular case. That proposition seems to me to be consistent, not only with the authorities to which I have just referred, but also with principle. The relationship between a chief constable and his officers is so closely analogous to that between an employer and his employees as to make it just in principle to hold that he owes the same duties to his officers as an employer does to his employees.

 Alert

10.2 Breach of Duty

Having established the existence of a non-delegable duty of care owed by the employer to the employee, we next need to ask if that duty has been breached. Just like standard negligence cases, it is necessary to establish the standard of care that the employer is required to meet.

Latimer v AEC LD [1953] AC 643

Panel: Lord Porter, Lord Oaksey, Lord Reid, Lord Tucker and Lord Asquith of Bishopstone

Facts: The claimant was an employee of the defendant and worked in the defendant's factory. During an unusually heavy rainstorm, the floor of the factory had been flooded and an oily industrial mixture that normally flowed in a channel set into the floor mixed with rain water and left the floor slippery after the flood water subsided. The employer spread sawdust on the floor to improve grip, but did not have sufficient supplies to cover the entire floor of the factory. The claimant was injured when he slipped on a part of the floor that had been sawdusted. The House of Lords held that the defendant had not been negligent, having done all that it was reasonably possible to do in the circumstances, and having regard to the level of risk.

LORD TUCKER

With regard to the alleged breach by the respondents of their common law duty to take reasonable care for the safety of their servants, I am in complete agreement with what was said by Singleton LJ in the Court of Appeal in his application of the standard required to the facts as found by the trial judge. I only venture to add a few observations out of respect for the careful judgment of Pilcher J., and because it appears to me desirable in these days, when there are in existence so many statutes and statutory regulations imposing absolute obligations upon employers, that the courts should be vigilant to see that the common law duty owed by a master to his servants should not be gradually enlarged until it is barely distinguishable from his absolute statutory obligations.

In the present case the respondents were faced with an unprecedented situation following a phenomenal rain storm. They set 40 men to work on cleaning up the factory when the flood subsided and used all the available supply of sawdust, which was approximately three tons. The judge has found that they took every step which could reasonably have been taken to deal with the conditions which prevailed before the night shift came on duty, and he has negatived every specific allegation of negligence as pleaded, but he has held the respondents liable because they did not close down the factory, or the part of the factory where the accident occurred, before the commencement of the night shift.

My Lords, I do not question that such a drastic step may be required on the part of a reasonably prudent employer if the peril to his employees is sufficiently grave, and to this extent it must always be a question of degree, but in my view there was no evidence in the present case which could justify a finding of negligence for failure on the part of the respondents to take this step. This question was never canvassed in evidence, nor was sufficient evidence given as to the condition of the factory as a whole to enable a satisfactory conclusion to be reached. The learned judge seems to have accepted the reasoning of counsel for the plaintiff to the effect that the floor was slippery, that slipperiness is a potential danger, that the defendants must be taken to have been aware of this, that in the circumstances nothing could have been done to remedy the slipperiness, that the defendants allowed work to proceed, that an accident due to slipperiness occurred, and that the defendants are therefore liable.

This is not the correct approach. The problem is perfectly simple. The only question was: Has it been proved that the floor was so slippery that, remedial steps not being possible, a reasonably prudent employer would have closed down the factory rather than allow his employees to run the risks involved in continuing work? The learned judge does not seem to me to have posed this question to himself, nor was there sufficient evidence before him to have justified an affirmative answer. The absence of any evidence that anyone in the factory during the afternoon or night shift, other than the plaintiff, slipped or experienced any difficulty or that any complaint was made by or on behalf of the workers all points to the conclusion that the danger was in fact not such as to impose upon a reasonable employer the obligation placed upon the respondents by the trial judge.

 Alert

So, as seems obvious, the standard of care expected of the employer is the standard of the reasonably competent employer.

Having established the standard, the next few cases look at instances where there has been a breach of duty. This will also exemplify breaches of the different constituent parts of the duty identified in *Wilsons*.

10.3 Competent Fellow Employees

Butler (or Black) v Fife Coal Company Limited [1912] AC 149

Panel: Earl Loreburn LC, Lord Kinnear, Lord Shaw of Dunfermline and Lord Ashbourne

Facts: The claimant, referred to in this judgment as the pursuer, was the widow of the deceased. The deceased had been an employee of the defendants and had worked at their colliery (coal mine). He was killed by poisonous gas (carbon monoxide) which escaped from a fire that had spontaneously started while working down the mine. The assistant manager and fireman on site were found negligent in their duties. The House of Lords held that the obligation on the defendants to provide competent fellow employees included those employees in a managerial capacity. These employees had been negligent, and therefore there had been a breach of duty.

LORD ASHBOURNE

It is found that there was negligence on the part of the assistant manager and the fireman, but that the respondents are not liable, as those officials were in a common employment with the deceased, and were appointed by the respondents after they were "satisfied that they were possessed of the qualifications and experience usually required of persons holding these offices." I do not think this is a very satisfactory statement that they were believed by the respondents to be entirely competent, but I believe, from the language used by Lord Low, that that was the opinion of the Second Division. ...

Whatever may have been the statutory duty of the respondents as to ventilation adequate to dilute and render harmless noxious gases, I think that when this connection was made with pit No. 11 the steps in the question remitted should have been taken, and it is to be regretted special warning was not circulated amongst their officials, drawing their attention to the new and deadly danger which might be thus introduced by the possible and insidious presence of this monoxide gas. I think that the question needed closer examination than the Second Division gave it at the first hearing and required the remit to ascertain a crucial fact. What is the effect of the finding in the remit? We must not allow ourselves to be hampered or embarrassed by other findings. Is it shewn that it is now open to the House to consider whether the defenders are liable? I think it clearly is; and that your Lordships are quite justified in holding that the defenders were guilty of neglect of their statutory duties in not taking any steps to deal with the special danger of the presence of noxious gases arising from the connection made.

I therefore think that the appeal should be allowed.

This case provides good authority for the proposition that a defendant employer will be liable if he fails to ensure that those in a management or supervisory role are competent. It is also another example of an employer's inability to delegate liability. If an employee in management acts incompetently, then the employer will be liable for any harm caused by that incompetence to other employees.

Hudson v Ridge Manufacturing Co. Ltd. [1957] 2 QB 348

Panel: Streatfeild J

Facts: The claimant was injured by a fellow employee who tripped him up as a practical joke. That employee was well known for engaging in horseplay and playing such practical jokes, having had a history of doing so for the previous four years. The claimant claimed that the defendants had breached their duty of care to him by failing to prevent the practical joker from tripping him up. The court held that, given the habitual nature of this employee's practical joking, and the fact that the defendants were well aware of the dangerous nature of this employee's activities, they had breached their duty of care to the claimant by failing to prevent his injury.

MR JUSTICE STREATFEILD

The plaintiff was injured, in the course of his work, on March 26, 1954, through a foolish prank practised upon him by one Harold Chadwick, a fellow servant who is not over-intelligent and appears to have grown to manhood with childish pranks still part of his make-up. Apparently over the course of some years, while he was employed by the defendants, he had repeatedly made a nuisance of himself, to say the least of it, to his fellow employees through his almost incurable habit of tripping people up, or otherwise engaging in horse-play and skylarking; the kind of thing which was not intended to do any injury, and which certainly could not be regarded as bullying. No doubt it was regarded as a bit of fun and almost harmless, but it was the kind of thing that is bound, one of these days, as the witnesses say, to lead to some injury.

That had been going on for some years and, notwithstanding repeated reprimands, Chadwick continued in his practice of teasing, not only the plaintiff, but other people with this kind of conduct, and on this particular occasion the inevitable at last happened. In the course of Chadwick's getting hold of the plaintiff from behind, as the plaintiff says, and then forcing him down onto the ground, the plaintiff put his hand out to save himself and fractured his right wrist. I accept the plaintiff's evidence as to how this accident happened.

Having been injured in that way during his work, the question arises whether the employers are responsible. As Mr. Leigh [counsel for the plaintiff] put it in his opening, he does not contend that the employers are vicariously liable for any negligent act of a fellow servant, but that they are primarily liable because they were guilty of a breach of their common law duty to take care for the safety of their employees.

This is an unusual case, because the particular form of lack of care by the employers alleged is that they failed to maintain discipline and to take proper steps to put an end to this skylarking which might lead to injury at some time in the future. As it seems to me, the matter is covered not by authority so much as principle. It is the duty of employers, for the safety of their employees, to have reasonably safe plant find machinery. It is their duty to have premises which are similarly reasonably safe. It is their duty to have a reasonably safe system of work. It is their duty to employ reasonably competent fellow workmen. All of those duties exist at common law for the safety of the workmen, and if, for instance, it is found that a piece of plant or part of the premises is not reasonably safe, it is the duty of the employers to cure it, to make it safe and to remove that source of danger. In the same way, if the system of working is found, in practice, to be beset with dangers, it is the duty of the employers to evolve a reasonably safe system of working so as to obviate those dangers, and upon principle it seems to me that if, in fact, a fellow workman is not merely incompetent but, by his habitual conduct, is likely to prove a source of danger to his fellow employees, a duty lies fairly and squarely on the employers to remove that source of danger.

Alert

... Here is a case where there existed, as it were in the system of work, a source of danger, through the conduct of one of the defendants' employees, of which they knew, repeated conduct which went on over a long period of time, and which they did nothing whatever to remove, except to reprimand and go on reprimanding to no effect. In my judgment, therefore, the injury was sustained as a result of the defendants' failure to take proper steps to put an end to that conduct, to see that it would not happen again and, if it did happen again, to remove the source of it. It was for that reason that this injury resulted. Under those circumstances, although it is an unusual type of case, I have come to the conclusion that Mr. Leigh is right in his contention and that the defendants are liable for the plaintiff's injuries.

This case establishes the principle that if an employer is aware, or should be aware, that an employee is an habitual practical joker, the employer will be liable for harm caused by that employee's actions. This can be contrasted with *Smith v Crossley Bros.* [1951] 95 SJ 655, in which the employee in question was not an habitual practical joker, but had engaged in dangerous conduct as a one-off. As such, the defendant employer was held *not* liable for the employee's conduct, as it was not reasonable to expect the employer to have known about, or prevented it.

10.4 Safe Place of Work

Joseph Smith v Charles Baker and Sons [1891] AC 325

Panel: Lord Halsbury LC, Lord Bramwell, Lord Watson, Lord Herschell, Lord Morris

Facts: The claimant was employed by the defendants to drill holes in rock near to where a crane was being used by other men employed by the defendant. A stone fell from the crane and hit the claimant, injuring him. He brought a claim against his employers alleging that they had negligently failed to provide him with a safe place of work. The House of Lords held that there had been a breach of duty, and that the defendants could not rely upon the defence of *volenti non fit injuria* or 'consent', since the claimant had not voluntarily agreed to run the risk of injury.

Link
See Chapter 8, General Defences

LORD WATSON

...Sometimes (as in the present case) when the danger is not constantly present, but recurs at intervals, the defect may be cured by giving the workmen timely warning of its approach. The employer may in such cases protect himself, either by removing the source of danger, or by making provision for due notice being given. Should he adopt the latter course, he will still be exposed to liability if injury results from failure to give warning through the negligence of himself or of his superintendent.

An employer is under a duty at common law to ensure that his employees have a safe place of work. This includes the equipment and facilities on site, as well as the premises themselves. It should be noted that what constitutes 'reasonable care' might be a lesser standard in instances where the work is being carried out on premises owned or occupied by a third party, as shown in the next case.

Wilson v Tyneside Window Cleaning Co [1958] 2 QB 110

Panel: Jenkins, Parker and Pearce LJJ

Facts: The claimant, a window cleaner of some 56 years' experience, was injured falling from a window he was cleaning at a third party's premises when a handle on the outside of the window by which he was supporting himself gave way. The court held that given the claimant's experience of dangerous situations, and given that the defendants could only assert a lesser amount of control over the premises of a third party, the defendants had not breached their duty to provide both a safe place and system of work.

LORD JUSTICE PEARCE

The accident (he says) shows that this place of work was not safe. That duty is always on the defendants, whether delegated or not, as is shown by the case (in particular) of *Wilsons & Clyde Coal Co. Ltd. v. English.* He relies on *Biddle v. Hart* and on a dictum of Denning LJ in *Christmas v. General Cleaning Contractors Ltd.* as showing that the employer's duty of care as to the safety of the place of work extends even to premises over which he has no control; and he argues that the decisions in *Taylor v. Sims & Sims and Cilia v. H. M. James & Sons* are wrong in so far as a contrary view was taken. On the basis that the responsibility for providing, a safe place of work remains on the master even though he has no control of the premises, Mr. Waller [counsel for the claimant] contends that at the least a preliminary inspection to ascertain the dangers is available to the master and that in this case the defendants were negligent in not so inspecting and in not providing a safe place of work for the plaintiff.

Further, in respect of premises out of the master's control Mr. Waller argues that the duty of providing safe premises is, as it were, delegated by the master to the occupier. The master is thus vicariously liable for the occupier's failure to provide safe premises. It is true that, if one can import such a notional delegation, that further argument would stand. But such a delegation necessitates a fiction which seems to me to have no justification in fact. The tradesman comes to the premises to do something to them. He does not thereby delegate to the owner something which he himself has no right to do and with which he has never been concerned. ...

Now it is true that in *Wilsons & Clyde Coal Co. Ltd. v. English* Lord Wright divided up the duty of a master into three main headings, for convenience of definition or argument; but all three are ultimately only manifestations of the same duty of the master to take reasonable care so to carry out his operations as not to subject those employed by him to unnecessary risk. Whether the servant is working on the premises of the master or those of a stranger, that duty is still, as it seems to me, the same; but as a matter of common sense its performance and discharge will probably be vastly different in the two cases. The master's own premises are under his control: if they are dangerously in need of repair he can and must rectify the fault at once if he is to escape the censure of negligence. But if a master sends his plumber to mend a leak in a respectable private house, no one could hold him negligent for not visiting the house himself to see if the carpet in the hall creates a trap. Between these extremes are countless possible examples in which the court may have to decide the question of fact: Did the master take reasonable care so to carry out his operations as not to subject those employed by him to unnecessary risk? Precautions dictated by reasonable care when the servant works on the master's premises may be wholly prevented or greatly circumscribed by the fact that the place of work is under the control of a stranger. Additional safeguards intended to reinforce the man's own knowledge and skill in surmounting difficulties or dangers may be reasonable in the former case but impracticable and unreasonable in the latter. So viewed, the question whether the master was in control of the premises ceases to be a matter of technicality and becomes merely one of the ingredients, albeit a very important one, in a consideration of the question of fact whether, in all the circumstances, the master took reasonable care. ...

Alert

Alert

The next case concerns the provision and use of safety equipment. An employer must provide safety equipment to employees if it is necessary. In *Bux v Slough Metals Ltd* [1973] 1 WLR 1358, it was made clear that the employer may also be held liable if he fails to encourage the use of such safety equipment. However, if the employee refuses to use such safety equipment then the employer may not be liable.

Bux v Slough Metals Ltd [1973] 1 WLR 1358

Panel: Edmund Davies, Stamp and Stephenson LJJ

Facts: The claimant worked as a die-caster for the defendants in their factory. During the course of his work, the claimant lifted molten metal using a ladle and poured it into a die. The goggles he was provided with misted up while he was working, and he told his supervisor, the superintendent on site, that he was no longer going to wear them. The defendants took no steps to ensure that he did wear the goggles. One day, while not wearing the goggles, molten metal splashed into the claimant's eyes, blinding him in one and severely restricting his sight in the other. The claimant alleged a breach of statute and negligence at common law. The Court of Appeal held that it was always open to the courts to impose a higher standard of care than that necessitated by statute, and that, at common law, there had been a breach of duty in that the defendants had failed to take any steps to ensure the claimant wore the goggles. The claimant was, however, found to be 40 per cent contributorily negligent.

Link
See Contributory Negligence in Chapter 8, General Defences

LORD JUSTICE EDMUND DAVIES

...The question of whether instruction or persuasion or even insistence in using protective equipment should be resorted to is, therefore, at large, the answer depending on the facts of the particular case. One of the most important of these is the nature and degree of the risk of serious harm resulting if it is not worn. Mr. Stuart Smith retorts that the plaintiff's own evidence showed that he regarded the risk as obvious and that accordingly no further instruction was called for, any more than, as this court held, it was reasonably to be expected on the facts of *Wilson v. Tyneside Window Cleaning Co. Ltd.* [1958] 2 QB 110, where this court drew a distinction between cases where the risk is obvious and those where it is insidious and hidden. I find it difficult to deal with this aspect of the case without also considering the question of causation, for Mr. Stuart Smith submits that the plaintiff's failure to use what the judge held to be suitable goggles indicates that the probability is that he would never have worn them, however much the employers tried (at the risk, testified to by the witnesses, of losing all their die-casters) to establish a rule that they must be. He therefore submitted that, even were there any obligation on the employers to exhort the plaintiff to wear his type 1 goggles, the irresistible inference here — as in *McWilliams v. Sir William Arrol & Co. Ltd.* [1962] 1 WLR 295 — was that the plaintiff would not have worn them.

I have found these the most difficult aspects of a somewhat troublesome case. But, basing himself on Mr. Bevan's evidence that the prudent employer "would not do nothing," the judge held negligence established. Having seen the type of man the plaintiff is and heard him, and despite his rejection of the plaintiff's evidence on several important points, the judge went on to say [...]

" He was not the type of man who would have disregarded instructions if they were given personally and in a reasonable and firm manner, and were followed up by supervision. I think he would have followed instructions and persistent advice. He was in no way a difficult or obstinate person."

And, as Stamp LJ pointed out during counsel's submissions, a reminder that all die-casters who disobeyed regulation 13 (4) were liable to be prosecuted could have fortified the employers' exhortation most effectively. The judge held that the plaintiff had discharged the onus of establishing on the balance of probabilities, that he would have worn goggles had the sort of system the judge described been instituted and followed. Whether I should have come to the same conclusion I cannot say, so much depending on the view formed by the court of the particular workman who was the plaintiff. This court is in a far less advantageous position in that respect than was Kerr J, and the conclusion I have come to is that we ought not to disturb his finding that the claim in common law succeeds.

There is a limit to how much safety equipment need be provided in order to discharge the duty to take reasonable care. What is reasonable will, as usual, depend on the circumstances of the case. There are instances in which it may not be reasonable to require an employer to provide a particular piece of safety equipment. It may be disproportionately expensive or inconvenient. Indeed, some employees may reject the equipment, as happened in *Yorkshire Traction Company Limited v Walter Searby* [2003] EWCA Civ 1856, a case in which the claimant bus driver, having been punched by an unidentified assailant, sued the defendants, claiming that they had negligently failed to fit the bus with a safety screen that would have prevented anyone from physically touching the driver. In regions where such screens had been installed, some drivers had objected to their presence, saying they made it harder to do their job. The court held that given the relatively low risk of an attack of that type, and the objections previously made by other drivers to the screens, there was no breach of duty on the facts.

10.5 Safe System of Work

General Cleaning Contractors LD v Christmas [1953] AC 180

Panel: Earl Jowitt, Lord Oaksey, Lord Reid and Lord Tucker

Facts: The claimant was a window cleaner who worked for the defendants. He was injured while cleaning a 'sash' type window that required a special cleaning technique in which he had not been trained. The window closed on the claimant's finger and caused him to lose his balance and fall to the ground. The court held that while there had been no breach of duty regarding provision of a safe *place* of work, there had been a breach of the obligation to provide a safe *system* of work, since the defendant had not trained the claimant in the appropriate technique, and had not provided safety devices to prevent the window closing on him.

EARL JOWITT

If, however, they [the defendants – the appellants in this appeal] are not liable thus to secure the safety of their workers they are under an obligation to make the system which they do employ reasonably safe. It is an undoubted fact that a sash does occasionally move down at the slightest touch and the system of work adopted by the appellants made the worker's safety entirely dependent on the sash not moving. It does not appear that the appellants had given any instructions to their workers to test the windows before cleaning them, or that they had applied their minds to the provision of wedges or blocks to prevent the window becoming closed. It is clear that any obstruction placed at the bottom of the window would have prevented the lower sash from closing, and would thus have avoided the jar on the fingers which caused the respondent to let go of his hold and thus produced the accident. That seems to have been the view of the trial judge, and was certainly the view of Lloyd-Jacob J., and with this view I am in agreement. I think the trial judge was entitled to find that the appellants were to blame in not taking all reasonable steps to see that the system of work which they required their men to adopt was made as safe as possible.

 Alert

LORD OAKSEY

...Workmen are not in the position of employers. Their duties are not performed in the calm atmosphere of a board room with the advice of experts. They have to make their decisions on narrow window sills and other places of danger and in circumstances in which the dangers are obscured by repetition. The risk that sashes may unexpectedly close, as the sashes in this case appear to have done, may not happen very often, but when it does, if the workman is steadying himself by a handhold, his fall is almost certain. If the possibility is faced the risk is obvious. If both sashes are closed there is no longer the handhold by which the workman steadies himself. If either sash is kept open the handhold is available and, on the evidence in this case, is, in my opinion, reasonably safe. But the problem is one for the employer to solve and should not, in my opinion, be left to the workman. It can be solved by general orders and the provision of appropriate appliances. The risk is undeniable and was not denied by the appellants' director, Mr. Mahoney...

The requirement to provide a safe system of work is a potentially very wide requirement, which can cover everything from training to the provision of equipment and the existence of procedures to assist with safety. It has also been made clear that providing a safe system of work is not of itself enough to discharge this aspect of the duty of care – the employer must also take reasonable steps to ensure that the system is implemented.

Clifford v Charles H Challen & Son LD [1951] 1 KB 495

Panel: Cohen, Asquith and Denning LJJ

Facts: The claimant worked for the defendants in their factory, where he was involved in the production of radio sets and pianos. In the course of his employment, he came into regular contact with a particular type of glue that was prone to causing dermatitis. Dermatitis could be avoided by the application of a "barrier" cream. This cream, however, was not made available in the workshop where the claimant worked. The foreman also discouraged its use, stating that he "did not have a great belief" in its effectiveness. The claimant developed dermatitis and brought an action against his employers. The court held that the failure to provide the cream in the workshop, coupled with the foreman's discouragement of its use, amounted to a failure to provide a safe system of work, and thus the defendants had breached their duty of care.

LORD JUSTICE DENNING

The question is whether the employers fulfilled their duty to the workman. The standard which the law requires is that they should take reasonable care for the safety of their workmen. In order to discharge that duty properly an employer must make allowances for the imperfections of human nature. When he asks his men to work with dangerous substances, he must provide proper appliances to safeguard them; he must set in force a proper system by which they use the appliances and take the necessary precautions; and he must do his best to see that they adhere to it. He must remember that men doing a routine task are often heedless of their own safety and may become slack about taking precautions. He must therefore, by his foreman, do his best to keep them up to

 Alert

the mark and not tolerate any slackness. He cannot throw all the blame on them if he has not shown a good example himself.

The first point concerns the barrier cream: did the employers fulfill [sic] their duty by keeping it in the store and leaving it for the men to fetch it from the store if they wished? No containers were provided for fetching it. If a man did not have a small tin or jar of his own, he could get the cream from the store on a piece of greaseproof paper and then take it back to the shop, and there apply it and so protect himself. But none of them did it in this shop. The foreman did not insist on it; as he said, he was not a great believer in it himself. In these circumstances, I cannot bring myself to believe that the employers fulfilled their duty to the men. They should at least have done in the fitting shop the same as they did in the radio shop, that is to say, provide the barrier cream in the shop itself; and the foreman should have seen, as far as he could, that the men used it. ...

I rest my judgment, therefore, on the barrier cream: it should have been provided in the shop itself, and a system should have been established whereby the men used it in accordance with the government notice. That not having been done, the employers were guilty of a breach of duty to their men; and it is a plain inference that that breach of duty was one of the causes of the dermatitis from which the plaintiff suffered.

The remaining question is whether the plaintiff was himself guilty of contributory negligence. The judge did not consider it, because he thought that the employers had not been guilty of any breach of duty. I think that the plaintiff was negligent: he knew that the glue was dangerous; he knew what precautions ought to have been taken; but he did not take them. He knew he could get the barrier cream by going to the store, yet he did not get it. The employers ought, no doubt, to have had it in the workshop; but I do not think that the workman can be acquitted of all responsibility on that account. The employers must take care of the men, but the men must also take care of themselves. The fact that all the men in the shop were negligent does not exempt any one of them from responsibility for his own negligence. The question then arises, in what proportion ought the plaintiff and the employer to share responsibility? On the whole, I think that they should share it equally. ...

Link

See Chapter 8 on General Defences

Here, there was a breach of duty in the lack of provision of cream that would have prevented the claimant developing dermatitis. There was also a breach in that the foreman actively discouraged the employees from using the cream. In such circumstances, the employer will be liable for the resulting injuries, albeit that there was some 50 per cent contributory negligence on the part of the claimant in this instance. This case can be contrasted, however, with the situation in the next case, where the employer provides and actively encourages the use of a similar cream, and makes known to the employee the consequences of failing to use it.

Woods v Durable Suites LD [1953] 1 WLR 857

Panel: Singleton and Morris LJJ and Harman J

Facts: The claimant worked for the defendants in their furniture factory. He regularly came into contact with a type of glue prone to causing dermatitis – a condition he developed. The protective cream, however, was provided, as were protective gloves. The defendants made clear that the workers were expected to use the cream and to wash their hands before and after work, and warned of the dangers should they fail to do so. The court held that, in the circumstances, the defendants had done all they could reasonably have been expected to do to ensure the workers used the protective measures provided, and thus they had not breached their duty. Employers are not to be regarded as being under an obligation to stand over every employee all the time and ensure compliance with safety procedures.

LORD JUSTICE MORRIS

...The obligation of an employer towards his servants includes an obligation to exercise due care and skill to provide a proper system of work and to provide effective supervision. If an employer allows safety precautions to lapse and to fade away into desuetude, it may well be that, on the facts of a particular case, there may be proof that there has been a failure to exercise due care and skill to provide a proper system of work, but each case must depend on its own exact facts.

The duty to exercise due care to provide effective supervision does not involve that an employer must provide a corps of overseers to ensure that some process, in regard to which there has been faithful and ample coaching, is at all times properly carried out. Again, each case must depend on its own facts. If a time comes when there is knowledge of the neglect of, or the rejection of, safety precautions, then, on the facts of the particular case, it may be that it can be established that there has been a failure to take reasonable care to supervise the smooth working of a safe system.

 Alert

On the facts of the present case in my judgment the judge came to a correct conclusion.

This established the principle that an employer need not take every step to ensure that the employee uses the safety equipment provided – he must only take reasonable steps to do so. In contrast to *Charles*, the employer in this case provided the safety equipment and encouraged the use of it. Such encouragement is clearly evidence that reasonable care has been taken.

That it is not enough, in order to discharge the duty of care, that the employer devise a safe system of work, but they must also take reasonable steps to *implement* it was also made clear in the case of *Mullaney*. Even if a safe system of work exists, it may well be that the employer has negligently failed to ensure that the system is implemented or *operated*.

10.6 Causation

Factual and legal causation in employers' liability follows the same structure and makes use of the same cases as general negligence. Thus reference should be made to the 'but for' test. The only extra case that ought to be considered and which is applicable only to employers' liability cases is that of *McWilliams v Sir William Arrol & Co Ltd and Another* [1962] 1 WLR 295.

 Link
to Chapter 6 on Causation

McWilliams v Sir William Arrol & Co Ltd and Another [1962] 1 WLR 295

Statute: Factories Act 1937 s 26(2)

Panel: Viscount Kilmuir LC, Viscount Simonds, Lord Reid, Lord Morris of Borth-y-Gest and Lord Devlin

Facts: The claimant was the widow of the deceased, M, who had been employed by the defendants. M had been killed when he fell seventy feet from a crane, having not been provided with a safety harness. The court took the view on the facts that there was an "irresistible inference" that M would not have worn a safety harness even if one had been provided. Thus, there was no causation in this case – the failure to provide a harness could not be said to have caused M's death.

VISCOUNT KILMUIR LC

…The evidence demonstrates to a high degree of probability that if safety belts had been available the deceased would, in any event, not have worn one. On this aspect the Lord Ordinary and the learned judges of the First Division found in favour of the respondents and rejected the appellant's contention. There were a number of witnesses called for the appellant and for these respondents with wide experience in structural steel operations including, in some instances, work on tower cranes such as that in which the deceased was engaged. The combined effect of evidence was that steel erectors never wear safety belts except in certain very special circumstances which do not include the erection of scaffolds for riveters on tower cranes. No witness deponed to having ever seen a safety belt worn in the course of such work, and there was ample evidence from these respondents' employees and from others that safety belts were not worn when such work was being carried out. One witness spoke of having seen the deceased wearing a safety belt on one or possibly two occasions, when doing an operation of a peculiar and special nature. The Lord Ordinary did not accept his evidence on that matter, which in any event was not corroborated. There was overwhelming evidence that the deceased did not normally wear a safety belt and in particular it was proved that he had been engaged in erecting riveters' scaffolds on the crane from which he fell, at heights greater than that from which he fell, and at times when safety belts were available, and that he had not on such occasions worn or asked for a safety belt. In my opinion, it was clearly open to a court to infer that the deceased would not have worn a safety belt even if it were available.

Finally, it was submitted that if the deceased's hypothetical refusal to wear a safety belt must be recognised as the effective cause of his not wearing one and hence of his death, the failure of the respondents to provide a safety belt should not be ignored as a causative factor. The answer in my view must be that there are four steps of causation: (1) a duty to supply a safety belt; (2) a breach; (3) that if there had been a safety belt the deceased would have used it; (4) that if there had been a safety belt the deceased would not have been killed. If the irresistible inference is that the deceased would not have worn a safety belt had it been available, then the first two steps in the chain of causation cease to operate.

McWilliams is an unusual case, and is rarely relied upon in practice. Only in circumstances where there is this "irresistible inference" that protective equipment would not have been used even if it had been provided, can it be said to prevent causation from being formed.

Further Reading

Bamber, Lawrence: 'Cases in Point', H & SW 2007, 29(1), 18 – 20

Patten, Keith: 'Do thy Duty', NLJ. 2009, 159 (7366), 579 – 580

11

Professional and Clinical Negligence

Topic List

Introduction

Professional negligence refers to negligence arising within a professional sphere such as the activities of accountants, lawyers, surveyors and architects. Clinical negligence refers to the negligence of doctors and other related medical professionals such as nurses, dentists and physiotherapists. The law relating to a claim against professionals in both of these fields is the same, and often the only real difference between this area and that of general negligence lies in establishing whether a particular professional duty of care has been breached. It is often difficult to bring successful claims in the context of professional and clinical negligence, for policy reasons (for example, because of the risk of creating a culture of fear among professionals who are recognised as doing a difficult job for the benefit of the public). It is on the field of clinical negligence that this chapter will focus, because the most useful authorities have been decided in this area, and their principles are in any event applicable to non-clinical professions.

Link
See Chapter 5 on Breach of Duty

This chapter will concentrate on the issues of duty of care and breach of duty, because these provide authorities and principles unique to this type of negligence, and which are not explored elsewhere in this Casebook. For discussion of, for example, causation in a clinical context, you should refer to Chapter 6.

11.1 Duty of Care

It is well established that a duty of care will arise where there is a relationship between professional and client (doctor and patient, for example). Note, however, that this relationship has to be *direct* for the duty to arise. Where a doctor provides advice for an occupational health report, for example, no duty would arise between the recipient and the doctor (*Kapfunde v Abbey National Plc* [1999] ICR 1).

Link
See Chapter 10 on Employers' Primary Liability; Chapter 9 on Vicarious Liability

The scope of duty is well illustrated by the case of *Cassidy v Ministry of Health* [1951] 2 KB 343. The case is a useful one for a number of reasons, in addition to illustrating the scope of the duty owed by doctor to patient. (For example, it also demonstrates that Health Authorities owe a duty of care in their primary capacity, and vicariously for the torts of their employees.)

Cassidy v Ministry of Health **[1951] 2 KB 343**

Panel: Denning, Somervell and Singleton LJJ

Facts: The plaintiff entered a hospital for an operation on his left hand, which necessitated post-operational treatment. While undergoing that treatment he was under the care of the following: the surgeon who performed the operation, a full time assistant medical officer of the hospital, the house surgeon and members of the nursing staff of the hospital, all of whom were employed under contracts of service. At the end of the treatment it was found that the plaintiff's hand had been rendered useless. It was suggested that his hand had been bandaged too tightly, that no heed or no sufficient heed had been paid to his complaints that he was suffering intense and excessive pain, and that the splint should have been loosened or his hand inspected to prevent the ensuring damage. The Court of Appeal held that the defendant Health Authority were liable for the negligence of doctors and surgeons employed by them under a contract of service arising in the course of the performance of their professional duties.

> **LORD JUSTICE DENNING**
>
> If a man goes to a doctor because he is ill, no one doubts that the doctor must exercise reasonable care and skill in his treatment of him: and that is so whether the doctor is paid for his services or not. But if the doctor is unable to treat the man himself and sends him to hospital, are not the hospital authorities then under a duty of care in their treatment of him? I think they are. Clearly, if he is a paying patient, paying them directly for their treatment of him, they must take reasonable care of him; and why should it make any difference if he does not pay them directly, but only indirectly through the rates which he pays to the local authority or through insurance contributions which he makes in order to get the treatment? I see no difference at all. Even if he is so poor that he can pay nothing, and the hospital treats him out of charity, still the hospital authorities are under a duty to take reasonable care of him just as the doctor is who treats him without asking a fee. In my opinion authorities who run a hospital, be they local authorities, government boards, or any other corporation, are in law under the selfsame duty as the humblest doctor; whenever they accept a patient for treatment, they must use reasonable care and skill to cure him of his ailment. The hospital authorities cannot, of course, do it by themselves: they have no ears to listen through the stethoscope, and no hands to hold the surgeon's knife. They must do it by the staff which they employ; and if their staff are negligent in giving the treatment, they are just as liable for that negligence as is anyone else who employs others to do his duties for him ... [T]he hospital authorities accepted the plaintiff as a patient for treatment, and it was their duty to treat him with reasonable care. They selected, employed, and paid all the surgeons and nurses who looked after him. He had no say in their selection at all. If those surgeons and nurses did not treat him with proper care and skill, then the hospital authorities must answer for it, for it means that they themselves did not perform their duty to him.

 Alert

Health Authorities and Trusts have a duty to provide the services of reasonably competent medical practitioners. A failure to do so amounts to a breach of their duty of care, which is an area to which we now turn.

11.2 Breach of the Duty of Care

In cases of professional and clinical negligence the reasonable man test is slightly modified. The standard of care appropriate to professionals is not judged according to the reasonable man, but rather is compared to the accepted standards of members of their profession. In order to establish a breach of the duty of care, the claimant must therefore show that the professional concerned has taken a course of action which would not have been acceptable to any reasonable body of medical opinion. This principle is known as the *Bolam* test and is named after the leading case of *Bolam v Friern Hospital Management Committee* [1957] 1 WLR 582.

Bolam v Friern Hospital Management Committee [1957] 1 WLR 582

Panel: McNair J and a jury

Facts: The plaintiff consented to and underwent electroconvulsive therapy as treatment for his mental illness. As a result he suffered severe injuries, including a fractured hip, and sued the defendants in negligence. He claimed that he should have been warned of the risk of injury, relaxant drugs should have been administered and he should have been physically restrained to eliminate that risk. At the time, medical opinion on these matters was divided. The court held that it is sufficient (in other words, there will be no breach of duty) if a skill is found to have been exercised in accordance with accepted practice by a 'responsible body of medical opinion' skilled in that particular art.

MR JUSTICE McNAIR

In the ordinary case which does not involve any special skill, negligence in law means a failure to do some act which a reasonable man in the circumstances would do, or the doing of some act which a reasonable man in the circumstances would not do; and if that failure or the doing of that act results in injury, then there is a cause of action. How do you test whether this act or failure is negligent? In an ordinary case it is generally said you judge it by the action of the man in the street. He is the ordinary man. In one case it has been said you judge it by the conduct of the man on the top of a Clapham omnibus. He is the ordinary man. But where you get a situation which involves the use of some special skill or competence, then the test as to whether there has been negligence or not is not the test of the man on the top of a Clapham omnibus, because he has not got this special skill. The test is the standard of the ordinary skilled man exercising and professing to have that special skill. A man need not possess the highest expert skill; it is well established law that it is sufficient if he exercises the ordinary skill of an ordinary competent man exercising that particular art. I do not think that I quarrel much with any of the submissions in law which have been put before you by counsel. [Counsel for the plaintiff] put it in this way, that in the case of a medical man, negligence means failure to act in accordance with the standards of reasonably competent medical men at the time. That is a perfectly accurate statement, as long as it is remembered that there may be one or more perfectly proper standards; and if he conforms with one of those proper standards, then he is not negligent.

[Counsel for the plaintiff] also was quite right, in my judgment, in saying that a mere personal belief that a particular technique is best is no defence unless that belief is based on reasonable grounds. That again is unexceptionable. But the emphasis which is laid by [counsel for the defendants] is on this aspect of negligence, that the real question you have to make up your minds about on each of the three major topics is whether the defendants, in acting in the way they did, were acting in accordance with a practice of competent respected professional opinion. [He] submitted that if you are satisfied that they were acting in accordance with a practice of a competent body of professional opinion, then it would be wrong for you to hold that negligence was established ... I myself would prefer to put it this way, that he is not guilty of negligence if he has acted in accordance with a practice accepted as proper by a responsible body of medical men skilled in that particular art ... Putting it the other way round, a

 Alert

> man is not negligent, if he is acting in accordance with such a practice, merely because there is a body of opinion who would take a contrary view. At the same time, that does not mean that a medical man can obstinately and pig-headedly carry on with some old technique if it has been proved to be contrary to what is really substantially the whole of informed medical opinion.

On the facts, the court held that the defendants were not liable as they had conformed to a practice that was approved by a responsible body of medical opinion.

A responsible body of medical opinion does not have to represent the majority of opinions, but merely an acceptable body, as is clearly demonstrated by the next case.

De Freitas v O'Brien [1995] PIQR P281

Panel: Leggatt, Swinton-Thomas and Otton LJJ

Facts: The plaintiff, Mrs Patricia De Freitas, had suffered from back problems for many years. A particular incident in July, 1988 was so bad that she went to see the defendant, John O'Brien, a consultant orthopaedic surgeon. She was in intense pain and the defendant performed an anterior lumbar fusion. She was discharged home on 7 August, but readmitted a few days later complaining of further pain and restricted leg movement. The defendant performed further surgery on 26 August. The plaintiff's condition did not improve. In October 1992, she alleged that Mr O'Brien was negligent in undertaking surgery on both July 15 and August 26 without any or sufficient radiological or clinical evidence to justify either operation. She also joined Mr Campbell-Connolly, a consultant neuro-surgeon, as a second defendant. (He was no longer a party by the time of the appeal.) On appeal, the only issue to be decided was whether the plaintiff had proved that the first defendant's decision to operate on August 26 was negligent.

> LORD JUSTICE OTTON
>
> It was submitted that the *Bolam* test was not designed to enable small numbers of medical practitioners, intent on carrying out otherwise unjustified exploratory surgery, to assert that their practices are reasonable because they are accepted by more than one doctor. If it appears from the evidence that the body of medical opinion relied upon by the defendant is both very small and diametrically opposed in its views to the conventional views of the vast majority of medical practitioners, the court should be vigilant in carrying out its duty to test whether the body of medical opinion relied upon by the defendant is a "responsible" body.
>
> Leading counsel referred us to the evidence that there are only eight or so orthopaedic surgeons in the country who came within the body of medical practitioners called "spinal surgeons"; there are only three neuro-surgeons in the country who come within this body. A body of 11 doctors out of a total of well over 1,000 orthopaedic surgeons and neuro-surgeons is very small. The experts called on behalf of the first defendants accepted that "normal medical opinion" would not have countenanced surgery in this case and that those who would have countenanced surgery were a very small body of "spinal surgeons". Accordingly, it was the learned judge's duty to analyse carefully

and with reservations the reasons put forward by the spinal surgeons for advocating a practice thought to be dangerous and unmerited by the vast majority of responsible practitioners. ...

My first observation is that the *Bolam* test does not impose any burden of proof upon the defendant to establish that his diagnosis or treatment would be acceptable to a responsible body of medical opinion. The burden of proof is upon the plaintiff. As the learned judge correctly put it at page 59F, "Has the plaintiff proved that the decision to operate on the basis was a decision that no reasonable doctor working within their specialism would take?" ...

Thus I do not consider the learned judge fell into error in not considering whether the body of spinal surgeons had to be substantial. It was sufficient if he was satisfied that there was a responsible body. Was the judge in this case justified in so holding? Mr Findlay is a consultant neuro-surgeon specialising exclusively in spinal surgery since 1985. He is a member of the International Society for the Study of the Lumbar Spine of which there are some 250 members world-wide, of whom four or five are neuro-surgeons. He has run spinal study training courses since 1984 and was editor of the textbook on spinal surgery published in 1992. He practices at the Walton Hospital in Liverpool, performing some 400 operations a year.

Mr John Webb is an orthopaedic surgeon whose training included a post at the Robert Jones and Agnes Hunt Orthopaedic Hospital, Oswestry. He is a Fellow of the British Orthopaedic Association and of the International Society for the Study of the Lumbar Spine. He considers himself a spinal surgeon pursuing this specialism at Queens Medical Centre, Nottingham, where 90 per cent of his time in surgery is spent on the spine. He either performs or is responsible for some 400–500 cases a year. I have already referred to the first defendant's qualifications and experience. Thus, on any basis, the witnesses called were a fair representation of specialists practising in that field.

The rule in *Bolam* was followed in *Maynard v West Midlands Regional Health Authority* [1984] 1 WLR 634.

Maynard v West Midlands Regional Health Authority [1984] 1 WLR 634

Panel: Lord Fraser of Tullybelton, Lord Elwyn-Jones, Lord Scarman, Lord Roskill and Lord Templeman

Facts: The plaintiff contracted an illness, the most likely diagnosis for which was held, according to the two consultants concerned, to be one of two things, either tuberculosis (the most likely) or Hodgkin's disease. Because Hodgkin's disease was fatal unless remedial steps were taken in its early stages, the consultants decided that, rather than await the result of a sputum test, which would involve some weeks' delay, the operation of mediastinoscopy should be performed. Mediastinoscopy involved a risk of damage to the left laryngeal recurrent nerve even if properly performed and that damage did in fact occur. It was subsequently confirmed that the plaintiff was suffering from tuberculosis and not Hodgkin's disease. The plaintiff brought an action against the defendant health authority, claiming that the decision to carry out the mediastinoscopy rather than await the result of the sputum test had been negligent. At the trial, a distinguished body of expert medical opinion was called approving of the action of the consultants in carrying out the operation, but the judge found for the plaintiff. The Court of Appeal reversed his decision.

LORD SCARMAN

...It is not enough to show that there is a body of competent professional opinion which considers that their [sic] was a wrong decision, if there also exists a body of professional opinion, equally competent, which supports the decision as reasonable in the circumstances. It is not enough to show that subsequent events show that the operation need never have been performed, if at the time the decision to operate was taken it was reasonable in the sense that a responsible body of medical opinion would have accepted it as proper. ...

I would only add that a doctor who professes to exercise a special skill must exercise the ordinary skill of his speciality. Differences of opinion and practice exist, and will always exist, in the medical as in other professions. There is seldom any one answer exclusive of all others to problems of professional judgment. A court may prefer one body of opinion to the other: but that is no basis for a conclusion of negligence. ...

The House of Lords chose not to become involved with preferring one professional opinion over another. Where there exist competing, equally reasonable opinions, it would seem that the defendant will not be in breach.

The *Bolam* test has been applied in a wide variety of medical scenarios, including, for example, the standard of handwriting on a prescription, the use of alternative medicine, and the duty to warn patients of risk.

11.3 Warnings as to Risk

On the issue of failure to warn of risk, the most important authority until recently was *Sidaway v Board of Governors of the Bethlem Royal Hospital* [1984] AC 871 in which the House of Lords, applying the *Bolam* test, found that the defendant surgeon had not breached his duty by his failure to warn the plaintiff of the particular spinal damage she sustained following surgery because the risk was below one per cent and a reasonable body of medical opinion would not have warned the patient of it. Lord Bridge regarded any risk of ten per cent or higher to be one that should be communicated because '...no reasonably prudent medical man would fail to make it.'

In other words, a claimant could not sue a doctor in negligence for failing to warn of risk if other reasonable doctors would also not have informed of that risk. Whilst that principle still has limited application, the following case has reversed the ruling as to informed consent.

Montgomery v Lanarkshire Health Board [2015] UKSC 11

Panel: Lord Neuberger, Lady Hale, Lord Kerr, Lord Clarke, Lord Wilson, Lord Reed, Lord Hodge

Facts: Mrs Nadine Montgomery gave birth to a baby boy on 1 October 1999, at Bellshill Maternity Hospital, Lanarkshire. Unfortunately, her son was starved of oxygen during the birth and sustained severe brain damage. The shoulders of the baby got stuck during delivery (a complication known as shoulder dystocia) and there was a 12 minute delay in freeing the shoulders, resulting in the brain damage. In addition, the baby sustained paralysis in one arm caused by the force used in pulling him out. Mrs Montgomery's principle claim was against her obstetrician for failing to give adequate warnings. The basis of her argument was that she, the mother, was small and diabetic, and that diabetes tends to lead to larger babies. Therefore, had she been warned of the risk of shoulder dystocia, she should also have been offered, and would have accepted, a caesarean section. The Supreme Court found for Mrs Montgomery, reversing the judgments at first instance and on appeal, and stating unequivocally that *Sidaway* should not be followed.

LADY HALE

We do not have a full transcript of the evidence, but in the extracts we do have Dr McLellan referred to explaining to a mother who requested a caesarean section "why it may not be in the mother's best interest" and later expressed the view that "it's not in the maternal interests for women to have caesarean sections". Whatever Dr McLellan may have had in mind, this does not look like a purely medical judgment. It looks like a judgment that vaginal delivery is in some way morally preferable to a caesarean section: so much so that it justifies depriving the pregnant woman of the information needed for her to make a free choice in the matter. Giving birth vaginally is indeed a unique and wonderful experience, but it has not been suggested that it inevitably leads to a closer and better relationship between mother and child than does a caesarean section...

A patient is entitled to take into account her own values, her own assessment of the comparative merits of giving birth in the "natural" and traditional way and of giving birth by caesarean section, whatever medical opinion may say, alongside the medical evaluation of the risks to herself and her baby. She may place great value on giving birth in the natural way and be prepared to take the risks to herself and her baby which this entails. The medical profession must respect her choice, unless she lacks the legal capacity to decide (*St George's Healthcare NHS Trust v S* [1999] Fam 26). There is no good reason why the same should not apply in reverse, if she is prepared to forgo the joys of natural childbirth in order to avoid some not insignificant risks to herself or her baby. She cannot force her doctor to offer treatment which he or she considers futile or inappropriate. But she is at least entitled to the information which will enable her to take a proper part in that decision.

The *Bolam* test also has wider application to other professions. The Court of Appeal in *Gold v Haringey Health Authority* [1998] QB 481 held that the test applied to any other profession or calling which requires special skill, knowledge or experience.

11.4 Criticisms of the *Bolam* Test

The *Bolam* test has attracted criticism for being too heavily weighted in favour of the defendant, and for allowing the professions to determine their own standards. In many Commonwealth jurisdictions, the test has been modified or rejected. Yet in this jurisdiction it prevails. The House of Lords had the opportunity to re-assess the *Bolam* test in the next case.

Bolitho v City & Hackney Health Authority [1998] AC 232

Panel: Lord Browne-Wilkinson, Lord Slynn of Hadley, Lord Nolan, Lord Hoffmann and Lord Clyde

Facts: A two year old child suffered severe brain damage and died after a paediatric registrar failed to attend to him. It was shown that even if the child had been attended to, he would not have been intubated. There were opposing expert opinions as to the reasonableness of the registrar's argument that, had she attended, she would not have intubated the child. The House of Lords held that if a professional opinion was not capable of withstanding logical analysis, the judge was entitled to hold that it could not provide the benchmark by reference to which the doctor's conduct fell to be assessed. In most cases, however, the fact that experts in the field were of a particular opinion would be a demonstration of the reasonableness of that opinion.

LORD BROWNE-WILKINSON

[Counsel for the appellant] submitted that the judge had wrongly treated the *Bolam* test as requiring him to accept the views of one truthful body of expert professional advice even though he was unpersuaded of its logical force. He submitted that the judge was wrong in law in adopting that approach and that ultimately it was for the court, not for medical opinion, to decide what was the standard of care required of a professional in the circumstances of each particular case.

My Lords, I agree with these submissions to the extent that, in my view, the court is not bound to hold that a defendant doctor escapes liability for negligent treatment or diagnosis just because he leads evidence from a number of medical experts who are genuinely of opinion that the defendant's treatment or diagnosis accorded with sound medical practice. In the *Bolam* case itself, McNair J ... stated that the defendant had to have acted in accordance with the practice accepted as proper by a "*responsible* body of medical men." Later he referred to "a standard of practice recognised as proper by a competent *reasonable* body of opinion." Again, in the passage which I have cited from [*Maynard's* case] Lord Scarman refers to a "*respectable*" body of professional opinion. The use of these adjectives - responsible, reasonable and respectable - all show that the court has to be satisfied that the exponents of the body of opinion relied upon can demonstrate that such opinion has a logical basis. In particular in cases involving, as they so often do, the weighing of risks against benefits, the judge before accepting a body of opinion as being responsible, reasonable or respectable, will need to be satisfied that, in forming their views, the experts have directed their minds to the question of comparative risks and benefits and have reached a defensible conclusion on the matter . ...

[I]n cases of diagnosis and treatment there are cases where, despite a body of professional opinion sanctioning the defendant's conduct, the defendant can properly be held liable for negligence (I am not here considering questions of disclosure of risk). In my judgment that is because, in some cases, it cannot be demonstrated to the judge's satisfaction that the body of opinion relied upon is reasonable or responsible. In the vast majority of cases the fact that distinguished experts in the field are of a particular opinion will demonstrate the reasonableness of that opinion. In particular, where there are questions of assessment of the relative risks and benefits of adopting a particular medical practice, a reasonable view necessarily presupposes that the relative risks and benefits have been weighed by the experts in forming their opinions. But if, in a rare case, it can be demonstrated that the professional opinion is not capable of withstanding logical analysis, the judge is entitled to hold that the body of opinion is not reasonable or responsible.

 Alert

I emphasise that in my view it will very seldom be right for a judge to reach the conclusion that views genuinely held by a competent medical expert are unreasonable. The assessment of medical risks and benefits is a matter of clinical judgment which a judge would not normally be able to make without expert evidence. As ... Lord Scarman makes clear, it would be wrong to allow such assessment to deteriorate into seeking to persuade the judge to prefer one of two views both of which are capable of being logically supported. It is only where a judge can be satisfied that the body of expert opinion cannot be logically supported at all that such opinion will not provide the benchmark by reference to which the defendant's conduct falls to be assessed.

Importantly, the House of Lords held that the paediatric registrar was *not* liable here, as there was a body of responsible medical opinion supporting her course of action. Therefore, while this decision challenges, in theory, the autonomy of the medical profession and reaffirms the role of the court in assessing whether treatment has been negligent, it will be rare for a court to hold that the views of a competent medical expert are unreasonable.

Further Reading

J Fanning, 'Uneasy lies the neck that wears a stethoscope: some observations on defensive medicine' *Professional Negligence* 2008, 24(2), pp 93 – 103

R Heywood, 'The logic of Bolitho' *Professional Negligence* 2006, 22(4), pp 225 – 235

M Hogg, 'Duties of care, causation, and the implications of Chester v Afshar' *Edinburgh Law Review* 2005, 9(1), pp 156 – 167

12

Product Liability

Topic List

Introduction

Liability for defective products is an area of law where a number of claims are available, in both contract law and tort law. This chapter concentrates on the potential claims in tort law. First, the position under the common law will be examined, concentrating on manufacturers' liability in negligence for defective products. Then the development of the law with the passing of the Consumer Protection Act 1987, the aim of which was to make producers of defective goods strictly liable for any harm caused by their products, will be considered

12.1 Liability at Common Law

The key point to note here is that this is not a separate area of law, but is an application of the normal rules of negligence. The case of *Donoghue v Stevenson* [1932] AC 562, established liability for a manufacturer of a defective product – this is what is referred to as the 'narrow ratio' of the case. Prior to *Donoghue*, a manufacturer was only liable for a dangerous product, rather than a defective one. The House of Lords (by a majority of 3 to 2) held that a manufacturer was under a duty to the final purchaser or consumer to take reasonable care to ensure the article was free from any defect which would be injurious.

Link
See Chapter 2 on Duty of Care for a full discussion of this case

Lord Atkin set out the duty owed to the ultimate consumer. This has been extended in later cases to include anyone within the foreseeable area of risk. Likewise, the person who owed the duty has been extended by later cases. This now covers not only the manufacturer, but also anyone who was involved with supplying, distributing, and possibly even repairing the product.

The case below illustrates how breach and causation are approached by the courts.

Grant v Australian Knitting Mills, Limited [1936] AC 85

Panel: Viscount Hailsham LC, Lord Blanesburgh, Lord Macmillan, Lord Wright, and Sir Lancelot Sanderson

Facts: The appellant had bought some woollen underpants which he wore without washing first. He contracted dermatitis due to a chemical which had been left in the garment from the manufacturing process, and which could not be detected by any reasonable examination of the product. His condition became acute and he ended up being hospitalized. He brought an action against the retailers for breach of contract and against the manufacturers for negligence.

LORD WRIGHT

… The facts set out in the foregoing show, in their Lordships' judgment, negligence in manufacture. According to the evidence, the method of manufacture was correct: the danger of excess sulphites being left was recognized and was guarded against: the process was intended to be fool proof. If excess sulphites were left in the garment, that could only be because someone was at fault. The appellant is not required to lay his finger on the exact person in all the chain who was responsible, or to specify what he did wrong. Negligence is found as a matter of inference from the existence of the defects taken in connection with all the known circumstances: even if the manufacturers could by apt evidence have rebutted that inference they have not done so.

On this basis, the damage suffered by the appellant was caused in fact (because the interposition of the retailers may for this purpose in the circumstances of the case be disregarded) by the negligent or improper way in which the manufacturers made the garments. But this mere sequence of cause and effect is not enough in law to constitute a cause of action in negligence, which is a complex concept, involving a duty as between the parties to take care, as well as a breach of that duty and resulting damage. It might be said that here was no relationship between the parties at all: the manufacturers, it might be said, parted once and for all with the garments when they sold them to the retailers, and were therefore not concerned with their future history, except in so far as under their contract with the retailers they might come under some liability: at no time, it might be said, had they any knowledge of the existence of the appellant: the only peg on which it might be sought to support a relationship of duty was the fact that the appellant had actually worn the garments, but he had done so because he had acquired them by a purchase from the retailers, who were at that time the owners of the goods by a sale which had vested the property in the retailers and divested both property and control from the manufacturers. It was said there could be no legal relationships in the matter save those under the two contracts between the respective parties to those contracts, the one between the manufacturers and the retailers and the other between the retailers and the appellant. These contractual relationships (it might be said) covered the whole field and excluded any question of tort liability: there was no duty other than the contractual duties. ...

It is clear that the decision treats negligence, where there is a duty to take care, as a specific tort in itself, and not simply as an element in some more complex relationship or in some specialized breach of duty, and still less as having any dependence on contract. All that is necessary as a step to establish the tort of actionable negligence is to define the precise relationship from which the duty to take care is to be deduced. It is, however, essential in English law that the duty should be established: the mere fact that a man is injured by another's act gives in itself no cause of action: if the act is deliberate, the party injured will have no claim in law even though the injury is intentional, so long as the other party is merely exercising a legal right: if the act involves lack of due care, again no case of actionable negligence will arise unless the duty to be careful exists. In *Donoghue's* case the duty was deduced simply from the facts relied on - namely, that the injured party was one of a class for whose use, in the contemplation and intention of the makers, the article was issued to the world, and the article was used by that party in the state in which it was prepared and issued without it being changed in any way and without there being any warning of, or means of detecting, the hidden danger ...

In *Donoghue's* case the thing was dangerous in fact, though the danger was hidden, and the thing was dangerous only because of want of care in making it; as Lord Atkin points out in *Donoghue's* case, the distinction between things inherently dangerous and things only dangerous because of negligent manufacture cannot be regarded as significant for the purpose of the questions here involved.

One further point may be noted. The principle of *Donoghue's* case can only be applied where the defect is hidden and unknown to the consumer, otherwise the directness of cause and effect is absent: the man who consumes or uses a thing which he knows to be noxious cannot complain in respect of whatever mischief follows, because it follows from his own conscious volition in choosing to incur the risk or certainty of mischance.

If the foregoing are the essential features of *Donoghue's* case, they are also to be found, in their Lordships' judgment, in the present case. The presence of the deleterious chemical in the pants, due to negligence in manufacture, was a hidden and latent defect, just as much as were the remains of the snail in the opaque bottle: it could not be detected by any examination that could reasonably be made. Nothing happened between the making of the garments and their being worn to change their condition. The garments were made by the manufacturers for the purpose of being worn exactly as they were worn in fact by the appellant: it was not contemplated that they should be first washed. It is immaterial that the appellant has a claim in contract against the retailers, because that is a quite independent cause of action, based on different considerations, even though the damage may be the same. ...

Mr. Greene, however, sought to distinguish *Donoghue's* case from the present on the ground that in the former the makers of the ginger-beer had retained "control" over it in the sense that they had placed it in stoppered and sealed bottles, so that it would not be tampered with until it was opened to be drunk, whereas the garments in question were merely put into paper packets, each containing six sets, which in ordinary course would be taken down by the shopkeeper and opened, and the contents handled and disposed of separately, so that they would be exposed to the air. He contended that though there was no reason to think that the garments when sold to the appellant were in any other condition, least of all as regards sulphur contents, than when sold to the retailers by the manufacturers, still the mere possibility and not the fact of their condition having been changed was sufficient to distinguish *Donoghue's* case: there was no "control" because nothing was done by the manufacturers to exclude the possibility of any tampering while the goods were on their way to the user. Their Lordships do not accept that contention. The decision in *Donoghue's* case did not depend on the bottle being stoppered and sealed: the essential point in this regard was that the article should reach the consumer or user subject to the same defect as it had when it left the manufacturer. That this was true of the garment is in their Lordships' opinion beyond question. At most there might in other cases be a greater difficulty of proof of the fact.

The case below, however, shows what happens if a manufacturer includes a warning to test the product or to use it only in a certain way, which the user fails to follow.

Kubach and Another v Hollands and Another (Frederick Allen & Son (Poplar) Ltd, Third Party) [1937] 3 All ER 907

Panel: Lord Hewart CJ

Facts: A schoolgirl was injured when carrying out an experiment in a chemistry laboratory. The suppliers of the chemical (the third defendants) had included a warning which stated that the product must be tested before use. The second defendants had bought the chemical, and sold it on to the school, without including the warning, carrying out the test, or informing the third defendants of the use it would be put to. The chemical was unsuitable for the experiment, although there was no way of ascertaining this without carrying out the test beforehand. The question for the court was whether the second defendants (who were held liable for negligence) could seek an indemnity from the third defendants.

LORD HEWART CJ

... Light is also, I think, thrown on the present case by the decision of the House of Lords in *M'Alister (or Donoghue) v Stevenson*, where it was held that the manufacturer of an article of food, medicine, or the like, sold by him to a distributor, in circumstances which prevent the distributor or the ultimate purchaser or consumer from discovering by inspection any defect, is under a legal duty to take reasonable care that the article is free from defect likely to cause injury to health. ...

The case which is there contemplated is, I think, in essential respects the opposite of the present case. The manganese dioxide which the third party ought to have supplied here to the second defendant might have been resold for a variety of purposes or in innocuous compounds or mixtures. The use of it for school experiments was only one of the many possible uses and the third party, unlike the second defendants, had no notice of the intended use. More than that, it was common ground that a very simple test, if it had been carried out, as the third party's invoice prescribed and as the first defendant was not warned, would immediately have exhibited the fact that antimony sulphide had erroneously been made up and delivered as manganese dioxide. The second defendants had ample and repeated opportunity of intermediate examination and, if they had taken the simple precaution which the invoice warned them to take, no mischief would have followed. ...

Note how Lord Hewart CJ distinguishes the previous caselaw here since in this case there was a note from the manufacturers specifying that an intermediate inspection should be made. There were also many ways in which the chemical in question could be used, and the manufacturers had no notice of the use to which it was being put.

12.2 Liability Under the Consumer Protection Act 1987 (Part 1)

Under the common law, litigants faced great difficulties when bringing an action for harm which was caused due to a design defect, and were only able to succeed in an action for a manufacturing defect if negligence could be established. There were calls for strict liability to be introduced in this area. In 1985 the European Community issued Directive 85/374, which required all member states to change their legislation with regards to product liability. This resulted in the Consumer Protection Act 1987. Part 1 deals with product liability.

12.3 Definitions of 'Product' and 'Defective'

The definition of a 'product' is contained in section 1(2) of the Act. The following case highlights some of the difficulties in defining a 'product' under the Act, setting out the courts' approach to standard and non-standard products. There is also a lengthy discussion of factors which should be taken into account when deciding whether the product was defective, including the application of the development risks defence.

A and Others v The National Blood Authority and Others [2001] 3 All ER 289

Panel: Burton J

Statute: Consumer Protection Act 1987 s 4(1)(e)

Facts: The claimants had been given blood transfusions which had used blood or blood products which had been taken from donors infected with Hepatitis C, a virus causing liver disease. The claimants had all been infected with the virus and sued. At the time the transfusions took place, it was virtually impossible to avoid the risk of any infection as it had either not yet been discovered, or there was no way of testing for it in the blood. The claims were brought under the Consumer Protection Act 1987.

MR JUSTICE BURTON

The claims in this trial have been that, pursuant to the CPA, those who received blood or blood products infected by Hepatitis C subsequent to 1 March 1988, when the Act came into effect, are entitled to recover damages: that is notwithstanding that: (i) the Hepatitis C virus itself had not been discovered or identified at the date when the claims commence on 1 March 1988; (ii) no screening test to discover the presence of such virus in a donor's blood was even known of, certainly not available, until Ortho's assay, first publicised in spring/summer 1989; and (iii) it is not sought to be alleged (at least not in this trial) that the United Kingdom blood authorities for whom the defendants are responsible were negligent in not introducing the screening tests until they did on 1 September 1991 (or now, as a result of the agreed concession, 1 April 1991) nor that they were negligent in not having introduced surrogate tests. The case which is put is that they are liable irrespective of the absence of any fault, under the directive and the CPA. ...

Were the infected bags of blood in this case non-standard products? The claimants say Yes—99 out of 100 are safe and uninfected as intended. The defendants say No—all blood, derived as it is from a natural raw material, albeit then processed, is inherently risky. But the claimants assert that persons generally are entitled to expect that all blood and blood products used for medical treatment are safe, and that they will not receive the unsafe one in 100. The claimants say that this will only not be the case if the public does know and expect that blood, like cigarettes or alcohol, is or may be defective, not because the public's expectation is limited to an expectation that legitimately expectable safety precautions will have been taken. ...

ARTICLE 7(e)

'The producer shall not be liable as a result of this Directive if he proves ... (e) that the state of scientific and technical knowledge at the time when he put the product into circulation was not such as to enable the existence of the defect to be discovered'.]

This defence, for such it is, being an escape clause for the producer, the onus being upon the producer, has been called by the claimants (as it is in most academic literature) the development risks defence, which is how it was usually described during the working through of the directive, as is apparent from the travaux préparatoires... . I propose, neutrally, simply to call it the 'art 7(e) defence'. ...

The issues between the parties

Must the producer prove that the defect had not been and could not be discovered in the product in question, as the defendants contend, or must the producer prove that the defect had not been and could not be discovered generally, ie in the population of products? If it be the latter, it is common ground here that the existence of the defect in blood generally, ie of the infection of blood in some cases by Hepatitis virus notwithstanding screening, was known, and indeed known to the defendants. The question is thus whether, in order to take advantage of the escape clause, the producer must show that no objectively assessable scientific or technical information existed anywhere in the world which had identified, and thus put producers potentially on notice of, the problem; or whether it is enough for the producer to show that, although the existence of the defect in such product was or should have been known, there was no objectively accessible information available anywhere in the world which would have enabled a producer to discover the existence of that known defect in the particular product in question. The crux of the dispute therefore is as follows. (i) The claimants say that once the defect in blood is known about, as it was, it is a known risk. A known but unavoidable risk does not qualify for art 7(e). It may qualify for art 6, not because it was unavoidable (see their contentions set out in [35] above) but if it could be shown that, because the risk is known, it was accepted, and lowered public expectations—like poison and alcohol. But otherwise once it is known, then the product cannot be supplied, or is supplied at the producer's risk and has no protection from art 7(e). Hence an art 7(e) defence is, as was intended, a development risks defence; for if it is not known that a particular product, perhaps a pioneering such product (such as a scrid), has or can have a harmful characteristic, whether by virtue of its inherent nature, its raw materials, its design or its method of manufacture, and then the defect materialises, or is published about, for the first time, it has prior to that time been a true development risk, and protection is available under art 7(e). However, once the risk is known, then if the product is supplied, and if the defect recurs, by then it is a known risk, and, even if undiscoverable in a particular example of the product, there is no escape. ...

 Decipher
Article 7(e) was enacted in the Consumer Protection Act 1987 as section 4(1)(e) – the development risks defence.

 Alert
This is the key question regarding the application of the development risks defence to the facts of this case.

Accordingly I am quite clear that the infected blood products in this case were non-standard products (whether on the basis of being manufacturing or design defects does not appear to me to matter). Where, as here, there is a harmful characteristic in a non-standard product, a decision that it is defective is likely to be straightforward, and I can make my decision accordingly. However, the consequence of my conclusion is that 'avoidability' is also not in the basket of circumstances, even in respect of a harmful characteristic in a standard product. So I shall set out what I consider to be the structure for consideration under art 6. It must be emphasised that safety and intended, or foreseeable, use are the lynchpins: and, leading on from these, what legitimate expectations there are of safety in relation to foreseeable use. (i) I see no difficulty, on that basis, in an analysis which is akin to contract or warranty. Recital 6 ('the defectiveness of the product should be determined by reference not to its fitness for use but to the lack of the safety which the public at large are entitled to expect') does not in my judgment counter-indicate an approach analogous to contract, but is concerned to emphasise that it is safety which is paramount. (ii) In the circumstances, there may in a simple case be a straightforward answer to the art 6 question, and the facts may be sufficiently clear. But an expert may be needed (and they were instructed in *Richardson's* case, the *'Cosytoes* case' and the *'German Bottle* case'). For art 6 purposes, the function of such expert would be, in my judgment, to describe the composition or construction of the product and its effect and consequence in use: not to consider what could or should have been done, whether in respect of its design or manufacture, to avoid the problem (that may be relevant in relation to art 7(e), if that arises). (iii) In the following analysis I ignore questions that may obviously arise, either by way of 'exoneration' in respect of other heads of art 7 or in respect of misuse or contributory negligence (art 8, set out in [16] above).

The first step must be to identify the harmful characteristic which caused the injury (art 4). In order to establish that there is a defect in art 6, the next step will be to conclude whether the product is standard or non-standard. This will be done (in the absence of admission by the producer) most easily by comparing the offending product with other products of the same type or series produced by that producer. If the respect in which it differs from the series includes the harmful characteristic, then it is, for the purpose of art 6, non-standard. If it does not differ, or if the respect in which it differs does not include the harmful characteristic, but all the other products, albeit different, share the harmful characteristic, then it is to be treated as a standard product. ...

But it seems to me that the primary issue in relation to a non-standard product may be whether the public at large accepted the non-standard nature of the product—ie they accept that a proportion of the products is defective (as I have concluded they do not in this case). That, as discussed, is not of course the end of it, because the question is of legitimate expectation, and the court may conclude that the expectation of the public is too high or too low. But manifestly questions such as warnings and presentations will be in the forefront. However, I conclude that the following are not relevant: (i) avoidability of the harmful characteristic—ie impossibility or unavoidability in relation to precautionary measures; (ii) the impracticality, cost or difficulty of taking such measures; and (iii) the benefit to society or utility of the product (except in the context of whether—with full information and proper knowledge—the public does and ought to accept the risk). ...

THE RESULT IN LAW ON ISSUE I

Unknown risks are unlikely to qualify by way of defence within art 6. They may, however, qualify for art 7(e). Known risks do not qualify within art 7(e), even if unavoidable in the particular product. They may qualify within art 6 if fully known and socially acceptable.

The blood products in this case were non-standard products, and were unsafe by virtue of the harmful characteristics which they had and which the standard products did not have.

They were not ipso facto defective (an expression used from time to time by the claimants) but were defective because I am satisfied that the public at large was entitled to expect that the blood transfused to them would be free from infection. There were no warnings and no material publicity, certainly none officially initiated by or for the benefit of the defendants, and the knowledge of the medical profession, not materially or at all shared with the consumer, is of no relevance. It is not material to consider whether any steps or any further steps could have been taken to avoid or palliate the risk that the blood would be infected. ...

 Alert

The conclusion of the court therefore was that the infected blood was a 'non-standard' product, and that the general public were entitled to expect a blood transfusion to be from blood that was completely free of infection. Therefore the blood was 'defective'.

There have been a few cases which examine the concept of defectiveness, defined rather loosely in s 3(1) as falling below the safety which persons generally are entitled to expect. Whether or not a product is defective depends, according to s 3(2), on all the circumstances of the case, including the presentation of the product, such as packaging, warnings, instructions and so on.

Richardson v LRC Products Ltd [2000] PIQR P164

Panel: Ian Kennedy J

Statute: Consumer Protection Act 1987 ss 3 and 4

Facts: The claimant claimed damages for personal injury from the defendant condom manufacturer. The condom, which was used by the claimant's husband failed as he was having sexual intercourse with the claimant. She then became pregnant as a result. After the act of sexual intercourse it was discovered that the condom had fractured. The claimant sought damages for breach of statutory duty under the CPA 1987.

MR JUSTICE IAN KENNEDY

The question of what persons are entitled to expect include, as one might suppose, all the circumstances including the manner in which and the purposes for which the product has been marketed, its get-up, the use of any mark in relation to the product and any instructions for, or warnings with respect to, doing or refraining from doing anything with or in relation to the product. Naturally enough the user's expectation is that a condom will not fail. There are no claims made by the defendants that one will never fail and no-one has ever supposed that any method of contraception intended to defeat nature will be 100 per cent effective. This must particularly be so in the case of a condom where the product is required, to a degree at least, to be "user friendly". So to the question "Does a fracture prove a defect?" I answer, "No, not by itself."…

For those reasons, I have reached the conclusion that the claimant has not established a breach of the section by either of the routes which she has sought to follow.

Further Reading

Howells Geraint and Mark Mildred, 'Infected Blood: Defect and Discoverability: A First Exposition of the EC Product Liability Directive' (2002) 65 *Modern Law Review* 95

Newdick, Christopher, 'The Development Risks Defence of the Consumer Protection Act 1987' (1988) 47 *Cambridge Law Journal* 455

13

Occupiers' Liability

Topic List

Introduction

The occupier of land or premises may be liable for injury or loss suffered on his premises. As such, occupiers' liability is an extension of the traditional rules of negligence. However, while general negligence requires the defendant to protect claimants from his negligent acts or omissions (sometimes called the 'activity duty') occupiers' liability requires defendant occupiers of land to keep claimants reasonably safe while on their premises (the 'occupancy duty'). In other words, it focuses on the state of the premises rather than activities carried out on those premises.

Link
see Chapters 2-8 on General Negligence

While the law of tort is largely reliant on case law, occupiers' liability is now governed mostly by statute, namely the Occupiers' Liability Act 1957 ('OLA 1957') and the Occupiers' Liability Act 1984 ('OLA 1984'). While the statutes are outside the scope of this chapter, it is necessary to be aware of them in order to put this area of the common law into context and when establishing if a cause of action has arisen. In any event, the Acts do not replace the common law but exist in parallel with it, and most claims will be pleaded both under statute and at common law.

Prior to 1957, the common law distinguished between different classes of entrants to premises, the occupier owing different levels of legal obligation to each. The subtleties that were required in order to draw distinctions between the various classes of entrant were the subject of much criticism and the matter was referred to the Law Reform Committee. As a result of the Committee's report, Parliament passed the OLA 1957. This Act did not however recognise a duty of care to trespassers, and no duty was owed to them unless the occupier was reckless as to their safety, for example by laying traps. The situation was altered through the common law and subsequently the OLA 1984 was passed which recognises a duty of care to trespassers.

13.1 Terminology

A claim in occupiers' liability begins with a visitor or trespasser seeking to bring an action against an occupier concerning the premises. Yet the terms 'occupier', 'visitor' and 'trespasser' are not defined in either Act. For that reason we look to the common law for assistance.

13.1.1 'Occupier'

Wheat v E. Lacon & Co. Ltd. [1966] AC 552

Panel: Lord Morris of Borth-y-Gest, Lord Pearce, Lord Pearson, Viscount Dilhorne and Lord Denning

Facts: The defendants were the owners of a pub. They granted Mr and Mrs Richardson, the manager and his wife, a licence to use the top floor of the premises for their private accommodation and to take in paying guests. The plaintiff and her husband were paying guests. The husband was fatally injured while using the staircase which had a faulty hand rail. He could not see this as the area had no lighting (the light bulb was missing). The question arose as to who was in occupation of the stairs on which the plaintiff was injured, for the purpose of a claim in occupiers' liability.

LORD DENNING

The case raises this point of law: did the brewery company owe any duty to Mr. Wheat to see that the handrail was safe to use or to see that the stairs were properly lighted? That depends on whether the brewery company was "an occupier" of the private portion of the "Golfers' Arms," and Mr. Wheat its "visitor" within the Occupiers' Liability Act, 1957: for, if so, the brewery company owed him the "common duty of care." ...

In the Occupiers' Liability Act, 1957, the word "occupier" is used in the same sense as it was used in the common law cases on occupiers' liability for dangerous premises. It was simply a convenient word to denote a person who had a sufficient degree of control over premises to put him under a duty of care towards those who came lawfully on to the premises. Those persons were divided into two categories, invitees and licensees: and a higher duty was owed to invitees than to licensees. But by the year 1956 the distinction between invitees and licensees had been reduced to vanishing point. The duty of the occupier had become simply a duty to take reasonable care to see that the premises were reasonably safe for people coming lawfully on to them: and it made no difference whether they were invitees or licensees: see *Slater v. Clay Cross Co. Ltd.* The Act of 1957 confirmed the process. It did away, once and for all, with invitees and licensees and classed them all as "visitors"; and it put upon the occupier the same duty to all of them, namely, the common duty of care. ... Translating this general principle into its particular application to dangerous premises, it becomes simply this: wherever a person has a sufficient degree of control over premises that he ought to realise that any failure on his part to use care may result in injury to a person coming lawfully there, then he is an "occupier" and the person coming lawfully there is his "visitor": and the "occupier" is under a duty to his "visitor" to use reasonable care. In order to be an "occupier" it is not necessary for a person to have entire control over the premises. He need not have exclusive occupation. Suffice it that he has some degree of control. He may share the control with others. Two or more may be "occupiers" and whenever this happens, each is under a duty to use care towards persons coming lawfully on to the premises, dependent on his degree of control. If each fails in his duty, each is liable to a visitor who is injured in consequence of his failure, but each may have a claim to contribution from the other.

 Alert

... There are other people who are "occupiers," even though they do not say "come in." If a person has any degree of control over the state of the premises it is enough. The position is best shown by examining the cases in four groups.

First, where a landlord let premises by demise to a tenant, he was regarded as parting with all control over them. He did not retain any degree of control, even though he had undertaken to repair the structure. Accordingly, he was held to be under no duty to any person coming lawfully on to the premises, save only to the tenant under the agreement to repair. ...

Secondly, where an owner let floors or flats in a building to tenants, but did not demise the common staircase or the roof or some other parts, he was regarded as having retained control of all parts not demised by him. Accordingly, he was held to be under a duty in respect of those retained parts to all persons coming lawfully on to the premises. ...

Thirdly, where an owner did not let premises to a tenant but only licensed a person to occupy them on terms which did not amount to a demise, the owner still having the right to do repairs, he was regarded as being sufficiently in control of the structure to impose on him a duty towards all persons coming lawfully on to the premises. ...

Fourthly, where an owner employed an independent contractor to do work on premises or a structure, the owner was usually still regarded as sufficiently in control of the place as to be under a duty towards all those who might lawfully come there. ...

In the light of these cases, I ask myself whether the brewery company had a sufficient degree of control over the premises to put them under a duty to a visitor. Obviously they had complete control over the ground floor and were "occupiers" of it. But I think that they had also sufficient control over the private portion. They had not let it out to Mr. Richardson by a demise. They had only granted him a licence to occupy it, having a right themselves to do repairs. That left them with a residuary degree of control ... They were in my opinion "an occupier" within the Act of 1957, Mr. Richardson, who had a licence to occupy, had also a considerable degree of control. So had Mrs. Richardson, who catered for summer guests. All three of them were, in my opinion, "occupiers" of the private portion of the "Golfer's Arms." There is no difficulty in having more than one occupier at one and the same time, each of whom is under a duty of care to visitors.

The court held that both the defendant owners *and* Mr and Mrs Richardson were occupiers and that both therefore owed a duty of care. In the event, neither were liable because the fatality was caused partly as a result of a light bulb having been removed by a third party, over which the occupiers had no control. So the claim failed at the legal causation stage. Lord Denning's description of the occupier being any person with a sufficient degree of control over the premises remains the key test for determining the occupier. Note the four specific examples of the occupier that Lord Denning provides. As to his fourth example, Lord Denning states that generally the occupier will remain responsible if he hires independent contractors. It is, however, possible for independent contractors to be occupiers or to be dual occupiers (*AMF International Ltd v Magnet Bowling Ltd* [1968] 1 WLR 1028).

Link
see Chapter 6 on Causation

Where no-one has sufficient control over the premises, the claim in occupiers' liability will necessarily fail, as it did in the next case.

Bailey v Armes (1999) 96(7) LSG 37

Panel: Beldam, Ward and Mantell LJJ

Facts: The appellant, when eight years old, was injured when he fell from a sloping roof behind premises used by Cullens Holdings plc, as a supermarket store. As a result of the fall he sustained serious head injuries. He commenced proceedings to recover damages against two defendants: Mr and Mrs Armes who occupied the flat overlooking the flat roof of the supermarket (and who had, on numerous occasions, allowed their own children to play on the flat roof, accessing it from their own roof), and against Cullens, as occupiers of the premises. Other defendants were later added, but these were in relation to the appellant's parallel claim in negligence and are not relevant here. The question was who was the occupier for the purpose of the claim under the OLA 1957, applying Lord Denning's test from *Wheat* (see above).

LORD JUSTICE BELDAM

Undoubtedly, as was made clear in the case of *Wheat v. Lacon* more than one person may in this sense exercise control over premises. The extent to which they are permitted to control either the condition of the premises or the things done upon the premises, may be expressly or impliedly circumscribed, but on the facts of this case, in my view, the judge came to the right conclusion in holding that the first and second defendants did not have a sufficient degree of control over who used the flat roof, and who was entitled to go upon it, to place them in occupation of it. That finding suffices to conclude the question whether either the first or second defendant was liable as an occupier of the roof

13.1.2 'Visitor'

This term also requires recourse to the common law for definition. It is essentially no different from the layman's definition, i.e. denoting that permission has been given to the person in question to enter the premises. Indeed, express permission is the most obvious way to demonstrate that one is a visitor ('Come in!'). However, in the context of occupiers' liability, a person can be classified as a visitor in a number of different ways, including by implied permission, by lawful authority, by contractual permission, and by virtue of the doctrine of allurement (whereby children are attracted onto land by things there that adults may not find so attractive, such as food, boats or machinery). Express permission can be limited in the following ways: by time, by area and by purpose. If the visitor goes beyond any of these, they become a trespasser for the purpose of any claim. The next case is useful authority on limiting permission by time.

13.2 Limiting Express Permission by Time

Stone v Taffe and Another [1974] 1 WLR 1575

Panel: Megaw and Stephenson LJJ and Sir Seymour Karminski

Facts: The second defendants were the owners and occupiers of a public house which was run for them by a manager, the first defendant. The manager permitted a social function to be held in an upstairs room on the premises and allowed guests to remain on the premises after closing time. On leaving the premises at about 1 am the plaintiff and her husband found that the staircase was unlit. While descending the staircase in the dark, the plaintiff's husband fell and sustained injuries from which he subsequently died. The question, among other things, was whether the plaintiff's permission to be on the premises had been limited by time. In other words, would the plaintiff be viewed as a visitor or trespasser?

LORD JUSTICE STEPHENSON

I would hold that ... the [defendants] still owed the deceased, at 1 a.m. or 1.15 a.m., the common duty of care. I reject the submission that the invitation admittedly extended earlier was a licence limited in time to opening hours and expired by effluxion of time at 10.30 p.m. or at latest about 11 p.m. without any calling of time by the manager or other indication that it was terminated. Although the analogy is imperfect, I think that those cases which hold that an occupier who wishes to limit the space of the area to which he invites or allows another to come must limit it clearly, apply to an occupier wishing to invite or permit another to enter and use his premises for a limited time. There was on the evidence no such clear delimitation of time by the [defendants], and before the accident no implied revocation of their invitation or permission ...

The plaintiff was construed as a visitor, thus afforded protection under the OLA 1957. While permission can be limited by time, any such limitation must be communicated clearly to the purported visitor.

13.2.1 'Trespasser'

This term was defined in the next case.

Robert Addie and Sons (Collieries) v Dumbreck [1929] AC 358

Panel: Lord Hailsham LC, Viscount Dunedin, Lord Shaw of Dunfermline, Lord Buckmaster and Lord Carson

Facts: The respondent in this appeal was the father of a four year old boy who was killed when he was crushed in the wheel of a haulage system belonging to the appellant colliery company. The field in which the wheel was situated was surrounded by a hedge, but it was well known that children would enter the field to use it as a play area. The colliery company were aware of this fact and warned children out of the area from time to time, but their warnings were disregarded. The wheel itself was inadequately protected and was attractive to children. The issue was whether the child would be seen as a visitor or trespasser.

VISCOUNT DUNEDIN

The trespasser is he who goes on the land without invitation of any sort and whose presence is either unknown to the proprietor or, if known, is practically objected to.

The boy was viewed as a trespasser and as such his father had no remedy in law for his loss. Even though the definition of trespasser remains unchanged, the law has moved on since this case was decided. Under the OLA 1984, a similar situation decided today would probably have afforded the boy some (albeit limited) protection.

13.3 Breach of the Duty of Care under the OLA 1957

Once a duty is established, the scope of which is set out under the Acts, it falls to determine whether the occupier has breached his duty. The principles derive from the common law tort of negligence, and will not be reiterated in this chapter. Suffice to say that the occupier has a duty to act as a reasonable occupier in all the circumstances. The OLA 1957 makes particular reference to the standard owed where the visitors are either children or professionals.

13.3.1 Children

Where the visitor is a child, the occupier may have to do more to satisfy their duty to keep that child visitor reasonably safe on the premises. In other words, the duty owed to children is higher than that owed to adult visitors. Occupiers must take into account that children are likely to be less careful than adults and that they may be attracted to areas which adults would have the experience to avoid.

Jolley v Sutton London Borough Council [2000] 1 WLR 1082

Panel: Lord Browne-Wilkinson, Lord Mackay of Clashfern, Lord Steyn, Lord Hoffman and Lord Hobhouse of Woodborough

Facts: A boat was left abandoned for over two years on land owned by the defendant council. The boat appeared sound but was completely rotten. The council was aware of the boat's presence and made plans to remove it, but never did so. Two boys, the plaintiff and a friend, who were then aged 14 and 13, started to repair the boat, using a car jack and some wood to prop it up. While the boys were working on the boat it fell off the prop, crushing the plaintiff, who suffered serious spinal injuries resulting in paraplegia. He brought an action against the council for damages in negligence and breach of statutory duty under the OLA 1957. One of the issues for the court was whether the OLA 1957 applied, and if so, whether the defendant had breached their duty under it.

LORD BROWNE-WILKINSON

The judgment at first instance

In a careful and detailed judgment the judge analysed the evidence and made detailed findings of fact. He then quoted the relevant statutory provisions. Section 2(2) of the Occupier's[sic] Liability Act 1957 defines the "common duty of care" as:

"a duty to take such care as in all the circumstances of the case is reasonable to see that the visitor will be reasonably safe in using the premises for the purposes for which he is invited or permitted by the occupier to be there."

Subsection (3) provides:

"The circumstances relevant for the present purpose include the degree of care, and of want of care, which would ordinarily be looked for in such a visitor, so that (for example) in proper cases—

(a) an occupier must be prepared for children to be less careful than adults..."

The judge observed that it has long been established that children are or may be attracted to meddle with objects on premises or property which constitute a danger when meddled with. He stated in very general terms that the occupier is under a duty to protect a child from danger caused by meddling with such an object by taking reasonable steps in the circumstances including, where appropriate, removing the object altogether so as to avoid the prospect of injury. He cited the well known case of *Hughes v Lord Advocate* [1963] AC 837, as well as a number of other decisions, illustrative of traps or allurements causing harm to children leading to liability by occupiers. ...

The judge summed up his conclusion as follows:

"I find that the type of accident and injury which occurred in this case was reasonably foreseeable (albeit that it involved significant meddling with the boat by two young teenage boys and that the injuries proved to be very severe) and that the actions of the plaintiff and/or Karl did not amount to a novus actus. Accordingly, I find the defendants in breach of their duty to the plaintiff as occupiers and (subject to the point on contributory negligence considered below) liable to the plaintiff for the injury, loss and damage which he has sustained."

The House of Lords restored the judgment of the judge at first instance, and allowed the plaintiff's appeal. This does not mean that children will always be given the protection of the OLA 1957. As so often in tort, the outcome turns on what is reasonable for an occupier to do in the circumstances. For example, where very young children are concerned, the court may take the view that they should have been supervised by their parents or guardians, and that it is not reasonable to expect the occupier to take on this parental role.

13.3.2 Professionals

Just as a higher standard is imposed on occupiers in respect of child visitors, so on occasion a lower standard will be imposed where the visitor is a professional in the exercise of their calling, for example, an electrician doing work on your property. The rationale is that skilled visitors should be able to guard against special risks associated with their profession. The leading case here is *Roles v Nathan (Trading as Manchester Assembly Rooms)* [1963] 1 WLR 1117.

Roles v Nathan (Trading as Manchester Assembly Rooms) [1963] 1 WLR 1117

Panel: Lord Denning MR, Harman and Pearson LJJ

Facts: The defendant owned assembly rooms which were heated by a coke burning boiler. Chimney sweeps were called in to clean out the flues. They tried to complete the work without extinguishing the boiler. The defendant warned them that the boiler room was dangerous and had at one point removed them by force. The sweeps ignored the warnings and both were found dead in the boiler room the next morning. The sweeps' widows in these proceedings claimed damages for the deaths of their husbands which they alleged were caused by the negligence or breach of statutory duty under the OLA 1957 of the defendant.

LORD DENNING MR

...The householder can reasonably expect the sweep to take care of himself so far as any dangers from the flues are concerned. These chimney sweeps ought to have known that there might be dangerous fumes about and ought to have taken steps to guard against them. They ought to have known that they should not attempt to seal up a sweep-hole whilst the fire was still alight. They ought to have had the fire withdrawn before they attempted to seal it up, or at any rate they ought not to have stayed in the alcove too long when there might be dangerous fumes about. All this was known to these two sweeps; they were repeatedly warned about it, and it was for them to guard against the danger. It was not for the occupier to do it, even though he was present and heard the warnings. When a householder calls in a specialist to deal with a defective installation on his premises, he can reasonably expect the specialist to appreciate and guard against the dangers arising from the defect. The householder is not bound to watch over him to see that he comes to no harm. I would hold, therefore, that the occupier here was under no duty of care to these sweeps, at any rate in regard to the dangers which caused their deaths. If it had been a different danger, as for instance if the stairs leading to the cellar gave way, the occupier might no doubt be responsible, but not for these dangers which were special risks ordinarily incidental to their calling.

 Alert

Even if I am wrong about this point, and the occupier was under a duty of care to these chimney sweeps, the question arises whether the duty was discharged by the warning that was given to them. This brings us to subsection (4) which states:

"In determining whether the occupier of premises has discharged the common duty of care to a visitor, regard is to be had to all the circumstances, so that (for example) —

(a) where damage is caused to a visitor by a danger of which he had been warned by the occupier, the warning is not to be treated without more as absolving the occupier from liability, unless in all the circumstances it was enough to enable the visitor to be reasonably safe." ...

Apply subsection (4) to this case. I am quite clear that the warnings which were given to the sweeps were enough to enable them to be reasonably safe. The sweeps would have been quite safe if they had heeded these warnings. They should not have come back that evening and attempted to seal up the sweep-hole while the fire was still alight. They ought to have waited till next morning, and then they should have seen that the fire was out before they attempted to seal up the sweep-hole. In any case they should not have stayed too long in the sweep-hole. In short, it was entirely their own fault. The judge held that it was contributory negligence. I would go further and say that under the Act the occupier has, by the warnings, discharged his duty.

I would therefore be in favour of allowing this appeal and entering judgment for the defendants.

The occupier was found not to be liable because he had not breached his duty of care to the chimney sweeps, and/or because the warnings he gave were adequate to keep the visitors reasonably safe on the premises, in accordance with the provisions of the OLA 1957. On the issue of warnings, subsequent case law has made clear that very obvious dangers (for example, slippery sea walls) may not require warnings at all. Again, this is because it is not reasonable to expect an occupier to warn of every conceivable possible danger. Of course, warnings suitable for adult visitors may not be appropriate for child visitors.

13.4 Duty Owed to Trespassers under the OLA 1984

The most important difference in terms of duty as regards visitors and trespassers is that under the OLA 1957, the duty to visitors is automatic, whereas under the OLA 1984, the duty owed to trespassers only arises where the claimant can satisfy three conditions, set out in s 1(3) of the Act.

Prior to the passing of the OLA 1984, the next case was decided. It set a precedent for the concept that a duty of care ought to be owed, albeit a limited duty, in certain circumstances, (for example, where the case concerned a child) even to trespassers. It formed the basis of the OLA 1984.

British Railways Board v Herrington [1972] AC 877

Panel: Lord Reid, Lord Morris of Borth-y-Gest, Lord Wilberforce, Lord Pearson and Lord Diplock

Facts: The defendants owned an electrified railway line. It was fenced off but the fence had been in a state of disrepair for several months and people often took a short cut across the line. The defendant's station master was notified that children had been seen playing on the line, but he did not arrange for the repair of the fence. The plaintiff, then aged six, got through the fence and was injured on the live railway line. Although a trespasser, he brought an action in negligence. The House of Lords had to decide whether he ought to be entitled to damages, despite his status as trespasser.

LORD REID

So it appears to me that an occupier's duty to trespassers must vary according to his knowledge, ability and resources. It has often been said that trespassers must take the land as they find it. I would rather say that they must take the occupier as they find him. ...

So the question whether an occupier is liable in respect of an accident to a trespasser on his land would depend on whether a conscientious humane man with his knowledge, skill and resources could reasonably have been expected to have done or refrained from doing before the accident something which would have avoided it. If he knew before the accident that there was a substantial probability that trespassers would come I think that most people would regard as culpable failure to give any thought to their safety. He might often reasonably think, weighing the seriousness of the danger and the degree of likelihood of trespassers coming against the burden he would have to incur in preventing their entry or making his premises safe, or curtailing his own activities on his land, that he could not fairly be expected to do anything. But if he could at small trouble and expense take some effective action, again I think that most people would think it inhumane and culpable not to do that. If some such principle is adopted there will no longer be any need to strive to imply a fictitious licence.

Alert

Note how this wording forms the basis of the test for a duty of care set out in the OLA 1984 s 1(3)(a)-(c).

It would follow that an impecunious occupier with little assistance at hand would often be excused from doing something which a large organisation with ample staff would be expected to do.

If I apply that test to the present case I think that the appellants must be held responsible for this accident. They brought onto their land in the live rail a lethal and to a young child a concealed danger. It would have been very easy for them to have and enforce a reasonable system of inspection and repair of their boundary fence. They knew that children were entitled and accustomed to play on the other side of the fence and must have known, had any of their officers given the matter a thought, that a young child might easily cross a defective fence and run into grave danger. Yet they did nothing. I do not think that a large organisation is acting with due regard to humane consideration if its officers do not pay more attention to safety. I would not single out the station master for blame. The trouble appears to have been general slackness in the organisation. For that the appellants are responsible and I think in the circumstances culpable. I would therefore hold them liable to the respondent and dismiss this appeal.

The next case is an example of the operation of the 1984 Act and the difference between it and the 1957 Act. (It also explores the defence of *volenti* in depth.)

Link
See Chapter 8 on General Defences

Tomlinson v Congleton Borough Council and Another [2004] 1 AC 46

Panel: Lord Nicholls of Birkenhead, Lord Hoffmann, Lord Hutton, Lord Hobhouse of Woodborough and Lord Scott of Foscote

Facts: The defendants owned and occupied a country park. A lake had formed in a disused quarry on the premises which was known to attract visitors to swim there. Swimming in the lake was prohibited and there were prominent signs to this effect. The defendants also hired rangers to warn people of the danger of swimming in the lake and to hand out safety leaflets. The plaintiff, who was 18 years old, dived into the shallow water of the lake. He hit his head and sustained very serious injury. He sued the defendants, alleging that the accident was caused by their breach of duty to him as a trespasser under the OLA 1984. The plaintiff was unsuccessful at first instance but won his appeal in the Court of Appeal. The defendants' appeal to the House of Lords was successful.

LORD HOFFMANN

The 1957 and 1984 Acts contrasted

...In the case of the 1984 Act, there is the additional consideration that unless in all the circumstances it is reasonable to expect the occupier to do something, that is to say, to "offer the other some protection" (section 1(3)(c)), there is no duty at all. One may ask what difference there is between the case in which the claimant is a lawful visitor and there is in principle a duty under the 1957 Act but on the particular facts no duty to do anything, and the case in which he is a trespasser and there is on the particular facts no duty under the 1984 Act. Of course in such a case the result is the same. But Parliament has made it clear that in the case of a lawful visitor, one starts from the assumption that there is a duty whereas in the case of a trespasser one starts from the assumption that there is none. ...

Alert

Free will

The second consideration, namely the question of whether people should accept responsibility for the risks they choose to run, is the point made by Lord Phillips of Worth Matravers MR in *Donoghue v Folkestone Properties Ltd* [2003] QB 1008, 1024, para 53 and which I said was central to this appeal. Mr Tomlinson was freely and voluntarily undertaking an activity which inherently involved some risk. By contrast, Miss Bessie Stone (*Bolton v Stone* [1951] AC 850), to whom the House of Lords held that no duty was owed, was innocently standing on the pavement outside her garden gate at 10 Beckenham Road, Cheetham when she was struck by a ball hit for six out of the Cheetham Cricket Club ground. She was certainly not engaging in any activity which involved an inherent risk of such injury. So compared with *Bolton v Stone*, this is an a *fortiori* case.

I think it will be extremely rare for an occupier of land to be under a duty to prevent people from taking risks which are inherent in the activities they freely choose to undertake upon the land. If people want to climb mountains, go hang-gliding or swim or dive in ponds or lakes, that is their affair. Of course the landowner may for his own reasons wish to prohibit such activities. He may ... think that they are a danger or inconvenience to himself or others. Or he may take a paternalist view and prefer people not to undertake risky activities on his land. He is entitled to impose such conditions, as the Council did by prohibiting swimming. But the law does not require him to do so.

Alert

... The fact that ... people take no notice of warnings cannot create a duty to take other steps to protect them. I find it difficult to express with appropriate moderation my disagreement with the proposition of Sedley LJ, ante, p 62b-c, para 45, that it is "only where the risk is so obvious that the occupier can safely assume that nobody will take it that there will be no liability". A duty to protect against obvious risks or self-inflicted harm exists only in cases in which there is no genuine and informed choice, as in the case of employees whose work requires them to take the risk, or some lack of capacity, such as the inability of children to recognise danger (*Herrington v British Railways Board* [1972] AC 877) or the despair of prisoners which may lead them to inflict injury on themselves: *Reeves v Comr of Police of the Metropolis* [2000] 1 AC 360 . ...

So this appeal gives your Lordships the opportunity to say clearly that local authorities and other occupiers of land are ordinarily under no duty to incur such social and financial costs to protect a minority (or even a majority) against obvious dangers. On the other hand, if the decision of the Court of Appeal were left standing, every such occupier would feel obliged to take similar defensive measures. Sedley LJ, ante, p 61g, para 42 was able to say that if the logic of the Court of Appeal's decision was that other public lakes and ponds required similar precautions, "so be it". But I cannot view this prospect with the same equanimity. In my opinion it would damage the quality of many people's lives. ...

My Lords, for these reasons I consider that even if swimming had not been prohibited and the council had owed a duty under section 2(2) of the 1957 Act , that duty would not have required them to take any steps to prevent Mr Tomlinson from diving or warning him against dangers which were perfectly obvious. If that is the case, then plainly there can have been no duty under the 1984 Act. The risk was not one against which he was entitled under section 1(3)(c) to protection. I would therefore allow the appeal and restore the decision of Jack J. ...

The House of Lords held that any risk of the plaintiff suffering injury had arisen not from any danger due to the state of the defendants' premises or to things done or omitted to be done on them, but from the plaintiff's own misjudgment in attempting to dive in too shallow water. That was held not to be a risk giving rise to any duty on the defendants. In addition, it had not been a risk which the defendants might reasonably have been expected to afford the plaintiff some protection under the OLA 1984s 1(3)(c). Note how this decision emphasises the difficulties faced by trespassers in establishing that they ought to be owed a duty.

Further Reading

Buckley, Richard: 'Occupiers' Liability in England and Canada' (2006) 35 CLWR 197

Macleod, Roddy: 'What do you mean it's my fault?' NLJ 2010, 160 (7414), 567 – 568

14

Defamation

Topic List

Introduction

The law of defamation in England and Wales is vast and complex. It is now governed largely by statute, namely the Defamation Act 2013. Therefore, whilst in this chapter we will introduce some of the key cases from different elements of the two defamation torts: slander and libel, these must be viewed in the context of the framework provided by statute. In the first part, we will look at the establishing of a *prima facie* case in both forms of defamation. In the second part of the chapter we will look at defences to defamation actions, which are unique to this area of the law.

14.1 Defamatory Material

The first issue is how we define 'defamatory'.

There are three classic phrases defining defamatory material. All three remain in regular use, and are broadly interchangeable. The best known of the three, however, comes from the following case.

Sim v Stretch [1936] 2 All ER 1237

Panel: Lord Atkin, Lord Russell of Killowen and Lord Macmillan

Facts: The facts of this case arise out of a neighbour dispute, involving a maid who had at one time been employed by both the claimant and the defendant. After a series of incidents, the defendant dictated a telegram at the local post office to be sent to the claimant. It read: "Stretch, The Twigs, Cookham Dean. Edith has resumed her service with us today. Please send her possessions and the money you borrowed also her wages to Old Barton. Sim." The claimant alleged that this contained the defamatory allegations that "… the plaintiff was in pecuniary difficulties, that by reason thereof he had been compelled to borrow and had in fact borrowed money from the … housemaid, that he had failed to pay the said housemaid her wages and that he was a person to whom no one ought to give any credit." The House of Lords held that, on the facts of the case, the words in the telegram were incapable of bearing the meaning that the claimant alleged, and were not defamatory.

LORD ATKIN

The question … is whether the words in their ordinary signification are capable of being defamatory. Judges and textbook writers alike have found difficulty in defining with precision the word "defamatory". The conventional phrase exposing the plaintiff to hatred, ridicule and contempt is probably too narrow. The question is complicated by having to consider the person or class of persons whose reaction to the publication is the test of the wrongful character of the words used. I do not intend to ask your Lordships to lay down a formal definition, but after collating the opinions of many authorities I propose in the present case the test: would the words tend to lower the plaintiff in the estimation of right-thinking members of society generally?

 Alert

The question of whether the material complained of tends to lower the claimant in the estimation of right-thinking members of society has become the best known test for

deciding whether the material is defamatory. The "exposing the [claimant] to hatred, ridicule and contempt" test, while rejected in *Sim v Stretch* for being too narrow is, however, still in use. This can be seen in the next case.

Berkoff v Burchill [1996] 4 All ER 1008

Panel: Neill, Millett and Phillips LJJ

Facts: The claimant, an actor, brought a claim in libel against the defendant who published, on two occasions, material that the claimant alleged bore the defamatory meaning that he was 'hideously ugly'. The defendant had published articles on the subject of films, one of which had contained the statement: "film directors from Hitchcock to Berkoff are notoriously hideous-looking people". The other, a review of the film *Mary Shelley's Frankenstein*, contained the statement that the 'creature' in the film was "a lot like Stephen Berkoff, only marginally better-looking". The Court of Appeal held that the words were capable of being defamatory.

LORD JUSTICE NEILL

It will be seen from this collection of definitions that words may be defamatory, even though they neither impute disgraceful conduct to the plaintiff nor any lack of skill or efficiency in the conduct of his trade or business or professional activity, if they hold him up to contempt, scorn or ridicule or tend to exclude him from society. On the other hand, insults which do not diminish a man's standing among other people do not found an action for libel or slander. The exact borderline may often be difficult to define.

The case for Mr Berkoff is that the charge that he is 'hideously ugly' exposes him to ridicule, and/or alternatively, will cause him to be shunned or avoided.

Counsel for Mr Berkoff ... contended that the present case fell into the ... class where words may be defamatory even though they do not involve an attack on a plaintiff's reputation in the conventional sense. Mr Berkoff, it was said, is an actor and a person in the public eye. It was submitted that it was necessary to look at all the circumstances. If this were done it was a matter for the jury to decide whether the words complained of had passed beyond mere abuse and had become defamatory by exposing Mr Berkoff to ridicule or by causing him to be shunned or avoided. It was suggested that these two passages would reduce the respect with which he was regarded. The words complained of might affect Mr Berkoff's standing among the public, particularly theatre-goers, and among casting directors.

 Alert

It may be that in some contexts the words 'hideously ugly' could not be understood in a defamatory sense, but one has to consider the words in the surroundings in which they appear. This task is particularly important in relation to the second article.

It is trite law that the meaning of words in a libel action is determined by the reaction of the ordinary reader and not by the intention of the publisher, but the perceived intention of the publisher may colour the meaning. In the present case it would, in my view, be open to a jury to conclude that in the context the remarks about Mr Berkoff gave the impression that he was not merely physically unattractive in appearance but actually repulsive. It seems to me that to say this of someone in the public eye who makes his living, in part at least, as an actor, is capable of lowering his standing in the estimation of the public and of making him an object of ridicule.

In the earlier case of *Youssoupoff v Metro-Goldwyn-Mayer Pictures Ltd* (1934) 50 TLR 581

it was held that alleging that the claimant had been raped could cause her to be "shunned or avoided".

Youssoupoff v Metro-Goldwyn-Mayer Pictures Ltd (1934) 50 TLR 581

Panel: Scrutton and Slesser LJ

Facts: The claimant was Princess Irina Alexandrovna Youssoupoff of Russia, who brought an action against the defendant film company relating to their film *Rasputin and the Empress*. She alleged that she was recognisable in the film's character, Natasha, and that the film bore the defamatory meaning that she had been seduced or raped. The defence argued, and the court at first instance agreed, that an allegation that someone had been raped was not capable of bearing a defamatory meaning. The Court of Appeal held, however, that such a meaning was capable of being defamatory, since it could cause the claimant to be shunned or avoided.

LORD JUSTICE SLESSER

...[N]ot only is the matter defamatory if it brings the plaintiff into hatred, ridicule, or contempt by reason of some moral discredit on [the plaintiff's] part, but also if it tends to make the plaintiff be shunned and avoided and that without any moral discredit on [the plaintiff's] part. It is for that reason that persons who have been alleged to have been insane, or to be suffering from certain diseases, and other cases where no direct moral responsibility could be placed upon them, have been held to be entitled to bring an action to protect their reputation and their honour. ...

This ruling reminds us that the "shunned or avoided" formulation may still be used, despite Lord Atkin's misgivings in *Sim v Stretch* (above). However, it is worth noting that *Youssoupoff* dates from 1934, when attitudes towards women were arguably substantially different from attitudes today. Whether in the 21st century such an allegation could be regarded as defamatory remains to be seen, but is highly unlikely.

14.2 Discerning Meaning

Another important question for us is how we are to discern the defamatory meaning. Some meanings are clear – they can be arrived at by the ordinary and natural meaning of words used, or pictures drawn and so on. However, sometimes a meaning is not clear on the face of the words used. In such instances, it may be that material does contain a defamatory meaning, but that meaning can only be arrived at by way of an innuendo. In defamation, there are two types of innuendo: a false innuendo, and a true innuendo (sometimes called a legal innuendo).

Rubber Improvement Ltd and Another v Daily Telegraph Ltd [1964] AC 234

Panel: Lord Morris of Borth-y-Gest, Lord Hodson, Lord Devlin, Lord Reid and Lord Jenkins

Facts: The defendants published articles that were defamatory of the claimant, in that they alleged that the claimant was being investigated by the police fraud squad. The claimant claimed that the defamatory meaning could be discerned from the ordinary and natural meaning of the words. However, the meaning that was complained of was not in fact clear on the face of the words themselves, but arose from an innuendo requiring an inference to be drawn from the words. The defendants pleaded justification in respect of the ordinary and natural meaning of the words. The House of Lords held that the jury in the original trial had been misdirected as to the manner in which the defamatory meaning could arise and ordered a new trial.

LORD HODSON

Whether the words are capable of defamatory meaning is for the judge, and where the words, whether on the face of them they are or are not innocent in themselves, bear a defamatory or more defamatory meaning because of extraneous facts known to those to whom the libel has been published, it is the duty of the judge to rule whether there is evidence of such extraneous facts fit to be left to the jury.

It is in conjunction with secondary meanings that much of the difficulty surrounding the law of libel exists. These secondary meanings are covered by the word "innuendo" which signifies pointing out what and who is meant by the words complained of. Who is meant raises no problem here but what is meant is of necessity divided into two parts much discussed in this case. Libels are of infinite variety and the literal meaning of the words even of such simple phrases as "X is a thief" does not carry one very far for they may have been spoken in play or other circumstances showing that they could not be taken by reasonable persons as imputing an accusation of theft. Conversely to say that a man is a good advertiser only becomes capable of a defamatory meaning if coupled with proof, for example, that he was a professional man whose reputation would suffer if such were believed of him.

The first subdivision of the innuendo has lately been called the false innuendo as it is no more than an elaboration or embroidering of the words used without proof of extraneous facts. The true innuendo is that which depends on extraneous facts which the plaintiff has to prove in order to give the words the secondary meaning of which he complains. ...

A pleader is entitled to allege in his statement of claim what the words in their natural and ordinary meaning convey, provided he makes it clear that he is not relying on a true innuendo, which gives a separate cause of action and requires a separate verdict from the jury. It is desirable that he should do so, for, where there is no true innuendo, the judge should define the limits of the natural and ordinary meaning of the libel and leave to the jury only those meanings which he rules are capable of being defamatory.

LORD DEVLIN

My Lords, the natural and ordinary meaning of words ought in theory to be the same for the lawyer as for the layman because the lawyer's first rule of construction is that words are to be given their natural and ordinary meaning as popularly understood. The proposition that ordinary words are the same for the lawyer as for the layman is, as a matter of pure construction, undoubtedly true. But it is very difficult to draw the line between pure construction and implication, and the layman's capacity for implication is much greater than the lawyer's. The lawyer's rule is that the implication must be necessary as well as reasonable. The layman reads in an implication much more freely; and, unfortunately, as the law of defamation has to take into account, is especially prone to do so when it is derogatory.

In the law of defamation these wider sorts of implication are called innuendoes. ... An innuendo had to be pleaded and the line between an ordinary meaning and an innuendo might not always be easy to draw. A derogatory implication may be so near the surface that it is hardly hidden at all or it may be more difficult to detect. If it is said of a man that he is a fornicator the statement cannot be enlarged by innuendo. If it is said of him that he was seen going into a brothel, the same meaning would probably be conveyed to nine men out of ten. But the lawyer might say that in the latter case a derogatory meaning was not a necessary one because a man might go to a brothel for an innocent purpose. An innuendo pleading that the words were understood to mean that he went there for an immoral purpose would not therefore be ridiculous. To be on the safe side, a pleader used an innuendo whenever the defamation was not absolutely explicit. That was very frequent since scandalmongers are induced by the penalties for defamation to veil their meaning to some extent. Moreover, there were some pleaders who got to think that a statement of claim was somehow made more forceful by an innuendo, however plain the words. So rhetorical innuendoes were pleaded, such as to say of a man that he was a fornicator meant and was understood to mean that he was not fit to associate with his wife and family and was a man who ought to be shunned by all decent persons and so forth.

The word "innuendo" is not used. But the effect of the language is that any meaning that does not require the support of extrinsic fact is assumed to be part of the ordinary meaning of the words. Accordingly, an innuendo, however well concealed, that is capable of being detected in the language used is deemed to be part of the ordinary meaning.

This might be an academic matter if it were not for the principle that the ordinary meaning of words and the meaning enlarged by innuendo give rise to separate causes of action. This principle, which orginated out of the old forms of pleading, seems to me in modern times to be of dubious value.

My lords, I think on the whole that this is the better solution though it brings with it a consequence that I dislike, namely, that at two points there is a divergence between the popular and the legal meaning of words. Just as the popular and legal meanings of "malice" have drifted apart, so the popular and legal meanings of "innuendo" must now be separated. I shall in the rest of my speech describe as a legal innuendo the innuendo that is the subject-matter of a separate cause of action. I suppose that it does not matter what terminology is used so long as it is agreed. But I do not care for the description of the popular innuendo as a false innuendo; it is the law and not popular usage that gives a false and restricted meaning to the word. The other respect is that the natural and ordinary meaning of words for the purposes of defamation is not their natural and ordinary meaning for other purposes of the law. There must be added to the implications which a court is prepared to make as a matter of construction all such insinuations and innuendoes as could reasonably be read into them by the ordinary man.

The opinions of Lords Hodson and Devlin usefully outline the different types of innuendo which can come into play when discerning meaning. Our next case makes clear that meaning can only be discerned when the material complained of is looked at and interpreted in context.

Charleston v News Group Newspapers **[1995] 2 AC 65**

Panel: Lord Goff of Chieveley, Lord Bridge of Harwich, Lord Jauncey of Tullichettle, Lord Mustill and Lord Nicholls of Birkenhead

Facts: The claimants were two actors who played the characters 'Harold' and 'Madge' in the Australian television soap *Neighbours*. The defendants published, on the front page of their newspaper, images that appeared to depict both claimants engaging in a sex act. In fact, the images had been electronically created and were taken from an online sex game that the article was being written about. The images were accompanied by text that, if read, made clear that the images were fake and were not true images of the claimants. The claimants brought an action in libel. The issue for the House of Lords was whether, when assessing the meaning to be attributed to the piece, the court should take into account the whole of the article or simply the images. Their Lordships held that the meaning could only be discerned by reading the article alongside the images, and that, when that was done, the combined piece was not capable of bearing a defamatory meaning.

LORD NICHOLLS OF BIRKENHEAD

I do not see how, consistently with this single standard, it is possible to carve the readership of one article into different groups: those who will have read only the headlines, and those who will have read further. The question, defamatory or no, must always be answered by reference to the response of the ordinary reader.

This is not to say that words in the text of an article will always cure a defamatory headline. It all depends on the context, one element in which is the layout of the article. Those who print defamatory headlines are playing with fire. The ordinary reader might not be expected to notice curative words tucked away further down in the article. The more so, if the words are on a continuation page to which a reader is directed. The standard of the ordinary reader gives a jury adequate scope to return a verdict meeting the justice of the case.

The present case is well on the other side of the borderline. The ordinary reader could not have failed to read the captions accompanying the pictures. These made clear that the plaintiffs' faces had been superimposed on other actors' bodies. The plaintiffs had not themselves been indulging in the activities shown in the pictures. The ordinary reader would see at once that the headlines and pictures could not be taken at their face value. And the reader's eye needed to travel no further than the "victims" caption to the smaller photographs, and to the second sentence of the article, to find confirmation that the plaintiffs were "unwitting" stars in the sordid computer game.

Accordingly, when the ordinary reader put down the "News of the World" on 15 March 1992, he or she would have thought none the worse of the two actors who are well known for their roles in the "Neighbours" television serial. The ordinary reader might have thought worse of the producers of the pornographic computer game, and of the "News of the World," but that is a different matter. I, too, would dismiss this appeal.

14.3 Reference to the Claimant

In order to be defamatory of the claimant, the material being complained of must refer to the claimant. Material may refer to, or identify, the claimant in the same ways as the overall meaning of the material can be discerned – either by identifying the claimant in the ordinary and natural meaning of the words, or by either type of innuendo. Because a claimant may be referred to by true innuendo, it is perfectly possible for a defendant to unintentionally defame a claimant. This happened in our next case.

E. Hulton & Co. v Jones [1910] AC 20

Panel: Lord Loreburn LC, Lord Atkinson, Lord Gorell and Lord Shaw of Dunfermline

Facts: The claimant was a barrister called Artemus Jones. The defendants published an article that was defamatory of a person called 'Artemus Jones'. The defendants did not intend the piece to refer to the claimant, but the claimant adduced evidence from his friends that they had read the article and thought it referred to him. The House of Lords held that the intention of the defendants was immaterial – they had published an article that referred to the claimant notwithstanding their lack of intent. As such, the defendants were liable.

LORD SHAW OF DUNFERMLINE

My Lords, with regard to this whole matter I should put my propositions in a threefold form, and, as I am not acquainted by training with a system of jurisprudence in which criminal libel has any share, I desire my observations to be confined to the question of civil responsibility.

In the publication of matter of a libellous character, that is matter which would be libellous if applying to an actual person, the responsibility is as follows: In the first place there is responsibility for the words used being taken to signify that which readers would reasonably understand by them; in the second place there is responsibility also for the names used being taken to signify those whom the readers

 Alert

would reasonably understand by those names; and in the third place the same principle is applicable to persons unnamed but sufficiently indicated by designation or description.

My Lords, I demur to the observation so frequently made in the argument that these principles are novel. Sufficient expression is given to the same principles by Abbott C.J. in *Bourke v. Warren*, in which that learned judge says: "The question for your consideration is whether you think the libel designates the plaintiff in such a way as to let those who knew him understand that he was the person meant. It is not necessary that all the world should understand the libel; it is sufficient if those who know the plaintiff can make out that he is the person meant." I think it is out of the question to suggest that that means "meant in the mind of the writer" or of the publisher; it must mean "meant by the words employed." ...

The intention of the defendant is irrelevant. If a claimant is in fact, albeit unintentionally, referred to then he/she will have a claim. It is for this reason that, in practice, the media routinely identify people as precisely as possible – often referring to them by age, profession, place of residence and so on.

Cassidy v Daily Mirror [1929] 2 KB 331

Panel: Scrutton, Greer and Russell LJJ

Facts: The defendants published, in their newspaper, a picture of a man and a woman, and identified them as having just announced their engagement. Unknown to the defendants, the man was in fact already married. The claimant was that man's wife, who alleged that the article had defamed her in that it cast an aspersion on her character. The Court of Appeal held (Greer LJ dissenting) that the article was capable of bearing a meaning that was defamatory of the claimant and that she was entitled to recover damages.

LORD JUSTICE SCRUTTON

In my view, the words published were capable of the meaning: "Corrigan is a single man," and were published to people who knew the plaintiff professed to be married to Corrigan; it was for the jury to say whether those people could reasonably draw the inference that the so-called Mrs. Corrigan [the claimant] was in fact living in immoral cohabitation with Corrigan, and I do not think their finding should be interfered with.

In my view, since *Hulton & Co v Jones* it is impossible for the person publishing a statement which, to those who know certain facts, is capable of a defamatory meaning in regard to A to defend himself by saying, "I never heard of A and did not mean to injure him." If he publishes words reasonably capable of being read as relating directly or indirectly to A and to those who know the facts about A capable of a defamatory meaning, he must take the consequences of the defamatory inferences reasonably drawn from his words.

It is said that this decision would seriously interfere with the reasonable conduct of newspapers. I do not agree. If newspapers, who have no more rights than private persons, publish statements which may be defamatory of other people, without inquiry as to their truth, in order to make their paper attractive, they must take the consequences if, on subsequent inquiry, their statements are found to be untrue or capable of defamatory and unjustifiable inferences. No one could contend that "M Corrigan, General in the Mexican Army," was "A source in whom we have full confidence." To publish statements first and inquire into their truth afterwards may seem attractive and up to date. Only to publish after inquiry may be slow, but at any rate it would lead to accuracy and reliability. In my opinion, the appeal should be dismissed with costs.

This is classic case of unintentional defamation – the claimant being referred to only by true innuendo. Only those people who knew that the claimant was the wife of the man referred to explicitly in the article could have thought it referred to her. This, however, is enough to found a cause of action in defamation.

14.4 Defences

Each of the following provides a complete defence to a defamation claim. The burden of proof is on the defendant (once the claimant has established that the material is defamatory, refers to him/her and has been published) to prove the existence of a valid defence. Please note that defences are now covered almost entirely by statute. We have concentrated here only on those for which there are cases to discuss. For a full understanding of the defences in their entirety you must refer to statute.

14.5 Truth

The first defence to look at is that of Truth (previously known as justification.) It is a complete defence for the defendant to prove the substantial truth of the defamatory allegations. This is governed by section 2 of the Defamation Act 2013.

Irving v Penguin Books Ltd [2001] EWCA Civ 1197

Panel: Pill, Mantell and Buxton LJJ

Facts: The appellant, the historian David Irving, sought permission from the Court of Appeal to appeal the decision of the judge at first instance to dismiss a claim for libel. The defendants were the publishers of a book that contained several defamatory allegations about the appellant, including that he was anti-semitic, a racist, a holocaust-denier and that he associated with right-wing extremists. The defendants pleaded justification and were able to prove the substantial truth of the majority of the defamatory allegations. The defendants were not, however, able to justify the allegation that Irving had agreed to appear at a conference at which members of various terrorist organisations were due to speak. The Court of Appeal dismissed Irving's application, holding that Defamation Act 1952 s 5 applied. (This has now been repealed and replaced by s. 2(3) of the DA 2013.) The defendants would not lose the defence of justification merely because they could not prove the substantial truth of each and every allegation if, having regard to the allegations that could be proved, those that remained unproven did not materially injure the appellant's reputation any further.

LORD JUSTICE PILL

The judge [at first instance] acknowledged that "there are certain defamatory imputations which I have found to be defamatory of Irving but which have not been proved to be true". With respect to those, the respondents seek to rely on section 5 of the 1952 [Defamation] Act. That provides:

"In an action for libel or slander in respect of words containing two or more distinct charges against the plaintiff, a defence of justification shall not fail by reason only that the truth of every charge is not proved if the words not proved be true do not materially injure the plaintiff's reputation having regard to the truth of the remaining charges".

With respect to one charge, Mr Davies [counsel for the appellant] strongly submits that the respondents are not entitled to rely on that defence. It is the unproved allegation that "on one occasion [the applicant] agreed to participate in a conference at which representatives of terrorist organisations were due to speak". The conference was "an anti-Zionist conference in Sweden in 1992 which was also to be attended by various representatives of terrorist organisations such as Hezbollah and Hamas". Mr Davies submits that not only is this a very grave allegation but it is of quite a different category from the charges against the applicant's historiography which have been the main issue in the case. Whatever the conclusion upon the applicant's historiography, Mr Davies submits, the applicant's reputation is materially injured by the allegation that he agreed to speak at a conference attended by terrorist organisations.

The judge concluded:

"The charges which I have found to be substantially true include the charges that Irving has for his own ideological reasons persistently and deliberately misrepresented and manipulated historical evidence; that for the same reasons he has portrayed Hitler in an unwarrantedly favourable light, principally in relation to his attitude towards and responsibility for the treatment of the Jews; that he is an active Holocaust denier; that he is anti-semitic and racist and that he associated with right wing extremists who promote neo-Nazism. In my judgment the charges against Irving which have been proved to be true are of sufficient gravity for it to be clear that the failure to prove the truth of the matters set out in paragraph 13.165 above does not have any material effect on Irving's reputation."

We agree with the judge. While the attack on the applicant's historiography was central and fundamental to the case, it was proved in the context described by the judge which involved anti-semitism and racism and association with right-wing extremists. In that context, the allegation that on one occasion he agreed to participate in a conference at which representatives of terrorist organisations were due to speak did not materially injure his reputation having regard to the truth of the charges proved.

The ruling further backs up the established principle at common law that, in order to succeed with a defence of justification, the defendants need only prove the substantial truth of the allegations. Of course, it will usually be up to a jury to decide whether the defendants have managed to prove the substantial truth of the allegations, something that introduces an element of uncertainty into the proceedings.

14.6 Qualified Privilege

Qualified privilege comes in two forms at common law:

- Traditional qualified privilege, covered by various provisions of both the Defamation Acts 1996 and 2013.
- Responsible publication on matter of public interest, governed by section 4 of the Defamation 2013 and replacing the old *Reynolds* defence.

Traditional qualified privilege focuses on the *occasion* on which defamatory material is published. If the occasion is privileged, then the defendant will have a complete defence that can only fail if the claimant can prove that, in publishing the material, the defendant acted with malice.

When, then, does an occasion of privilege arise? When certain conditions are fulfilled, the courts will find that, at common law, an occasion of privilege exists. These conditions are best set out in the case of *Adam v Ward* [1917] AC 309. It should be remembered that we are, from now on, considering defences for defamatory material that is, in the eyes of the law, untrue.

Adam v Ward [1917] AC 309

Panel: Lord Finlay LC, Earl Loreburn, Lord Dunedin, Lord Atkinson and Lord Shaw of Dunfermline

Facts: The claimant, a Member of Parliament and former cavalry officer, made false allegations of dishonesty against his former commanding officer. The claimants' former commanding officer referred the matter to the Army Council. Having considered the matter, the Army Council wrote back, vindicating the former commanding officer and making defamatory allegations about the claimant. The defendant published this letter in the British and Colonial Press. Their Lordships held that the letter was published on an occasion of privilege and there was no evidence of malice to defeat the defence.

LORD FINLAY LC

My Lords, this is an action for libel, and the questions that arise in this appeal are whether the occasion was privileged, and, if so, whether there was evidence of express malice. ...The law of privilege is well settled.

Malice is a necessary element in an action for libel, but from the mere publication of defamatory matter malice is implied, unless the publication was on what is called a privileged occasion. If the communication was made in pursuance of a duty or on a matter in which there was a common interest on the party making and the party receiving it, the occasion is said to be privileged. This privilege is only qualified and may be rebutted by proof of express malice. It is for the judge, and the judge alone, to determine as a matter of law whether the occasion is privileged, unless the circumstances attending it are in dispute, in which case the facts necessary to raise the question of law should be found by the jury. It is further for the judge to decide whether there is any evidence of express malice fit to be left to the jury - that is, whether there is any evidence on which a reasonable man could find malice. Such malice may be inferred either from the terms of the communication itself, as if the language be unnecessarily strong, or from any facts which show that the defendant in publishing the libel was actuated by spite or some indirect motive. The privilege extends only to a communication upon the subject with respect to which privilege exists, and it does not extend to a communication upon any other extraneous matter which the defendant may have made at the same time. The introduction of such extraneous matter may afford evidence of malice which will take away protection on the subject to which privilege attaches, and the communication on the extraneous matter is not made upon a privileged occasion at all, inasmuch as the existence of privilege on one matter gives no protection to irrelevant libels introduced into the same communication.

So, where there are reciprocal duties between the publisher and the audience to impart and receive the information, respectively, the law will impose an occasion of privilege. Only if the claimant can prove that the defendant acted with malice will the defence be lost. This privilege covers any situation where there are these reciprocal duties, but beware that the *reciprocity* of the duties is a necessity.

The problem with traditional qualified privilege is that it afforded no defence for the media. While it could be said that the media are under a duty to impart information to their audience, there is no reciprocal duty on the part of the audience to receive it. For example, there is no duty on the public to go out and buy a newspaper, or turn on a news channel on the television. Faced with this problem, the House of Lords sought to rectify it and provide the media with a defence in the seminal case of *Reynolds v Times Newspapers* [2001] 2 AC 127.

Reynolds v Times Newspapers [2001] 2 AC 127

Panel: Lord Nicholls of Birkenhead, Lord Steyn, Lord Cooke of Thorndon, Lord Hope of Craighead and Lord Hobhouse of Woodborough

Facts: The former Irish Taoiseach (Prime Minister) claimed in libel against the defendants, who had published an article alleging that he had misled the Irish Parliament in the run-up to his resignation as Taoiseach. The version of the newspaper published in Ireland had contained the claimant's side of the story. The version published in the United Kingdom did not. The House of Lords created a new defence and held that while the subject matter of the article was in the public interest, the defendants had not acted as responsible journalists – evidenced by the difference between the Irish and British versions of the newspaper.

LORD NICHOLLS OF BIRKENHEAD

My starting point is freedom of expression. The high importance of freedom to impart and receive information and ideas has been stated so often and so eloquently that this point calls for no elaboration in this case. At a pragmatic level, freedom to disseminate and receive information on political matters is essential to the proper functioning of the system of parliamentary democracy cherished in this country.

Likewise, there is no need to elaborate on the importance of the role discharged by the media in the expression and communication of information and comment on political matters. It is through the mass media that most people today obtain their information on political matters. Without freedom of expression by the media, freedom of expression would be a hollow concept. The interest of a democratic society in ensuring a free press weighs heavily in the balance in deciding whether any curtailment of this freedom bears a reasonable relationship to the purpose of the curtailment. In this regard it should be kept in mind that one of the contemporary functions of the media is investigative journalism. This activity, as much as the traditional activities of reporting and commenting, is part of the vital role of the press and the media generally.

My conclusion is that the established common law approach to misstatements of fact remains essentially sound. The common law should not develop 'political information' as a new 'subject-matter' category of qualified privilege, whereby the publication of all such information would attract qualified privilege, whatever the circumstances. That would not provide adequate protection for reputation. Moreover, it would be unsound in principle to distinguish political discussion from discussion of other matters of serious public concern. The elasticity of the common law principle enables interference with freedom of speech to be confined to what is necessary in the circumstances of the case. This elasticity enables the court to give appropriate weight, in today's conditions, to the importance of freedom of expression by the media on all matters of public concern.

Depending on the circumstances, the matters to be taken into account include the following. The comments are illustrative only.

 Alert

1. The seriousness of the allegation. The more serious the charge, the more the public is misinformed and the individual harmed, if the allegation is not true.

2. The nature of the information, and the extent to which the subject-matter is a matter of public concern.

3. The source of the information. Some informants have no direct knowledge of the events. Some have their own axes to grind, or are being paid for their stories.

4. The steps taken to verify the information.

5. The status of the information. The allegation may have already been the subject of an investigation which commands respect.

6. The urgency of the matter. News is often a perishable commodity.

7. Whether comment was sought from the plaintiff. He may have information others do not possess or have not disclosed. An approach to the plaintiff will not always be necessary.

8. Whether the article contained the gist of the plaintiff's side of the story.

9. The tone of the article. A newspaper can raise queries or call for an investigation. It need not adopt allegations as statements of fact.

10. The circumstances of the publication, including the timing.

This list is not exhaustive. The weight to be given to these and any other relevant factors will vary from case to case. Any disputes of primary fact will be a matter for the jury, if there is one. The decision on whether, having regard to the admitted or proved facts, the publication was subject to qualified privilege is a matter for the judge. This is the established practice and seems sound. A balancing operation is better carried out by a judge in a reasoned judgment than by a jury. Over time, a valuable corpus of case law will be built up.

In general, a newspaper's unwillingness to disclose the identity of its sources should not weigh against it. Further, it should always be remembered that journalists act without the benefit of the clear light of hindsight. Matters which are obvious in retrospect may have been far from clear in the heat of the moment. Above all, the court should have particular regard to the importance of freedom of expression. The press discharges vital functions as a bloodhound as well as a watchdog. The court should be slow to conclude that a publication was not in the public interest and, therefore, the public had no right to know, especially when the information is in the field of political discussion. Any lingering doubts should be resolved in favour of publication.

The House of Lords created an entirely new defence. It is, in reality, a defence that is completely different from traditional qualified privilege. For, in protecting information that is on a matter in the public interest, the defence does not seek to privilege the *occasion* on which it is published, but the *content* of the material itself. So, when the defamatory material is on a matter in the public interest, the media will have a defence as long as there has been 'responsible journalism'. As outlined above, 'responsible journalism' is assessed by the courts using a ten-point list of considerations, which must be weighed and balanced against each other. The key point about this non-exhaustive list, the factors on which may not all be relevant in every case, is that the more serious the allegation made, the more responsible the journalism must have been in order to legitimise the publication. It was also emphasised, and has subsequently been re-emphasised, that any lingering doubts as to the responsible nature of the journalism "should be resolved in favour of publication".

NOTE that s.4 (6) of the DA 2013 abolishes the Reynolds defence but many of the provisions of it suggest that this section of the statute seeks to put the old defence on a statutory footing, therefore it is definitely worth being aware of Reynolds, above. To succeed with this defence, the defendant must show that the material was on a matter of public interest and that the defendant reasonably believed that publishing the statement at that time was in the public interest.

S.4(3) is probably an attempt to codify Jameel (below).

Jameel v Wall Street Journal Europe [2007] 1 AC 359

Panel: Lord Bingham of Cornhill, Lord Hoffmann, Lord Hope of Craighead, Lord Scott of Foscote and Baroness Hale of Richmond

Facts: The defendants published an article which contained defamatory allegations that the claimant's company was being financially investigated in its native Saudi Arabia, at the request of the United States' government, for suspected links to terrorist organisations. The defendants pleaded the *Reynolds* defence, arguing that the matter was in the public interest and that they had engaged in responsible journalism. Their Lordships ruled in favour of the defendants, allowing the *Reynolds* defence to succeed.

LORD HOFFMANN

Although Lord Nicholls [in Reynolds] uses the word 'privilege', it is clearly not being used in the old sense. It is the material which is privileged, not the occasion on which it is published. There is no question of the privilege being defeated by proof of malice because the propriety of the conduct of the defendant is built into the conditions under which the material is privileged. The burden is upon the defendant to prove that those conditions are satisfied. I therefore agree with the opinion of the Court of Appeal in Loutchansky v Times Newspapers Ltd (No 2)), Loutchansky v Times Newspapers Ltd (Nos 2, 3 and 5) that the 'Reynolds privilege' is 'a different jurisprudential creature from the traditional form of privilege from which it sprang'. It might more appropriately be called the Reynolds public interest defence rather than privilege.

Alert

...In Reynolds, Lord Nicholls gave his well-known non-exhaustive list of ten matters which should in suitable cases be taken into account. They are not tests which the publication has to pass. In the hands of a judge hostile to the spirit of *Reynolds*, they can become ten hurdles at any of which the defence may fail. That is how Eady J [at first instance] treated them. The defence, he said (at [32]), can be sustained only after 'the closest and most rigorous scrutiny' by the application of what he called 'Lord Nicholls' ten tests'. But that, in my opinion, is not what Lord Nicholls meant. As he said in Bonnick's case (2002) 12 BHRC 558 at [24] the standard of conduct required of the newspaper must be applied in a practical and flexible manner. It must have regard to practical realities.

Alert

Instead, Eady J rigidly applied the old law. Building upon some obiter remarks of Lord Cooke of Thorndon in *McCartan Turkington Breen (a firm) v Times Newspapers Ltd* [2000] 4 All ER 913 at 932, [2001] 2 AC 277 at 301 to which he referred seven times in the course of his judgment (the case was actually about statutory privilege), the judge insisted that Reynolds had changed nothing. It was not in his opinion sufficient that the article concerned a matter of public interest and was the product of responsible journalism. It was still necessary to show, in the words of Parke B in *Toogood v Spyring* (1834) 1 Cr M & R 181 at 193, 149 ER 1044 at 1049, that the newspaper was under a social or moral duty to communicate to the public at large not merely the general message of the article (the Saudis were co-operating with the United States Treasury) but the particular defamatory statement that accounts associated with the claimants were being monitored. A 'useful cross-check', he suggested (at [33]), was 'whether the journalists concerned might be the subject of legitimate criticism if they withheld the ex hypothesi false allegations'. In my opinion this approach, equating a responsible journalist reporting on matters of public interest with an employer who has a moral duty to include in his reference the fact that his former employee was regularly drunk on duty, is quite unrealistic. Its use by Eady J on two previous occasions had already been criticised by the Court of Appeal in *Loutchansky's case* [2002] 1 All ER 652 at [49. In my opinion it is unnecessary and positively misleading to go back to the old law on classic privilege. It is the principle stated in Reynolds and encapsulated by Lord Nicholls in Bonnick's case which should be applied. ...

S.4(4) is probably an attempt to codify Flood (below).

Flood v Times Newspapers Ltd [2012] UKSC 11

Panel: Lord Phillips PSC, Lord Brown, Lord Mance, Lord Clarke and Lord Dyson JJSC

Facts:

The appellant, TNL, appealed against a Court of Appeal decision holding that it could not succeed with a *Reynolds* defence in respect of an article it published that was defamatory of the respondent, Flood. Flood was, at all material times, an officer of the Metropolitan Police. TNL published an article effectively naming Flood as an officer under investigation for suspected corrupt practices. Flood was at no time in fact under any such investigation. The article was conceded to be defamatory of Flood but TNL sought to rely on the *Reynolds* defence. It argued that the subject of its article (corrupt practices within the police) was a matter of public interest. Moreover, it argued, the publication of Flood's name was integral to the story. Flood argued that there was no need to identify him as the officer under suspicion in order to satisfy the public interest; the story had gone further than was necessary. TNL countered that a key aim of the story was to spur the police into properly investigating its allegations and that this required that the article have maximum impact upon its audience. TNL also argued that the story would not have been publishable unless it identified Flood, for it would have appeared speculative.

The Supreme Court held, unanimously, that TNL were entitled to rely upon the defence of *Reynolds* privilege. In so doing, the Court reversed the Court of Appeal's ruling and reinstated the first instance decision of Tugendhat J.

LORD PHILLIPS PSC

Mr Price QC for Sergeant Flood has argued that, as a matter of principle, *Reynolds* privilege should not normally protect publication of accusations of criminal conduct on the part of a named individual made to the police, at least if they are accompanied by details of matters alleged to support those allegations. This raises the "public interest issue".

The public interest issue is whether, and in what circumstances, it is in the public interest to refer to the fact that accusations have been made, and in particular that accusations have been made to the police, that a named person has committed a criminal offence. This issue embraces the question of whether, if it is in the public interest to report the fact of the accusation, it is also in the public interest to report the details of the accusation.

The third issue of principle raised by this appeal is the "verification issue". As I shall show when I come to examine *Reynolds* in detail, one relevant element in the approach of a responsible journalist was held to be "the steps taken to verify the information".

Where the publication alleges that accusations have been made of misconduct on the part of the claimant, or alternatively that there are grounds to suspect him of misconduct, the question arises of what, if any, "verification" is required on the part of the responsible journalist? In particular, is the journalist required to take steps to check whether the accusations that have been made are well founded, or is his duty to do no more than verify that the accusations reported were in fact made?

Reynolds privilege arises not simply because of the circumstances in which the publication is made, although these can bear on the test of responsible journalism. *Reynolds* privilege arises because of the subject matter of the publication itself. Furthermore, it arises only where the test of responsible journalism is satisfied, and this requirement leaves little or no room for separate consideration of malice.

As to the formulation of the test of public interest, different opinions were expressed [by the House of Lords in *Jameel v Wall Street Journal Europe*]. Lord Bingham at para 30 referred, with approval, to the adoption by Lord Nicholls in *Reynolds* of the "duty-interest test" or the simpler test of "whether the public was entitled to know the particular information". Lord Hoffmann at para 50 said that he did not find it helpful to apply the classic test of whether there was a duty to communicate the information and an interest in receiving it. These requirements should be taken as read where the publication was "in the public interest". Lord Hope at para 107 commented that the "duty-interest test, based on the public's right to know, which lies at the heart of the matter, maintains the essential element of objectivity". Lord Scott at paras 130 and 135, like Lord Bingham, endorsed Lord Nicholls' adaption of the duty/interest test. Lady Hale at para 146 observed that the *Reynolds* defence sprang from "the general obligation of the press, media and other publishers to communicate important information upon matters of general public interest and the general right of the public to receive such information. " She added at para 147 that "there must be some real public interest in having this information in the public domain". I doubt if this formulation could be bettered.

Reynolds privilege is not reserved for the media, but it is the media who are most likely to take advantage of it, for it is usually the media that publish to the world at large. The privilege has enlarged the protection enjoyed by the media against liability in defamation. The decisions to which I have referred contain frequent emphasis on the importance of freedom of speech and, in particular, the freedom of the press. That importance has been repeatedly emphasised by the European Court of Human Rights when considering article 10 of the Convention. There is, however, a conflict between article 10 and article 8, and the Strasbourg Court has recently recognised that reputation falls within the ambit of the protection afforded by article 8 – see *Cumpana and Mazare v Romania* (2004) 41 EHRR 200 (GC) at para 91 and *Pfeifer v Austria* (2007) 48 EHRR 175 at paras 33 and 35. In *Reynolds* Lord Nicholls at p 205 described adjudicating on a claim to *Reynolds* privilege as "a balancing operation". It is indeed. The importance of the public interest in receiving the relevant information has to be weighed against the public interest in preventing the dissemination of defamatory allegations, with the injury that this causes to the reputation of the person defamed.

There is a danger in making an exact comparison between this balancing exercise and other situations where article 8 rights have to be balanced against article 10 rights. Before the development of *Reynolds* privilege, the law of defamation, as developed by Parliament and the courts, already sought to strike a balance between freedom of expression and the protection of reputation. Thus a fair and accurate report of court proceedings is absolutely privileged. Publication is permitted even though this may involve publishing allegations that are clearly defamatory. The balance in respect of the reporting of such proceedings is heavily weighted in favour of freedom of speech. The public interest in favour of publication is firmly established. The judge has, however, jurisdiction to make an anonymity order, thereby tilting the balance back. Decisions in relation to the exercise of this power cannot be automatically applied to a situation where the publication of defamatory allegations has no statutory protection. In the former case one starts with a presumption in favour of protected publication; in the latter one starts with a presumption against it.

There is thus a need for care when applying to the law of defamation decisions on the tension between article 8 and article 10 in other contexts. The fact remains, however, that the creation of *Reynolds* privilege reflected a recognition on the part of the House of Lords that the existing law of defamation did not cater adequately for the importance of the article 10 right of freedom of expression. Their Lordships had well in mind the fact that Convention rights were about to be introduced into our domestic law as a consequence of the Human Rights Act 1998.

In developing the common law the courts as public authorities are obliged to have regard to the requirements of the Convention. Article 10.2 provides that the right of freedom of expression may be subject to restrictions "for the protection of the reputation or rights of others" and the Strasbourg Court has had to address the tension between articles 8 and 10 in the context of the publication of statements by the press that prove to be defamatory.

Reynolds privilege exists where the public interest justifies publication notwithstanding that this carries the risk of defaming an individual who will have no remedy. This requires a balance to be struck between the desirability that the public should receive the information in question and the potential harm that may be caused if the individual is defamed. In *Reynolds* at pp 200-201 Lord Nicholls dwelt at some length both on the importance of freedom of expression and on the importance of the protection of reputation. As to the latter, he rightly observed that it is not simply the individual but also society that has an interest in ensuring that a reputation, and particularly the reputation of a public figure, is not falsely besmirched. Lord Nicholls at p 205 commented that the more serious the charge, the more the public is misinformed and the individual harmed, if the allegation is not true. But, turning the coin over, the more serious the allegation the greater is likely to be the public interest in the fact that it may be true. Either way, it may be a critical matter in striking the right balance.

Both Tugendhat J and the Court of Appeal considered that the subject matter of the article was of sufficient public interest to render publication of it justified in the public interest provided that the test of responsible journalism was satisfied. This was in the context of a concession by Mr Price that the report of the statement of the Metropolitan Police reported at para 7 of the Article was subject to statutory qualified privilege pursuant to section 15(1) of the Defamation Act 1996 and that Sergeant Flood could not have complained had TNL simply reported that he was the officer under investigation. That latter concession Mr Price withdrew, without objection from Mr Rampton. Mr Price's primary grounds for complaint were not, however, that TNL had named Sergeant Flood as the person who was the subject of the police investigation, but that they had published the details of the "supporting facts" that had been placed before the police in support of the accusation that the police were investigating.

It follows that two matters have to be considered in relation to public interest. (i) Was it in the public interest that the details of the "supporting facts" should be published and (ii) was it in the public interest that Sergeant Flood should be named?

I have reached the conclusion that, subject to the issue of verification, it was in the public interest that both the accusation and most of the facts that supported it should be published. The story, if true, was of high public interest. That interest lay not merely in the fact of police corruption, but in the nature of that corruption. The object of the Extradition Unit of the Metropolitan Police was to assist in the due process of extradition. The accusation was that there were grounds for suspecting the respondent of selling sensitive information about extradition for the benefit of Russian oligarchs who might be subject to it. What was suggested was not merely a corrupt breach of confidentiality, but the betrayal of the very object of his employment by the police. The story told was a story of high public interest and, as Moore-Bick LJ remarked, "the allegations *were* the whole story".

Tugendhat J accepted evidence given by Michael Gillard to the effect that he had doubts as to whether the police were exercising due diligence in investigating the information provided to them by the ISC Insider. He explained that one motive in publishing the Article was to ensure that the police investigation was carried out promptly. This finding has not been directly challenged, albeit that some of Mr Price's oral submissions verged upon such a challenge and Moore-Bick LJ at para 106 said that he was unable to accept this. The judge's finding was based upon his assessment of the oral evidence given by Michael Gillard – see para 38 – and there is no valid basis for challenging it. Lord Neuberger observed at para 54 that the journalists' motives for publishing were of little relevance. In this instance I do not agree. Tugendhat J considered that Michael Gillard's motive was relevant both because it constituted a legitimate aim of publishing - para 200, and because it was in the public interest to ensure that the investigation was carried out promptly- para 216. I consider that there is force in these points. Michael Gillard had good reason to doubt whether the investigation was being pursued with diligence. In fact, there is no evidence that there had been any investigation before the police reacted to TNL's intervention on 26 April. Michael Gillard's concern, coupled with the high public interest in the story, justified its publication. There was, in the words of Lady Hale in *Jameel* at para 147, "real public interest in having this information in the public domain".

Tugendhat J at para 218 held that the naming of Sergeant Flood was within the range of judgments open to TNL, partly because it gave the story the interest referred to by

Lord Steyn in *In re S (A Child) (Identification: Restrictions on Publication)* [2004] UKHL 47; [2005] 1 AC 593, para 34, but more importantly because not naming the claimant would not have saved his reputation entirely. Rather it would have spread the damage to reputation to all the officers in the extradition unit.

On the facts of this case, however, it was impossible to publish the details of the Article without disclosing to those close to the respondent that he was the officer to whom it related. He would be identified as such by the other members of the Extradition Unit and anyone else who knew that he had been removed from that unit. There is also force in the point that, if he were not named, other members of the Extradition Unit might come under suspicion. Having regard to these matters, I have concluded that naming the respondent was not, of itself, in conflict with the test of responsible journalism or with the public interest.

Although the judge considered, on the basis of *Jameel*, that responsible journalism did not require verification of the accusation made by the Article, his careful analysis of the evidence involved consideration of the evidential base of the allegations made in the Article. The judge concluded that the case against Sergeant Flood was not strong on the facts known to the journalists, but found it significant that the police appeared to have sufficient evidence to justify obtaining a search warrant and the other action that they took. There is a danger of using hindsight in a case such as this. My initial reaction on reading the facts of this case was that the journalists had been reasonably satisfied, on the basis both of the "supporting facts" and of the action of the police that there was a serious possibility that Sergeant Flood had been guilty of corruption. After a detailed analysis of the case I remain of that view. Contrary to the decision of the Court of Appeal, I consider that the requirements of responsible journalism were satisfied. I would allow this limb of the appeal.

LORD MANCE

in a line of recent cases including *Reynolds v Times Newspapers Ltd* [2001] 2 AC 127, *Bonnick v Morris* [2002] 1 AC 300 (PC) and *Jameel Mohammed v Wall Street Journal Europe Sprl* [2006] UKHL 44; [2007] 1 AC 359. Its basic elements are "the public interest of the material and the conduct of the journalists at the time". Whether the material is true is a "neutral circumstance". In contrast, whether at the time the relevant journalists believed it to be true is (other than in cases of purely neutral reportage of allegations) highly material when considering their conduct. See, on these points, Jameel, para 62, per Lord Hoffmann.

Although the words I have cited from *Jameel* treat the conduct of the journalists as a separate element of the test, an alternative approach subsumes the second element within the first. It will not be, or is unlikely to be, in the public interest to publish material which has not been the subject of responsible journalistic enquiry and consideration. The alternative approach appears in Lord Nicholls's speech in *Reynolds*, listing a series of matters as being of potential relevance to an overall decision whether publication was in the public interest.

Lord Nicholls did not regard any of these factors as a pre-condition which must always be satisfied. In particular, he viewed the steps taken to verify the information as one factor among all others.

In determining the public interest of material, the court considers both its subject matter and content and the appropriateness of publishing it as and when it was (or is to be) published. The speeches in *Jameel* [2007] 1 AC 359 discuss the extent to which it remains helpful to view the privilege in terms of the test (traditionally applied in cases of qualified privilege) of a reciprocal duty on the part of the press to publish and an interest on the part of the public to know. It is a truism that "what engages the interest of the public may not be material which engages the public interest": para 31 per Lord Bingham. Lord Bingham, with whom Lord Hope agreed, thought that a duty/interest test still underpinned public interest privilege: paras 31, 92 and 105-106. But Lord Hoffmann thought at para 50 that it should be regarded as a proposition of law that, where there is a public interest in publishing, the duty and interest are taken to exist. Lady Hale said at para 147 that "there must be a real public interest in communicating and receiving the information" and "in having [it] in the public domain", but that was "less than a test of what the public 'need to know', which would be far too limited". Lord Scott engaged in a detailed discussion at paras 128-138, concluding that the duty was the press's professional duty to publish information of "real and unmistakeable" public interest to the public, and the interest was the public's in free expression, both of which only existed provided that the press satisfied the test of responsible journalism. In so far as there was any difference between the speeches of the members of the House, he agreed with Lord Hoffmann's.

Like Lord Phillips at para 44, I find Lady Hale's formulation helpful. It also seems consistent with both Lord Hoffmann's succinct and Lord Scott's more detailed discussion of the point.

The courts (...) give weight to the judgment of journalists and editors not merely as to the nature and degree of the steps to be taken before publishing material, but also as to the content of the material to be published in the public interest. The courts must have the last word in setting the boundaries of what can properly be regarded as acceptable journalism, but within those boundaries the judgment of responsible journalists and editors merits respect. This is, in my view, of importance in the present case.

I agree in this connection with what I understand to be Lord Phillips' view that the defence of public interest privilege involves a spectrum. At one end is pure reportage, where the mere fact of a statement is itself of, and is reported as being of, public interest. Higher up is a case like the present, where a greater or lesser degree of suspicion is reported and the press cannot disclaim all responsibility for checking their sources as far as practicable, but, provided the report is of real and unmistakeably public interest and is fairly presented, need not be in a position to produce primary evidence of the information given by such sources.

Taking first the naming of DS Flood (about which no issue was raised in the Court of Appeal: para 148 above), his identification did not underline a central aspect of the article's message in quite the same way as the naming of Mr Jameel and his company in *Jameel*. But the naming was still in my judgment central to any publication. Without names, there would have been little to publish at all. Any article would have been "very much disembodied": see para 135 above. The allegations of corruption made by the ISC insider touched Mr Beresovsky, ISC and Mr Hunter as much as DS Flood. To avoid the risk of identification of all or any of them, all would have had to have been anonymised. An article excluding all names, and consisting of a general and anonymised report of investigation into possible corruption in the extradition unit at the instance of unidentified foreigners at risk of extradition, would have been unlikely to be readable or publishable. It would also have been unlikely to fulfil the purpose of stimulating and ensuring diligent pursuit by the police of their investigation, which the judge found that Mr Gillard junior intended.

As to the detail of the allegations, TNL could have reproduced the police statement of 28 April 2006, together with a bare statement identifying DS Flood as the officer under investigation. But, as the Master of the Rolls acknowledged (Court of Appeal, para 68), it is doubtful how publishable any article would then have been. Again, it is also doubtful whether it would have achieved the purpose which the journalists had in mind. Here too, journalistic judgment and editorial freedom are entitled to weight.

These considerations do not however themselves determine the question whether it was in the public interest to publish an article with the names and detail in fact included, or whether, if without such names and detail there was no publishable article, TNL should not simply have awaited the outcome of the police investigation before contemplating any publication.

More fundamental though is the point noted by Lord Phillips, that the House of Lords in *Reynolds* – and later also in *Jameel* – has reconsidered the weight to be attached to protection of reputation and freedom of the press, and reached decisions of which the effect is to "liberalise" and to redress the balance "in favour of greater freedom to publish matters of genuine public interest": *Jameel*, para 35, per Lord Bingham and para 38, per Lord Hoffmann.

It follows from the analysis in paragraphs 154 to 178 above that in my view the Court of Appeal erred in its approach and in the reasons it gave for reaching conclusions differing from the judge. Balancing the competing interests in this case, the judge was in my view justified in the present case in regarding the article concerning DS Flood as covered by the public interest defence recognised in *Reynolds* and *Jameel*. The starting point is that the investigation into possible police corruption in the area of extradition of a Russian oligarch to Russia informed the public on a matter of great public interest and sensitivity. TNL journalists were motivated by a concern to ensure that the investigation was being or would be properly pursued. They had themselves investigated the sources and nature of the allegations exhaustively over a substantial period as far as they could. The article would have been unlikely to be publishable at all without details of the names and transactions involved in the alleged corruption. The facts regarding such transactions were accurately stated.

. The article, although undoubtedly damaging to DS Flood's immediate reputation, was balanced in content and tone (certainly much more so, I add in parenthesis, than the articles in issue in *White v Sweden*: paras 140-141 above). It did not assert the truth of the reported allegations of impropriety made by the ISC insider, but it identified them as the basis of an investigation in progress to establish whether there had been any impropriety. DS Flood and all others implicated in the allegations of impropriety were given the opportunity of

commenting, and their denials in that regard were in each case recorded. Such omissions as there may have been in the reporting were in the overall context minor. The judgment of the journalists and editors of TNL as to the nature and content of the article merits respect: paras 127-137 above. All these and other relevant factors fell and fall to be weighed in the balance.

181. On this basis, there was, in my judgment, no good reason for the Court of Appeal to depart from the judge's overall assessment that publication of the article was in the public interest, despite its immediate adverse effect on DS Flood's reputation. On the contrary, I agree with the judge's assessment.

Whilst this obviously does not mean that the press will have *carte blanche* to publish unnecessarily intrusive levels of detail that result in harm to a claimant's reputation, it does indicate that the Court is prepared to give the press a margin of appreciation when it comes to *how* a story is presented.

14.7 Innocent Dissemination

The final defence we shall consider is that of innocent dissemination. This is largely unchanged by the new Defamation Act 2013 and is still governed therefore by the Defamation Act 1996, and the Electronic Commerce (EC Directive) Regulations 2002, but there are instances where reference must still be had to case law. This is particularly true where the defendant is an Internet Service Provider (ISP), or similar operator of an Internet domain.

Godfrey v Demon Internet Ltd [2001] QB 201

Panel: Morland J

Statute: Defamation Act 1996 s 1

Facts: The defendants were an ISP that hosted a website upon which a third party posted material defamatory of the claimant. The claimant wrote to the defendants, demanding that the material be removed. The defendants did not respond and took no action. The material disappeared from the website ten days after the claimant had written to the defendants, when the time the material could have remained lapsed naturally due to the way the website was designed. The judge held that an ISP such as the defendants were not a publisher for the purposes of the Defamation Act 1996 s 1, but that in this instance the failure to remove the offending material from the website meant that the defendants had not acted reasonably and therefore could not rely on s 1 as a defence. Accordingly, the defendants' attempt to rely upon s 1 was struck out.

MR JUSTICE MORLAND

In my judgment the defendants were clearly not the publisher of the posting defamatory of the plaintiff within the meaning of section 1(2) and (3) and incontrovertibly can avail themselves of section 1(1)(a). However the difficulty facing the defendants is section 1(1)(b) and (c). After 17 January 1997, after receipt of the plaintiff's fax, the defendants knew of the defamatory posting but chose not to remove it from their Usenet news servers. In my judgment this places the defendants in an insuperable difficulty so that they cannot avail themselves of the defence provided by section 1. ...

The situation is analogous to that of the bookseller who sells a book defamatory of the plaintiff ... I do not accept [counsel for the defendants'] argument that the defendants were merely owners of an electronic device through which postings were transmitted. The defendants chose to store [website] postings within their computers. Such postings could be accessed on that newsgroup. The defendants could obliterate and indeed did so about a fortnight after receipt.

This case, however, now needs to be reconsidered in the light of the Electronic Commerce (EC Directive) Regulations 2002, which is designed to afford a greater degree of protection to ISPs.

Bunt v Tilley [2006] EWHC 407 (QB), [2007] 1 WLR 1243

Panel: Eady J

Facts: The claimant brought an action against the defendant Internet Service Provider, in respect of defamatory material that was posted on the internet by a third party. The defendant claimed that it had not been aware of the complaint until the claim form was served at the commencement of the libel proceedings. The defendant provided evidence to the effect that as an Internet Service Provider, it engaged only passively in the publication of the defamatory material, through a process known as 'caching', and argued it should be able to rely on an innocent dissemination defence. The judge held that the defendants were merely passive in the publication of the defamatory material and were thus entitled to the defence.

MR JUSTICE EADY

...In so far as the claimant seeks support in *Godfrey v Demon Internet Ltd* [2001] QB 201, there are plainly significant distinctions. Morland J deprived the ISP in that case from protection under section 1 of the 1996 Act because it had continued publication of the same defamatory statements after Mr Godfrey's letter had been received, asking for them to be removed from the Usenet news server. Here, by contrast, the claimant is relying upon separate postings. ... There are no pleaded facts to suggest any knowing participation by AOL in the publication of *these* words.

There is thus no sustainable case on the claimant's part to support the proposition that BT knowingly authorised, sanctioned or participated in any of the relevant publications. Despite written requests, it was only upon receipt of the amended particulars of claim that BT was made aware of the postings actually complained of.

> In all the circumstances I am quite prepared to hold that there is no realistic prospect of the claimant being able to establish that any of the corporate defendants, in any meaningful sense, knowingly participated in the relevant publications. ... More generally, I am also prepared to hold as a matter of law that an ISP which performs no more than a passive role in facilitating postings on the Internet cannot be deemed to be a publisher at common law. I would not accept the claimant's proposition that this issue "can only be settled by a trial", since it is a question of law which can be determined without resolving contested issues of fact. ...

 Alert

This judgment did not overrule *Godfrey*, rather Eady J explicitly distinguished it. However, reference made by the judge to the importance of The European Convention on Human Rights art 10 may indicate a move away from the *Godfrey* position to one where, as a matter of law, an ISP is highly unlikely to be regarded as a publisher unless it has taken some active step to facilitate the publishing of the particular libel complained of. In this sense, *Bunt* should now be regarded as the leading case on liability for ISPs in defamation.

Further Reading

Coad, Jonathan: 'Reynolds and public interest – what about truth and human rights?' Ent. L.R. 2007, 18(3), 75 – 85

Johnson, Howard: 'Investigating Corruption – the article and the archive, and the Reynolds defence in action: Flood v Times Newspapers Ltd.' Comms.L.R. 2009, 14(5), 157 – 160

15

Torts Relating to Land – Nuisance

Topic List

Introduction

Nuisance is the generic term for a number of torts that protect a person's use of and/or enjoyment of their land. It comprises private nuisance, public nuisance and the rule in *Rylands v Fletcher* (the tort is known by the name of the case). Private nuisance actions involve a person claiming that either their use of or enjoyment of land has been interfered with by the behaviour of a neighbour in using their land. Such behaviour can include: making excessive noise or creating an offensive odour or producing smoke or fumes. Public nuisances differ in that the activity affects a class of person rather then just one individual and there is no need to establish a connection with the land. A public nuisance is a crime as well as being actionable in the law of tort. The strict liability tort of *Rylands* concerns the isolated escape of a dangerous, non-natural substance from one piece of land to another, resulting in foreseeable damage, for example, a chemical leaking from the defendant's storage tanks on to the claimant's land. Though the elements to be proven are very different from private nuisance, the two torts are similar in many ways. They share the same criteria in determining who can be a claimant, for example.

15.1 Private Nuisance

In an action for private nuisance, the claimant must establish that the defendant has been carrying out an activity or state of affairs on their land that causes the claimant a substantial interference with their land or, the use or enjoyment of their land. Case authorities tend to emphasise the effect on the claimant caused by the defendant's unreasonable activity.

15.1.1 Who Can Sue?

As this tort relates to the use and enjoyment of land, traditionally, only those claimants with some interest in the land (either possessionary or proprietary) can bring an action.

Malone v Laskey and Another [1907] 2 KB 141

Panel: Sir Gorell Barnes P, Fletcher Moulton and Kennedy LJJ

Facts: The plaintiff, the wife of the landowner, was injured when a lavatory cistern fell on her head whilst she was using the toilet. The brackets holding the cistern to the wall had become loose because of vibrations caused by the defendant's industrial process next door. As the plaintiff lacked any interest in the land, her claim for a private nuisance failed.

SIR GORELL BARNES P

...The two main questions argued before us were (1.) whether the plaintiff had a cause of action arising from the nuisance alleged, which question involves the consideration of the first three questions left to the jury; and (2.) whether there was a cause of action based on the negligence of the defendants in undertaking to do the work and doing it in such an improper manner that injury resulted to the plaintiff. As to the first question, I must confess to feeling some doubt whether there was any substantial evidence that the fall of the bracket was due to the alleged vibration, but that would only affect the question of whether there should be a new trial. I doubt whether the findings of the jury can be correct; the plaintiff contended that the use of oil in the engine had made a change, but the defendants reverted from January to May to the use of coal; and further, as the engine had been working for years, it is not likely to have done this damage in three months. The main question, however, on this part of the case is whether the plaintiff can maintain this action on the ground of vibration causing the damage complained of, and in my opinion the plaintiff has no cause of action upon that ground. Many cases were cited in the course of the argument in which it had been held that actions for nuisance could be maintained where a person's rights of property had been affected by the nuisance, but no authority was cited, nor in my opinion can any principle of law be formulated, to the effect that a person who has no interest in property, no right of occupation in the proper sense of the term, can maintain an action for a nuisance arising from the vibration caused by the working of an engine in an adjoining house. On that point, therefore, I think that the plaintiff fails, and that she has no cause of action in respect of the alleged nuisance.

 Alert

This rule has more recently been confirmed by the seminal House of Lords case of *Hunter and Others v Canary Wharf Ltd* [1997] AC 655.

Hunter and Others v Canary Wharf Ltd [1997] AC 655

Panel: Lord Goff of Chieveley, Lord Lloyd of Berwick, Lord Hoffmann, Lord Cooke of Thorndon and Lord Hope of Craighead

Facts: This case actually involves two separate, though interrelated actions. In the first, the claimants claimed for interference to their television reception caused by the defendant's construction of the Canary Wharf Tower in the London Docklands. The dimensions of the tower (250 meters high and over 50 meters square) combined with the specific materials used, namely reflective glass, caused, it was argued, interference to broadcasting transmissions to the local community. In the second action, claimants argued that the excessive amount of dust created during the construction period (and specifically, in the building of the 1800 metres long Limehouse Link Road) seriously disrupted their enjoyment in using their property. The Docklands area had been designated, by the Secretary of State, an Economic Development and Enterprise Zone under his statutory powers. A preliminary matter arose for the House of Lords to consider: was it necessary for claimants to have some interest in the property before commencing a nuisance action?

LORD GOFF OF CHIEVELEY

…I turn next to the question of the right to sue in private nuisance. In the two cases now under appeal before your Lordships' House, one of which relates to interference with television signals and the other to the generation of dust from the construction of a road, the plaintiffs consist in each case of a substantial group of local people. Moreover they are not restricted to householders who have the exclusive right to possess the places where they live, whether as freeholders or tenants, or even as licensees. They include people with whom householders share their homes, for example as wives or husbands or partners, or as children or other relatives. All of these people are claiming damages in private nuisance, by reason of interference with their television viewing or by reason of excessive dust.

Judge Havery held that the right to sue in private nuisance did not extend to include so wide a class of plaintiffs, but was limited to those with a right to exclusive possession of the relevant property. His decision on this point was however reversed by the Court of Appeal who, in the judgment delivered by Pill L.J., held, ante, p. 675B-C:

"A substantial link between the person enjoying the use and the land on which he or she is enjoying it is essential but, in my judgment, occupation of property, as a home, does confer upon the occupant a capacity to sue in private nuisance."

Against that decision, the defendants in both actions now appeal to your Lordships' House.

...Since the tort of nuisance is a tort directed against the plaintiff's enjoyment of his rights over land, an action of private nuisance will usually be brought by the person in actual possession of the land affected, either as the freeholder or tenant of the land in question, or even as a licensee with exclusive possession of the land (see *Newcastle-under-Lyme Corporation v Wolstanton Ltd* [1947] Ch 92, 106-108, *per* Evershed J); though a reversioner may sue in respect of a nuisance of a sufficiently permanent character to damage his reversion. It was however established, in *Foster v Warblington Urban District Council* [1906] 1 KB 648, that, since *jus tertii* is not a defence to an action of nuisance, a person who is in exclusive possession of land may sue even though he cannot prove title to it. ...

...[I]t has for many years been regarded as settled law that a person who has no right in the land cannot sue in private nuisance. For this proposition, it is usual to cite the decision of the Court of Appeal in *Malone v Laskey* [1907] 2 KB 141. In that case, the manager of a company resided in a house as a licensee of the company which employed him. The plaintiff was the manager's wife who lived with her husband in the house. She was injured when a bracket fell from a wall in the house. She claimed damages from the defendants in nuisance and negligence, her claim in nuisance being founded upon an allegation, accepted by the jury, that the fall of the bracket had been caused by vibrations from an engine operating on the defendants' adjoining premises. The Court of Appeal held that she was unable to succeed in her claim in nuisance.

Alert

...The decision in *Malone v Laskey* on nuisance has since been followed in many cases ... Recently, however, the Court of Appeal departed from this line of authority in *Khorasandjian v. Bush* [1993] QB 727, a case which I must examine with some care.

The plaintiff, a young girl who at the time of the appeal was 18, had formed a friendship with the defendant, then a man of 28. After a time the friendship broke down and the plaintiff decided that she would have no more to do with the defendant, but the defendant found this impossible to accept. There followed a catalogue of complaints against the defendant, including assaults, threats of violence, and pestering the plaintiff at her parents' home where she lived. As a result of the defendant's threats

Decipher
This case seemed to suggest that a claimant may be able to sue in private nuisance, even without proprietary interest in land. *Hunter* distinguishes this case, though (see below).

259

and abusive behaviour he spent some time in prison. An injunction was granted restraining the defendant from various forms of activity directed at the plaintiff, and this included an order restraining him from "harassing, pestering or communicating with" the plaintiff. The question before the Court of Appeal was whether the judge had jurisdiction to grant such an injunction, in relation to telephone calls made to the plaintiff at her parents' home. The home was the property of the plaintiff's mother, and it was recognised that her mother could complain of persistent and unwanted telephone calls made to her; but it was submitted that the plaintiff, as a mere licensee in her mother's house, could not invoke the tort of private nuisance to complain of unwanted and harassing telephone calls made to her in her mother's home. The majority of the Court of Appeal (Peter Gibson J. dissenting) rejected this submission ...

...If a plaintiff, such as the daughter of the householder in *Khorasandjian v. Bush*, is harassed by abusive telephone calls, the gravamen of the complaint lies in the harassment which is just as much an abuse, or indeed an invasion of her privacy, whether she is pestered in this way in her mother's or her husband's house, or she is staying with a friend, or is at her place of work, or even in her car with a mobile phone. In truth, what the Court of Appeal appears to have been doing was to exploit the law of private nuisance in order to create by the back door a tort of harassment which was only partially effective in that it was artificially limited to harassment which takes place in her home. I myself do not consider that this is a satisfactory manner in which to develop the law, especially when, as in the case in question, the step so taken was inconsistent with another decision of the Court of Appeal, viz. *Malone v Laskey* [1907] 2 KB 141, by which the court was bound. In any event, a tort of harassment has now received statutory recognition: see the Protection from Harassment Act 1997. We are therefore no longer troubled with the question whether the common law should be developed to provide such a remedy. For these reasons, I do not consider that any assistance can be derived from *Khorasandjian v. Bush* by the plaintiffs in the present appeals.

Decipher
This is why the case was distinguished.

It follows that, on the authorities as they stand, an action in private nuisance will only lie at the suit of a person who has a right to the land affected. Ordinarily, such a person can only sue if he has the right to exclusive possession of the land, such as a freeholder or tenant in possession, or even a licensee with exclusive possession. ...

Alert

The question therefore arises whether your Lordships should be persuaded to depart from established principle, and recognise such a right in others who are no more than mere licensees on the land. At the heart of this question lies a more fundamental question, which relates to the scope of the law of private nuisance. Here I wish to draw attention to the fact that although, in the past, damages for personal injury have been recovered at least in actions of public nuisance, there is now developing a school of thought that the appropriate remedy for such claims as these should lie in our now fully developed law of negligence, and that personal injury claims should be altogether excluded from the domain of nuisance. ... In any event, it is right for present purposes to regard the typical cases of private nuisance as being those concerned with interference with the enjoyment of land and, as such, generally actionable only by a person with a right in the land. Characteristic examples of cases of this kind are those

Alert

concerned with noise, vibrations, noxious smells and the like. The two appeals with which your Lordships are here concerned arise from actions of this character. ...

15.1.2 Elements of a Private Nuisance Claim

After considering those who can be a party to a private nuisance action, we now move on to the elements required to impose liability on the defendant. There are three elements the claimant must establish, namely: indirect interferences to the claimant's land (if direct, the correct course of action is trespass to land); damage to the claimant's property or use thereof; and unlawful (by which we mean 'unreasonable') interference. The first element is very much a question of fact demarcating the various actions available in the law of tort. The second element involves proving damage to the claimant's property or an interference with the use or enjoyment of the property. This can be in the form of damage to property or interference with a claimant's servitude (such as an easement). More usually, however, it takes the form of damage to a claimant's use or enjoyment of their land.

15.2 Damage to Property or Sensible Personal Discomfort

St. Helen's Smelting Company v William Tipping [1865] 11 HL Cas 642

Panel: Lord Westbury LC

Facts: The plaintiffs claimed both damage to vegetation and interference to their use of land as a direct result of the defendant's industrial activity next door. The smoke and fumes form the defendant's copper smelting plant caused damage to the plaintiff's property and prevented the use and enjoyment of their own property. This was the occasion in which the courts coined the phrase 'Sensible Personal Discomfort' ('SPD') in describing interference or damage to a person's use or enjoyment of their land.

LORD WESTBURY LC

My Lords, in matters of this description it appears to me that it is a very desirable thing to mark the difference between an action brought for a nuisance upon the ground that the alleged nuisance produces material injury to the property, and an action brought for a nuisance on the ground that the thing alleged to be a nuisance is productive of sensible personal discomfort. With regard to the latter, namely, the personal inconvenience and interference with one's enjoyment, one's quiet, one's personal freedom, anything that discomposes or injuriously affects the senses or the nerves, whether that may or may not be denominated a nuisance, must undoubtedly depend greatly on the circumstances of the place where the thing complained of actually occurs.

Alert

Here is the definition of SPD

15.2.1 The Reasonable Use of Land

The courts do not, in fact, assess whether the use of land is 'unlawful' (although that terminology remains) but whether it is unreasonable. In determining this, the judiciary refer to a number of factors, effectively balancing the competing interests between adjacent landowners. The weighting given to each element depends on the circumstances of each case.

One of the most useful judgments in this area is that of *Sturges v Bridgman* (1879) LR 11 Ch D 852. In this case, the Court of Appeal made reference to a number of factors involved in deciding if an activity on the land would be regarded as unlawful, including both the locality and the plaintiff's consent in moving to the area.

Sturges v Bridgman [1879] LR 11 Ch D 852

Panel: James, Baggallay and Thesiger LJJ

Facts: The plaintiff doctor had his consulting rooms extended in to his garden. The defendant was a confectioner with property adjacent to the plaintiff's land. Unfortunately, both the noise and vibrations from the defendant's manufacturing process meant the doctor was unable to use his newly constructed consulting rooms. The plaintiff brought an action for an injunction based on the defendant's alleged nuisance. The defendant had operated their business, in the largely residential area (Wigmore Street in London), for over 20 years.

LORD JUSTICE THESIGER

...[I]t may be answered that whether anything is a nuisance or not is a question to be determined, not merely by an abstract consideration of the thing itself, but in reference to its circumstances; what would be a nuisance in *Belgrave Square* would not necessarily be so in *Bermondsey*; and where a locality is devoted to a particular trade or manufacture carried on by the traders or manufacturers in a particular and established manner not constituting a public nuisance, Judges and juries would be justified in finding, and may be trusted to find, that the trade or manufacture so carried on in that locality is not a private or actionable wrong.

It was held that the defendant's conduct amounted to a nuisance.

15.2.2 Abnormal Sensitivity

In determining whether the activity on the land is unlawful and, therefore, unreasonable the courts adopt an objective test. A claimant, with an abnormally sensitive disposition, or with abnormally sensitive property, is unlikely to succeed in establishing that a defendant has been using their property unreasonably.

Robinson v Kilvert [1889] LR 41 Ch D 88

Panel: Cotton, Lindley and Lopes LJJ

Facts: The plaintiff was a dealer in twine and paper, whose premises were directly above a cellar. The cellar was in due course leased to the defendants, who manufactured paper boxes there, for which they required warm and dry air. They set up pipes to heat the cellar, but the heat dried and ruined the plaintiff's stock of brown paper. He brought an action against the defendants in private nuisance, and the issue for the court was whether his property (the paper) was abnormally sensitive.

LORD JUSTICE COTTON

...It was first argued as a case of nuisance. Now the heat is not excessive, it does not rise above 80°F at the floor, and in the room itself it is not nearly so great, If a person does what in itself is noxious, or which interferes with the ordinary use and enjoyment of a neighbour's property, it is a nuisance. But no case has been cited where the doing something not in itself noxious has been held a nuisance, unless it interferes with the ordinary enjoyment of life, or the ordinary use of property for the purposes of residence or business. It would, in my opinion, be wrong to say that the doing something not in itself noxious is a nuisance because it does harm to some particular trade in the adjoining property, although it would not prejudicially affect any ordinary trade carried on there, and does not interfere with the ordinary enjoyment of life. Here it is shown that ordinary paper would not be damaged by what the Defendants are doing, but only a particular kind of paper, and it is not shown that there is heat such as to incommode the workpeople on the Plaintiff's premises. I am of opinion, therefore, that the Plaintiff is not entitled to relief on the ground that what the Defendants are doing is a nuisance.

 Alert

LORD JUSTICE LOPES

I am of the same opinion. I think the Plaintiff cannot complain of what is being done as a nuisance. A man who carries on an exceptionally delicate trade cannot complain because it is injured by his neighbour doing something lawful on his property, if it is something which would not injure anything but an exceptionally delicate trade.

Note that the test for abnormal sensitivity is an objective one: if the 'ordinary' (hypothetical reasonable) man or property would not have been affected by the interference complained of, then the claimant will not be able to claim for damage to themselves or their property, because they will be construed as abnormally sensitive. Only if the ordinary man/property *would* have been affected, will the claimant be able to claim, for the full extent of their loss.

15.2.3 Public Benefit

In a number of cases, the courts have had to consider whether the public benefit (or social utility) provided by the defendant in their use of the land, should outweigh a claimant's right to the enjoyment of their land. It would appear that this argument has not found favour with the majority of the judiciary. Public benefit cannot be used to justify the unlawful use of land.

Adams v Ursell [1913] 1 Ch 269

Panel: Swinfen Eady J

Facts: The plaintiff was a local resident living close by to a fish and chip shop leased by the defendant landlord. The fish and chip shop was situated in a largely residential and working class area. The plaintiff complained that the smell emanating from the shop constituted a private nuisance, even though, as the defendant argued, both the neighbours and customers benefited from the service provided. The issue for the court was whether the defence of social utility outweighed the fact of the smell coming from the shop.

> MR JUSTICE SWINFEN EADY
>
> I must accept the plaintiff's evidence that the smell caused by the frying of fish pervades the house and makes it very uncomfortable. In *Tod-Heatly v Benham* Bowen LJ said: "If guided strictly by the common law, we know what nuisance is ... that is in the language of Vice-Chancellor Knight Bruce in *Walter v Selfe* 'an inconvenience materially interfering with the ordinary comfort physically of human existence, not merely according to elegant or dainty modes and habits of living, but according to plain and sober and simple notions among the English people.'" Applying that rule here I have no doubt that the plaintiff has proved that having the odour pervading his house is an intolerable inconvenience, and in my judgment he has made out a case of nuisance at common law. It was urged that an injunction would cause great hardship to the defendant and to the poor people who get food at his shop. The answer to that is that it does not follow that the defendant cannot carry on his business in another more suitable place somewhere in the neighbourhood. It by no means follows that because a fried fish shop is a nuisance in one place it is a nuisance in another. The evidence shows that the defendant supplies fresh fish and has the most approved appliances; but a case is none the less made out, and I must grant an interlocutory injunction restraining the defendant from carrying on his fried fish business on the premises which he now occupies. It will not extend to the whole street as asked.

Not every member of the judiciary is convinced that this approach, as illustrated in *Adams*, is correct. A powerful (and some would state, passionate) advocate of the opposite view can be seen in the dissenting judgment of Lord Denning MR in *Miller and Another v Jackson and Others* [1977] QB 966.

Miller and Another v Jackson and Others [1977] QB 966

Panel: Lord Denning MR, Geoffrey Lane and Cumming-Bruce LJJ

Facts: The plaintiff moved into a recently built house next to the defendant's cricket pitch. He commenced an action for nuisance as a result of cricket balls being frequently hit into his garden. The defendants cited both public benefit and the fact the defendant had moved to the area, in their defence. The majority of the Court of Appeal rejected these arguments and found an actionable nuisance. Lord Denning MR, however, provided a compelling dissenting judgment.

LORD DENNING MR

In summertime village cricket is the delight of everyone. Nearly every village has its own cricket field where the young men play and the old men watch. In the village of Lintz in County Durham they have their own ground, where they have played these last 70 years. They tend it well. The wicket area is well rolled and mown. The outfield is kept short. It has a good club house for the players and seats for the onlookers. The village team play there on Saturdays and Sundays. They belong to a league, competing with the neighbouring villages. On other evenings after work they practise while the light lasts. Yet now after these 70 years a judge of the High Court has ordered that they must not play there any more. He has issued an injunction to stop them. He has done it at the instance of a newcomer who is no lover of cricket. This newcomer has built, or has had built for him, a house on the edge of the cricket ground which four years ago was a field where cattle grazed. The animals did not mind the cricket. But now this adjoining field has been turned into a housing estate. The newcomer bought one of the houses on the edge of the cricket ground. No doubt the open space was a selling point. Now he complains that when a batsman hits a six the ball has been known to land in his garden or on or near his house. His wife has got so upset about it that they always go out at week-ends. They do not go into the garden when cricket is being played. They say that this is intolerable. So they asked the judge to stop the cricket being played. and the judge, much against his will, has felt that he must order the cricket to be stopped: with the consequence, I suppose, that the Lintz Cricket Club will disappear. The cricket ground will be turned to some other use. I expect for more houses or a factory. The young men will turn to other things instead of cricket. The whole village will be much the poorer. and all this because of a newcomer who has just bought a house there next to the cricket ground.

...The cricket club have offered to remedy all the damage and pay all expenses. They have offered to supply and fit unbreakable glass in the windows, and shutters or safeguards for them. They have offered to supply and fit a safety net over the garden whenever cricket is being played. In short, they have done everything possible short of stopping playing cricket on the ground at all. But Mrs. Miller and her husband have remained unmoved. Every offer by the club has been rejected. They demand the closing down of the cricket club. Nothing else will satisfy them. They have obtained legal aid to sue the cricket club.

It would seem that in such cases, the issue of public benefit will be considered only in reference to the granting of a suitable remedy and not in determining liability upon the defendant.

15.2.4 Malice

A number of authorities have focused on the malicious behaviour of the defendant in determining the reasonable use of land. Authorities have indicated that, if a defendant acts with a bad or malicious motive, behaviour that would normally be regarded as reasonable will become unlawful and, therefore, constitute a nuisance.

Hollywood Silver Fox Farm, Limited v Emmett [1936] 2 KB 468

Panel: Macnaghten J

Facts: The plaintiff owned and operated a fox breeding farm. The defendant, after a dispute over a property sign, instructed his son to fire shot near the plaintiff's land with the intention of seriously frightening the vixen (and disturbing their breeding). The plaintiff's action succeeded despite the defendant arguing he had an absolute right to carry out such an activity on his own land.

MR JUSTICE MACNAGHTEN

...[T]here is authority for the view that in an action for nuisance by noise the intention of the person making the noise must be considered. In the case of *Gaunt v Fynney* Lord Selborne, delivering the judgment of the Court, said: "A nuisance by noise (supposing malice to be out of the question) is emphatically a question of degree." The parenthetical statement, "supposing malice to be out of the question," clearly indicated that his Lordship thought that in the case of an alleged nuisance by noise where the noise was made maliciously different considerations would apply from those applicable where the defendant had in the words of Lord Holt "occasion" to make the noise. In *Christie v Davey* the plaintiffs, Mr. and Mrs. Christie, and the defendant lived side by side in semi-detached houses in Brixton. Mrs. Christie was a teacher of music, and her family were also musical, and throughout the day sounds of music pervaded their house and were heard in the house of their neighbour. The defendant did not like the music that he heard, and by way of retaliation he took to making noises himself, beating trays and rapping on the wall. The action came on for trial before North J., who delivered judgment in favour of the plaintiffs and granted an injunction restraining the defendant from causing or permitting any sounds or noises in his house so as to vex or annoy the plaintiffs or the occupiers of their house. In the course of his judgment, he said at page 326, after dealing with the facts as he found them, "The result is that I think I am bound to interfere for the protection of the plaintiffs. In my opinion the noises which were made in the defendant's house were not of a legitimate kind. They were what, to use the language of Lord Selborne in *Gaunt v. Fynney*, 'ought to be regarded as excessive and unreasonable.' I am satisfied that they were made deliberately and maliciously for the purpose of annoying the plaintiffs." Then come the significant words: "If what has taken place had occurred between two sets of persons both perfectly innocent, I should have taken an entirely different view of the case. But I am persuaded that what was done by the defendant was done only for the purpose of annoyance, and in my opinion it was not a legitimate use of the defendant's house to use it for the purpose of vexing and annoying his neighbours."

 Alert

...I think ... that in the circumstances an injunction should be granted restraining the defendant from committing a nuisance by the discharge of firearms or the making of other loud noises in the vicinity of the Hollywood Silver Fox Farm during the breeding season ...

15.3 Defences and Remedies

A defendant can utilise all the general defences available including both *volenti* and contributory negligence. In addition, there is the specific defence of prescription. This defence can be raised if an activity has been carried out by the defendant for 20 years or more and the claimant has not sought to bring a nuisance action within that time. The usual remedy sought by a claimant in nuisance claims is either a full or partial injunction; though damages will be awarded in appropriate cases.

Link
See Chapter 8 on General Defences

15.3.1 Public Nuisance

Actions for public nuisance are fundamentally different in nature from those of a private nuisance. Such actions represent crimes as well as torts and, as such, are usually dealt with by public enforcement agencies, such as the police and local authority Environmental Health Departments.

The classic definition of a public nuisance was given by Romer LJ in *Attorney-General v P. Y. A. Quarries Ltd.* [1957] 2 QB 169

Attorney-General v P. Y. A. Quarries Ltd [1957] 2 QB 169

Panel: Denning, Romer and Parker LJJ

Facts: The defendants were involved in quarry blasting which caused severe vibrations, a high level of noise and resulted in dust and stones being thrown off the land. The action involved over 30 households within the local area. The Court of Appeal held that this activity could amount to a public nuisance.

LORD JUSTICE ROMER

…I do not propose to attempt a more precise definition of a public nuisance than those which emerge from the textbooks and authorities to which I have referred. It is, however, clear, in my opinion, that any nuisance is "public" which materially affects the reasonable comfort and convenience of life of a class of Her Majesty's subjects. The sphere of the nuisance may be described generally as "the neighbourhood"; but the question whether the local community within that sphere comprises a sufficient number of persons to constitute a class of the public is a question of fact in every case. It is not necessary, in my judgment, to prove that every member of the class has been injuriously affected; it is sufficient to show that a representative cross-section of the class has been so affected for an injunction to issue.

Alert

Many activities have been classified as public nuisance including: obstruction of Her Majesty's highway, organising a pop festival and making obscene phone calls. Unlike private nuisances, the activity can be a single, isolated event. Claimants bringing such actions do not need to establish an interest in the land but merely that they have suffered **special damage** over and above the other persons affected by the defendant's activity.

15.3.2 Special Damage

Lyons, Sons & Co. v Gulliver [1914] 1 Ch 631

Panel: Cozens-Hardy MR, Swinfen Eady and Phillimore LJJ

Facts: The plaintiff was successful in an action for public nuisance against a defendant who caused a queue to form outside his theatre, blocking access to the plaintiff's tea rooms. Though everyone using the highway was affected by the queue, the plaintiff established special damage in that his café trade was severely disrupted.

COZENS-HARDY MR

...Another peculiarity of this case is that the queue which is formed is not, to any appreciable extent, in front of the theatre premises; the Palladium people keep their own front clear, and leave the queue to stretch down to, and in front of, Messrs. Lyons' property. Then there is this to be mentioned, which seems to me not to be unimportant. The queue sometimes is on the footpath, and sometimes on the street itself, and it is said that the customers can make their way, elbowing their way through the crowd, or politely asking them to make way, or inviting the able assistance of the policemen who may happen to be there; or, if not, the defendants say, "Let them go round, down Argyll Place and up the other way, and get in, if they can, at the back of the queue." I cannot bring myself to doubt that this is a serious nuisance and annoyance, by which the plaintiffs are specially affected, and that it is not a case in which it is at all necessary for them to say "We can prove that we have lost 1l., 2l., or 3l., by reason of this."

There is evidence by customers themselves that they avoided going there because of the inconvenience and trouble caused by this long queue twice a day right in front of the plaintiffs' house. I really think that, on that part of the case, the evidence speaks for itself. One must take one's own common knowledge of the world in a thing of this kind, and I say deliberately that I think it is quite obvious that a queue, more or less permanent, lasting not for a few minutes, but lasting for sometimes more than an hour, in front of this house, must be calculated to deter customers from coming to the shop. I should have come to that conclusion, I think, in default of any evidence, but there is evidence of customers, and there is evidence by the plaintiffs' managers and representatives that many complaints have been made to them by customers.

15.3.3 *The Rule in Rylands v Fletcher*

The tort of *Rylands* concerns isolated escapes of dangerous, non-natural substances from the defendant's land on to the claimant's land causing foreseeable damage. The tort is most often used in situations involving industrial pollution. The tort has strict liability in that there is no requirement of fault on the part of the defendant. The elements necessary to found a claim come from the case itself.

John Rylands and Jehu Horrocks v Thomas Fletcher [1868] LR 3 HL 330

Panel: Lord Cairns LC, Lord Cranworth

Facts: The defendant, a mill owner, engaged some independent contractors to construct a reservoir on his land in order to supply water for his mill. Unfortunately, the builders failed to block off a number of disused mineshafts and, as a result, when the reservoir was filled, water escaped and flooded the plaintiff's adjoining mine. The plaintiff commenced an action to recover the cost of the flood damage (i.e. £937). There was no evidence of negligence by the defendant (as he had not known of the mineshafts) and an action for trespass to land was not possible as there was no intent.

LORD CAIRNS LC

...On the other hand if the Defendants, not stopping at the natural use of their close, had desired to use it for any purpose which I may term a non-natural use, for the purpose of introducing into the close that which in its natural condition was not in or upon it, for the purpose of introducing water either above or below ground in quantities and in a manner not the result of any work or operation on or under the land,—and if in consequence of their doing so, or in consequence of any imperfection in the mode of their doing so, the water came to escape and to pass off into the close of the Plaintiff, then it appears to me that that which the Defendants were doing they were doing at their own peril; and, if in the course of their doing it, the evil arose to which I have referred, the evil, namely, of the escape of the water and its passing away to the close of the Plaintiff and injuring the Plaintiff, then for the consequence of that, in my opinion, the Defendants would be liable. ...

The same result is arrived at on the principles referred to by Mr. Justice Blackburn in his judgment, in the Court of Exchequer Chamber, where he states the opinion of that Court as to the law in these words:

Alert

"We think that the true rule of law is, that the person who, for his own purposes, brings on his land and collects and keeps there anything likely to do mischief if it escapes, must keep it in at his peril; and if he does not do so, is primâ facie answerable for all the damage which is the natural consequence of its escape. He can excuse himself by showing that the escape was owing to the Plaintiff's default; or, perhaps, that the escape was the consequence of vis major, or the act of God; ... and it seems but reasonable and just that the neighbour who has brought something on his own property (which was not naturally there), harmless to others so long as it is confined to his own property, but which he knows will be mischievous if it gets on his neighbour's, should be obliged to make good the damage which ensues if he does not succeed in confining it to his own property. But for his act in bringing it there no mischief could have accrued, and it seems but just that he should at his peril keep it there, so that no mischief may accrue, or answer for the natural and anticipated consequence. And upon authority this we think is established to be the law, whether the things so brought be beasts, or water, or filth, or stenches."

In the more recent decision of *Cambridge Water Co. v Eastern Counties Leather plc* [1994] 2 AC 264 the House of Lords stated that any damage caused to the claimant's property must be foreseeable.

Cambridge Water Co. v Eastern Counties Leather plc [1994] 2 AC 264

Panel: Lord Templeman, Lord Goff of Chieveley, Lord Jauncey of Tullichettle, Lord Lowry and Lord Woolf

Facts: The defendants operated a leather manufacturing business. Part of the tanning process involved using a particular chemical solvent called PCE. Over many years, this chemical seeped through the concrete floor contaminating the water table below. The polluted water was detected by the plaintiff's pumping station approximately three miles away. As a result of this, the plaintiff water company was forced to relocate their pumping station at a cost of over a million pounds. Their claim for these costs failed as the House of Lords regarded such damage as not being foreseeable and, therefore, too remote. Liability would only arise if the damaged caused was either foreseen or ought to have been foreseen by the defendant.

LORD GOFF OF CHIEVELEY

... It is against this background that it is necessary to consider the question whether foreseeability of harm of the relevant type is an essential element of liability either in nuisance or under the rule in *Rylands v. Fletcher*. I shall take first the case of nuisance. In the present case, as I have said, this is not strictly speaking a live issue. Even so, I propose briefly to address it, as part of the analysis of the background to the present case.

Foreseeability of damage under the rule in Rylands v. Fletcher

...Blackburn J. spoke of "anything *likely* to do mischief if it escapes;" and later he spoke of something "which he *knows* to be mischievous if it gets on his neighbour's [property]," and the liability to "answer for the natural *and anticipated* consequences." Furthermore, time and again he spoke of the strict liability imposed upon the defendant as being that he must keep the thing in at his peril; and, when referring to liability in actions for damage occasioned by animals, he referred, at p. 282, to the established principle that "it is quite immaterial whether the escape is by negligence or not." The general tenor of his statement of principle is therefore that knowledge, or at least foreseeability of the risk, is a prerequisite of the recovery of damages under the principle; but that the principle is one of strict liability in the sense that the defendant may be held liable notwithstanding that he has exercised all due care to prevent the escape from occurring.

...However, quite apart from the indications to be derived from the judgment of Blackburn J. in *Fletcher v. Rylands*, LR 1 Ex 265 itself, to which I have already referred, the historical connection with the law of nuisance must now be regarded as pointing towards the conclusion that foreseeability of damage is a prerequisite of the recovery of damages under the rule. I have already referred to the fact that Blackburn J. himself did not regard his statement of principle as having broken new ground; furthermore,

Professor Newark has convincingly shown that the rule in *Rylands v. Fletcher* was essentially concerned with an extension of the law of nuisance to cases of isolated escape. Accordingly since, following the observations of Lord Reid when delivering the advice of the Privy Council in *The Wagon Mound (No. 2)* [1967] 1 AC 617, 640, the recovery of damages in private nuisance depends on foreseeability by the defendant of the relevant type of damage, it would appear logical to extend the same requirement to liability under the rule in *Rylands v. Fletcher*.

Further Reading

Amirthalingam, K [2004] *'Rylands Lives'* 63 CLJ 273

Buckley, RA [1996], *The Law of Nuisance*, Butterworths

Cane, P [1997], 113 LQR 515 [Hunter]

Campbell, D [2000] *'Of Coase and Corn; A (sort of) Defence of Private Nuisance'* 63 MLR 197

English, R [1996] *'The tenant, his wife, the lodger and their telly: a spot of nuisance in Docklands'* 59 MLR 726

Gearty, C [1989], *'The Place of Nuisance in the Modern Law of Torts'* CLJ 214

Markesinis, B. [1989], *'Negligence, Nuisance and Affirmative Duties of Action'* 105 LQR 104

Murphy, J [2004] *' The Merits of Rylands v Fletcher'* 24 OJLS 643

Nolan, D [2005] *'The Distinctiveness of Rylands v Fletcher'* 24 MLR 557

O'Sullivan, J [2000], *'Nuisance, Local Authorities and Neighbours from Hell'* 59 CLJ 11

Rodgers, C [2001] *'Nuisance and the unruly tenant'* 60 CLJ 382

Spencer, J [1989], *'Public Nuisance: A Critical Examination'* CLJ 55

Steele, J [1995], *'Private Law and the Environment'* LS 236

Wightman, J [1998], *'Nuisance – the Environmental Tort'* 61 MLR 870